For the City Yet to Come

AbdouMaliq Simone

For the City Yet to Come

Changing African Life in Four Cities

Duke University Press   Durham and London   2004

© 2004 Duke University Press

All rights reserved

Printed in the United States of America

on acid-free paper ∞

Designed by CH Westmoreland

Typeset in Sabon with Helvetica Neue display

by Keystone Typesetting, Inc.

Library of Congress Cataloging-in-Publication

Data appear on the last printed page of

this book.

For Karin, Zaira, and Na'ilah

Contents

Acknowledgments

I offer much gratitude to the following persons, who contributed a great deal to my work on this project: Mohamed Soumaré, acting executive secretary of Environment Developmental Action in the Third World and former coordinator of the African NGO Habitat Caucus; my colleagues at the caucus, particularly Jérome Gérard and Mohamadou Abdoul Diop, as well as members of the caucus network; and Marilyn Douala-Bell Schaub, Cecilia Kinuthia-Njenga, Maria Rosario, Mario Rosario, Ousman Dembele, Malick Gaye, and Pauline Biyong.

For many years of institutional, professional, and personal support, I thank my colleagues at the Isandla Institute of South Africa and the Foundation for Contemporary Research: Edgar Pieterse, Dominique Woolridge, Frank Mentjies, Kam Chetty, Paul Thulare, and Sue Parnell. For the opportunity to intersect with a wide range of African scholarship on urban issues, I am particularly grateful for the support offered to me by colleagues at the Council for the Development of Social Science Research in Africa, particularly Ebrahim Sall, Thandika Mkandawire, Mamadou Diouf, Moumar Coumba Diop, Mahmood Mamdani, and Tade Aina. For the opportunity to complete a draft of this book, I am particularly indebted to the International Center for Advanced Studies at New York University, the Institute of African Studies at Columbia University, and the Center for International Studies at Yale University. Key colleagues and friends who have provided both substantial intellectual and moral support include Achille Mbembe, Sarah Nuttall, Deborah Posel, Jennifer Robinson, Jean-Charles

Tall, Graeme Gotz, Filip de Boeck, Peter Geschiere, Dominique Malaquais, Wambui Mwangi, David Hecht, Alan Mabin, Michael Cohen, Jonathan Bach, Eric Worby, Donald Moore, Marcello Balbo, Alain Durand-Lasserve, and Adam Ashforth. My closest colleague and my wife, Karin Santi, provided countless ideas, framings, and ways of thinking about things, in addition to the immeasurable support needed for this project. Finally, I wish to acknowledge the memory of Tshikala Kayembe Biaya, who in my estimation was perhaps one of the most creative and daring urbanists who ever lived, and whose commitment to finding life in the bleakest of urban situations is the spirit without which this book could never have been written.

For the City Yet to Come

Introduction

Remaking African Cities

African cities don't work, or at least their characterizations are conventionally replete with depictions ranging from the valiant, if mostly misguided, struggles of the poor to eke out some minimal livelihood to the more insidious descriptions of bodies engaged in near-constant liminality, decadence, or religious and ethnic conflict. A more generous point of view concedes that African cities are works in progress, at the same time exceedingly creative and extremely stalled. In city after city, one can witness an incessant throbbing produced by the intense proximity of hundreds of activities: cooking, reciting, selling, loading and unloading, fighting, praying, relaxing, pounding, and buying, all side by side on stages too cramped, too deteriorated, too clogged with waste, history, and disparate energy, and sweat to sustain all of them. And yet they persist. Sony Labou Tansi, the Congolese writer and one of the continent's renowned observers of urban life, talks about the African love affair with the "hodgepodge"—the tugs and pulls of life in all directions from which provisional orders are hastily assembled and demolished, which in turn attempt to "borrow" all that is in sight. It may be that such a making use of whatever comes along as well as keeping hundreds of diversities in some kind of close attachment give many African cities their appearance of vitality.

But as Tansi also implies in his novel *The Antipeople*, as well as in much of his theater, the very sense of throwing things together does not necessarily make a society more flexible or productive.[1] Sometimes the hodgepodge freezes the elements in place and makes cultures static and slow to adapt to changing conditions. At other times, they may adapt all too well and forget that adaptation or accommodation is not essentially what the society is, or is capable of becoming. In this way, while there are many ways in which urban Africans have reinvented traditions and have made them dynamic interlocutors between pasts and futures in their everyday lives, enormous creative energies have been ignored, squandered, and left unused.

For a long time I have been involved in various kinds of efforts to understand what is at work in African cities. I have pursued investigations about how they work — both in some normative sense of efficacy and in a broadened series of notions about what cities can and should do — in order to use these understandings as a platform for more innovative and incisive institutional engagements with urban processes and residents. Much of this effort has entailed often very hit-or-miss attempts to look at how African cities become a locus for the elaboration of translocal economies unfolding and deployed within logics and practices that stand aside the usual notions of growth and development. Far from being marginal to contemporary processes of scalar recomposition and the reimagination of political communities, African cities can be seen as a frontier for a wide range of diffuse experimentation with the reconfiguration of bodies, territories, and social arrangements necessary to recalibrate technologies of control. For example, there is a burgeoning interest within several European Union ministries as to what the apparent ungovernability, yet ongoing survival, of cities like Lagos and Kinshasa may have to say about the future of urban governance in general.

Here, what we may know conventionally as legality and illegality, war and peace, the corporeal and the spiritual, the formal and the informal, and movement and home are brought into a proximity that produces a highly ambiguous sense of place. These ambiguities do occasion intense struggles over which identities have legitimate access to and rights over specific places and resources. But they also amplify the historical capacity of many African societies to configure highly mobile social formations. These formations emphasize the construction of multiple spaces of operation embodying a broad range of tactical abilities aimed at maximizing economic opportunities through transversal engagements across territories and disparate arrangements of power.

In this book I have chosen to concentrate on specific social, political, and economic practices that I think are crucial in the making of these capacities of social formations. In other words, I look at what happens in fairly circumscribed spaces and times that may help to prepare specific actors to reach and extend themselves across a larger world and enact these possibilities of urban becoming.

Specifically, I focus on the following problematic: in cities where livelihood, mobility, and opportunity seem to be produced and enacted through the very agglomeration of different bodies marked and situated in diverse ways, how can permutations in the intersection of their given physical existence, their stories, networks, and inclinations, produce specific value and capacity? If the city is a huge intersection of bodies in need, and with desires in part propelled by the sheer number of them, how can larger numbers of bodies sustain themselves by imposing themselves in critical junctures, whether these junctures are discrete spaces, life events, or sites of consumption or production?

The task is a daunting one in that it is difficult to ascertain with any precision just what kind of urban possibilities and futures are being made. For cities are full of stories of sudden and inexplicable transformations and resurrections — of people who have nothing suddenly accumulating significant amounts of wealth, only to lose it overnight and then have it "resurrected" at a later time. These oscillations are embedded in a context where the horizons of a reasonably attainable future and the capacity to imagine them have disappeared for many youth — now the region's largest population group. Urban Africans also appear increasingly uncertain how to spatialize an assessment of their life chances — that is, questions such as where they will secure livelihood, where they can feel protected and looked after, and where they will acquire the critical skills and capacities to do so.

The accumulated years of popular disillusionment with African states, the labor-intensive demands of securing basic needs, the entrenched "negotiability" of justice, and the effects of internationally mandated and supervised economic reform processes have largely overwhelmed the effectiveness of urban practices prioritizing social reciprocity and the continuous interaction of complementary diversity.

The urban environment is increasingly one where it is difficult to ascertain just what social practices, alliances, and knowledge can be mobilized sufficiently enough to produce probable outcomes conceived in advance.

Similarly, the rapidity through which impressions can be fixed in the popular imagination, unanticipated resourcefulness organized, and the dispositions of behavior transformed often doesn't permit any certainty as to the identities of the ingredients or processes involved.

The pressures for maintaining functional cohesion within the framework of extended family systems and the practices of resource distribution that go with it are enormous. There is a preoccupation on the part of many residents in African cities with the extent to which they are tied to the fates of others who they witness "sinking" all around them. At the same time, they hope that the ties around them are sufficiently strong to rescue them if need be.

The very acts of mooring and taking apart social ties become the locus of intense contestation and concern — that is, who can do what with whom under what circumstances becomes a domain so fraught with tension and even violence that clear demarcations are deferred and made opaque. It is not clear just what is taking place. This ambiguity is not only a reality faced by urban residents but one that they also seem to bring about. In many cities, the very layout of quarters is meant to always confound and unhinge clear assessments about what is going on in face of often overwhelming uncertainty.[2]

Another way to look at this dynamic is to consider the ambiguity that ensues in the relationship between how cities are ruled and the responses to this rule on the part of the majority of urban residents. For many urban residents, life is reduced to a state of emergency.[3] What this means is that there is a rupture in the organization of the present. Normal approaches are insufficient. What has transpired in the past threatens the sustenance of well-being at the same time as it has provided an inadequate supply of resources in order to deal with this threat. Emergency leaves no time for accounting, no time to trace out the precise etiology of the crisis, for the sequence of causation is suspended in the urgency of a moment where recklessness may be as important as caution. The past brings the community to the brink, and at this precipice, what can there be to remember?

At the same time, emergency describes a process of things in the making, of the emergence of new thinking and practice still unstable, still tentative in terms of the use of which such thinking and practice will be put. This is a present, then, able to seemingly absorb any innovation or experiment; a temporality characterized by a lack of gravity that would hold meanings to specific expressions and actions. There are no bearings and disorientation is guaranteed. Yet, the experience of crisis can be dissipated in that there is no normality to refer to, no feeling of something unraveling, even though there is also no guarantee that the community will not return to the very place from which it started. Thus emergency connotes both the end of a certain flexibility of interpretation, of the ability to put off until another day a reckoning of commitment and conviction now found to have been the wrong way to go. At the same time, this state of emergence enables, however fleetingly, a community to experience its life, its experiences and realities, in their own terms: this is our life, nothing more, nothing less.

Even when a certain degree of amelioration, rationalization, or "development" takes place, this double-edged experience of emergency sets in motion a specific way of seeing, of envisioning the environment that will inform how people, things, places, and infrastructure will be used. Self-responsibility for urban survival has opened up spaces for different ways of organizing activities. Communities have become increasingly involved in one or more aspects of the provision of essential services, while advocating for more effective urban planning and management. Many local associations have been formed to improve sanitation, provide shelter, improve marketing, extend microfinance, and advocate for a broad range of rights. Also, more diffuse forms of social mobilization and coordination have come to the fore. But what I also want to show in this discussion is how these efforts are sometimes engaged as platforms extending to elaborate ways of using the city and ways for urban residents to use each other that are more difficult to pin down, account for, or contain.

As a result of these histories and dynamics, the mechanisms through which local economies expand in scale and coalesce into new political formations are often unclear, as well as often murky and problematic. They can entail highly tenuous and frequently clandestine articulations among, for example, religious and fraternal networks, public officials operating in private capacities, clientelist networks mobilizing very cheap labor, foreign political parties, and transnational corporations operating outside of conventional procedures. With these economic scenarios come more flexible configurations of associational life, more deterritorialized frameworks of social reproduction and political identity, as well as autochthonous preoccupations with belonging. Consequently, the efforts to "juggle" contradictory scenarios of well-being become more volatile and uncertain.

In response, residents pursue ways of collaborating with people often very different from themselves, operating in different parts of the city, and with whom they work out highly particularized relationships and ways of dealing with each other. These networks are not constructed in terms of conventional organizations or grassroots associations, but often involve large numbers of people who implicitly coordinate their behavior in the pursuit of objectives that have both individual definition but mutual coherence among participants. In this book I seek to document and analyze these shifting forms of social collaboration. I also set out to provide a historical, political, and socioeconomic context for the emergence of such forms and their importance in the remaking of a broad range of African cities.

Dealing with Constraints

In part, emergent forms of social collaboration are related to the proliferation of certain constraints on how urban Africans are able to secure livelihood and maneuver through the city in general. The social support systems rooted in extended family connections, local reciprocity, and various compositions of shared ties, once relied on to sustain the semblance of dynamic and stable urban quarters, are becoming increasingly strained.[4] These strains are sometimes political as quarters are given more official responsibility to manage different urban services.[5] This responsibility generates new modalities of collaboration but also intensifies competition.[6] In some instances, communities have become polarized along lines of social stratification that in the past were more open ended.[7]

The strains are also economic in that employment of any kind — formal and informal — is increasingly difficult to access.[8] As a result, formerly highly elaborated extended family and residential support systems find themselves overburdened.[9] It is estimated that roughly 75 percent of basic needs are provided informally in the majority of African cities, and that processes of informalization are expanding across discrete sectors and domains of urban life.[10] Whereas unemployment has long been a persistent reality for African cities, available compensations now require more drastic action.[11] Floods of cheap imports made possible through trade liberalization are shrinking local productions systems.[12] At the same time, various components of economic rationalization have opened up possibilities for the appropriation of formerly public assets — land, enterprises, services — by private interests, particularly for the emerging elite who are well positioned in the apparatuses that manage structural adjustment.

Possibilities of social reproduction are foreclosed for increasing numbers of youths. As such, the actions, identities, and social composition through which individuals attempt to eke out daily survival are more provisional, positioning them in a proliferation of seemingly diffuse and discordant times. Without structured responsibilities and certainties, the places that young people inhabit and the movements they undertake become instances of disjointed geographies — that is, subsuming places into mystical, subterranean, or sorceral orders, prophetic or eschatological universes, highly localized myths that capture the allegiances of large social bodies, or daily reinvented routines that have little link to anything.

At the extreme, as the material underpinnings of the confidence in once-reliable local institutions dissipates, larger numbers of Africans "disappear" very visibly into a receding interior space — a kind of collective hallucination of moving away from the world. This can be a highly volatile space, for even if marked by intricate geographies of spirit worlds, it can upend "civil life" in an inchoate mix of cruelty and tenderness, indifference and generosity. At the same time, new relational webs are pieced together with different cultural strands and references. These webs promote a capacity for residents to be conversant with sites, institutions, and transactions at different scales — in other words, a capacity to know what to do in order to gain access to various kinds of instrumental resources.

The survival of these cities is also increasingly predicated on the extent of their connections to a broad range of international organizations, as well as bilateral and multilateral agreements that provide the funds for many of the basic urban services that are delivered. Thus, cities remain, at least "officially," inscribed in a narrative of development. But development as a specific modality of temporality is not simply about meeting the needs of citizens. It is also about capturing residents to a life aesthetic defined by the state so that they can be citizens. It is about making ethical beings; about holding people in relations that makes them governable. As such, development is about assisting residents to meet their needs in a "good" way or a "moral" way.[13] Yet, within African cities, the sustainability of communities largely means sustaining ways of associating and moving that are not conducive to such citizenship nor to the production of the moral beings of the type needed by states and other "supervisory" and/or donor bodies. As such, their salience of these local practices, and even their efficacy, must often be masked.

Cities and Structural Adjustment

In constrast to such precarious realities, Thandika Mkandawire has argued incisively that African states performed reasonably well in the first decade of independence. They expedited development, not only in the delivery of development products but in their attempts to transform national political and administrative apparatuses ill-suited for the tasks of modernization. The scope of this work forced governments to push their budgets to the limit in order to address both the costs of needed physical and social infrastructures and to configure viable social contracts in order to provide at least temporary frameworks of social cohesion.[14] In attempting to recalibrate the financial viability of development, the political capacities of societies have eroded, resulting in the imposition of disciplinary regimes that establish enclaves of fiscal administrative capacity distanced from real engagements with either local social processes or institutions.

Thus structural adjustment comes not only to refer to policies that restructure the economy but also to the restructuring of the time and space of African lives.[15] Many states no longer even make symbolic efforts to demonstrate concern with the welfare of their populations, and discourses of participatory governance or local entrepreneurship largely become performances deployed to attract donor interest. The city that emerges out of crises in the political field occasioned by constantly fluctuating monetary values or insurmountable debts is one where considerations about what it is important to do, about what has value or efficacy, become increasingly opaque.

In some instances, seemingly the entirety of the material resources of many African nations is owed to foreign interests that, in the process, become owned by them as well. As Juan Obarrio points out, spaces of transaction are effectively eroded, as whatever a nation possesses, its material, human, and cultural resources, is consumed in what increasingly becomes a spectral conception of value—that is, the values of virtual financial capital.[16] The volatility of African postcolonial societies in the making is thus submitted to the volatility of price fluctuations. This volatility constitutes the standard through which derivatives and other financial instruments are priced and by which African resources, such as gold or cotton, are leveraged to an indeterminable future. Oscillations between stability and instability, such as the on-again, off-again waging of low-intensity warfare have become highly profitable for those managing, for example, the commodity circuits of cocoa, gems, and minerals. At the same time, the political ability of states to regulate or to service fractured populations diminishes, as does the capacity of the nation to serve as locus of references through which "citizens" can locate their prospects and develop some kind of assessment about what is likely to happen to them.

This era of structural adjustment then frames the intense preoccupation across the region with the question of how urban residents can work and collaborate with each other—most particularly how connections are best forged and maintained; how visible and known these connections can and should be. For if a discernible future and a life outside of incessant misery have become unthinkable for many, then Africans must operate through various forms of the spectral in order to proffer some counterreality.[17]

Making Use of the City

The city is the conjunction of seemingly endless possibilities of remaking. With its artifice of architectures, infrastructures, and sedimentation channeling movement, transaction, and physical proximity, bodies constantly are "on the line" to affect and be affected, "delivered up" to specific terrain and possibilities of recognition or coalescence.[18] Take, for example, precarious structures such as roads, often flooded and potholed, areas often inaccessible, torn shacks, fragile businesses, hawkers, tailors, and artisans amassed in provisional locations and dispersed. Even in their supposedly depleted conditions, all are openings onto somewhere, textures that punctuate and steer. They are the products of specific spatial practices and complex interactions of variously located actors that reflect maneuvers on the part of city residents to continuously resituate themselves in broader fields of action.[19]

There has been an enormous range of studies on African urban informal economic sectors, land markets, and livelihoods. But most of this work has focused on informalities as a compensation for the lack of successful urbanization, particularly in terms of deferring heightened levels of spatial, economic, and social integration within the city. Other studies have looked at informal or "real" economies as instruments through which sustainable and viable processes of a "normative" urbanization might be consolidated. For the most part, these studies have not examined the ways in which such economies and activities themselves might act as a platform for the creation of a very different kind of sustainable urban configuration than we have yet generally to know.[20]

In one sense, shrinking public sector employment, overcrowding in informal sectors,[21] increased competition for resources and services, and a growing survivalist orientation on the part of many urban residents relocalizes the ways people structure everyday work relationships. Firms deal with those most familiar to them. Transactions are conducted with those with whom one is in regular contact. For all of its problems — mutual resentments, obligations, and loss of autonomy — family relations become the basis of business relations. This is especially the case when particular sectors are unable to effectively absorb any new entrants.[22]

But there are also large elements of dissimulation and masking involved in this process. In other words, what appears to be increasingly parochial, narrowly drawn identities and practices may actually operate as markers in a complex social economy where actors attempt to participate in many different identities at the same time.[23] This is a "game" where individuals become different kinds of actors for different communities and activities. On the one hand, a largely kinship, neighborhood-based solidarity is reiterated at home. At the same time, social actors are involved in very different ways of associating, doing business, gaining support, sharing information, or performing their identities in other neighborhoods across the city. In addition, there is often a proliferation of "officially" clandestine (but in actuality, highly visible) economic arrangements.[24]

Here, actors from different religious, ethnic, regional, or political affiliations collaborate on the basis that no one expects such collaborations either to take place or to work. As a result, resources can often be put together and deployed with great speed and effectiveness. This is because the process is not excessively deliberated, scrutinized, or subject to the demands and obligations usually inherent in kin and neighborhood-based solidarity systems.

In most African cities, policy and programmatic interventions have focused on the need for the enhanced integration of cities. This is often pursued without coming to grips with the ways in which fragmented urban space — that is, highly divergent characteristics of quarters and their relationships with each other — embodies the heterogeneity of urban opportunities and offers possibilities for the elaboration of livelihoods that don't easily correspond to imposed normative frameworks. There is often the assumption that urban quarters — of varying histories and capacities — are primarily interested in consolidating local social fields into representational structures that can act as a platform for accessing and influencing power arrangements at larger scales. There is often the assumption that this consolidation inevitably takes the form of at least the semblance of well-cohered organizations and roles. But popular investments in time and energy are often elsewhere; that is, focused on piecing together larger spaces of action — larger both in terms of territory and social interdependencies across status, class, ethnicity, generation, social position, and so forth.

The city is also the locus of potentially irreparable harm, where those navigating it never can be sure how their own existence may be implicated in the narratives and behaviors of others; in other words, where they can never be sure whether their immediate positions and actions inadvertently place them in some "line of fire" — on a trajectory of some conveyance capable of doing them serious harm. As the possibilities of mediation diminish — that is, institutional frameworks able to organize differences of intensity and inclination into clearly defined locations, entities, sectors, and fields of reliable interpretation — the sense of potential harm increases. Nonetheless, urban residents must come up with some means of connection, usually implicit and out of their conscious awareness, that set them toward each other in ways that keep them in play. At the same time, these connections provide the basis for their conviction that they can keep each other within arm's length and out of harm's way.[25] Who can be in the streets under what circumstances; who can have recourse to protected spaces without having to figure out ways of dealing with others; who can have access to what kinds of spaces? These are all questions with great immediacy and meaning in most African cities.

In states with precarious or nonexistent welfare systems and safety nets, much has been made about the ability of individuals to fall back on extended family systems and forms of social capital to get through prolonged periods of unemployment, illness, and old age. But often the process of falling back on these ties results in a falling into harm, as dependency turns individuals into frequently easy objects of manipulation and blame.

Cities are densities of stories, passions, hurts, revenge, aspiration, avoidance, deflection, and complicity. As such, residents must be able to conceive of a space sufficiently bounded so as to consolidate disparate energies and make things of scale happen. But at the same time, they must conceive of a fractured space sufficiently large enough through which dangerous feelings can dissipate or be steered away. Urban residents are thus concerned about what kinds of games, instruments, languages, sight lines, constructions, and objects can be put in play in order to anticipate new alignments of social initiative and resources, and thus capacity. The question is how people from different walks of life can be engaged in each other's lives without necessarily obliging specific transactions and obligations. How do the subsequent permutations resuscitate mutual interest in social collaborations, even when the discernible benefits may not be clear or when participants are faced with inconclusive evidence of their own positions within them?[26]

Reaffirming Collaboration

Many of the sounds emerging from African cities are rendered inaudible or inexplicable. Speech is often violently foreclosed or relentless in its mimicry, its promises or its desperate fear of taking pause. Urban politics must thus concern the invention of a platform or scene on which the cacophony of urban voices are audible and become understood, and on which speakers are made visible. What is given as an objective status is put into question through making visible that which has not, under the optics of a given perceptive field, been visible.[27] It is given a "name," not necessarily a "right name" but, nevertheless, a designation. This name is a technique and an instrument that allows something to affect and be affected.

Here I am concerned with how affective bonds are revitalized and how a desire for social interchange and cooperation might contain the seeds of social economies that extend themselves through scale, time, and reach. But this is not directly about civil society organizations and nongovernmental organizations (NGOs), microcredit associations or people's associations. Rather, I am interested here in more diffuse but no less concrete ways in which diverse urban actors are assembled and act. What are some of the ways in which urban residents are building a particular emotional field in the city, trying to restore a very physical sense of connection to one another? This is a micropolitics of alignment, interdependency, and exuberance. This is not the work of detailed ethnographic examinations of new social movements, new living arrangements, or new forms of urban productivity. It is a practice of being attuned to faint signals, flashes of important creativity in otherwise desperate maneuvers, small eruptions in the social fabric that provide new texture, small but important platforms from which to access new views.

For knowledgeable action is largely a practical activity involving the construction of new relations in the gaps that always open up in the process of conducting existing relations — of acting, gesturing, moving, and aligning. Urban collaboration does not simply reflect and institutionalize clearly identifiable social processes and forms. There are gaps and openings, room for negotiation and provocation, and thus collaboration can take many forms. Sometimes people coalesce in organizations that have names, but where it is unclear to almost everyone what precisely the organization is and what it does. At other times, an event may trigger an entire neighborhood into apparently unfamiliar courses of action, but with a synchronicity that makes it appear as if some deep-seated logic of social mobilization is being unleashed. At still other times, the ways in which localities both activate and resist change in relationship to the decisions of government authorities construct tentative platforms for people to collaborate in "silent" but powerful ways. These collaborations have the potential of substantially altering the position of the locality within the larger urban system.

Recombining Contingency

The thrust of this book is that a wide range of provisional, highly fluid, yet coordinated and collective actions are being generated that run parallel to, yet intersect with, a growing proliferation of decentralized local authorities, small-scale enterprises, community associations, and civil society organizations. These actions are, in turn, replete with locally generated moral and social economies, compelled, nevertheless, from a more expansive engagement with a broad range of external processes and actors. If African cities do, at some level, work, then I contend that these practices play a major role in making them work.

The core of this book, then, is a series of case studies that attempt to demonstrate the complex interweaving of resources and problems in a wide range of efforts to piece together viable forms of urban life. I will discuss at length several "cases" — from Pikine (Senegal), Winterveld (South Africa), Douala (Cameroon), and Jidda (Saudi Arabia). Each of the four cases will be prefaced and framed by one of four distinct notions: the informal, the invisible, the spectral, and movement. These notions are not used as conceptual structures that steer and account for urban behavior but rather are heuristic entry points into describing varied capacities of diverse urban residents to operate in concert without discernible infrastructures, policy frameworks, and institutional practices in which to do so. They are used to help make sense of what otherwise appear simply as disparate and irrational dimensions of urban life.

These notions are deployed to posit processes of urban operation that may not necessarily have an empirical coherence but rather elaborate a possible field through which residents from various walks of life pay attention to, approach, and coordinate their actions with one another. They serve as ways of bringing the city into some kind of focus and for leveraging access to the effects of urban forces and practices otherwise not easy to apprehend. In other words, to find ways of making visible urban possibilities that have been crowded out or left diffuse or opaque in the concentration on analytical languages that attempt to account for urban life through a specific delineation of social identities, sectors, and institutions.

Urban landscapes come to refract various layers of sedimentation — of past uses and organization — as well as to embody a range of possible meanings and actions falling outside the shifting levels of specification brought to bear on these landscapes by the prevailing and, in Africa, often fragmentary apparatuses of control. The question I am interested in by exploring these case studies is how residents can read their environments in ways that propel them outward from the everyday navigation to which they are accustomed. What chances and opportunities are opened? How are various possibilities viewed as foreclosed? How are residents assuming various identities and positions included in different efforts at collaboration? How are these collaborations spatialized and assessed in such a way as to manage oscillating patterns of inclusion and exclusion?

African urban institutions in the past have been called on to provide platforms that facilitate independent action yet try to ensure a sense of equanimity that resonates with deeply felt cultural values. But as these institutions weaken and centers of social gravity dissipate, new forms of urban livelihood and sociality are potentially fraught with the dangers of parasitism, manipulation, and incessant provisionality. Therefore, in order for new transactions to ensue, their constituent elements — people, resources, places, and mobilities — must often be assembled in ways that deflect publicity, scrutiny, and comparison. This process of assembling proceeds not by a specific logic shared by the participants but rather can be seen as a recombination of contingency. In other words, a coincidence of perspectives, interpretations, engagements, and practices that enable different residents in different positions to, either incrementally or radically, converge and/or diverge from one another and, in the process of doing so, remake what is considered possible to do.

These framing notions — informality, invisibility, spectrality, and movement — are used here as tactical operational fields constituting an analytical site or locus through which different capacities, practices, and interpretations can be intersected and through which the more ephemeral ways residents of different backgrounds collaborate can be visualized. Again, these notions are not posited here as some overarching logic structuring action; rather, they simply provide a mechanism through which diverse practices and tendencies at work in each case study can be seen to coincide.

In order to appreciate what African urban residents are up against, as well as the context in which emergent forms of social collaboration have come to the fore, make sense, or get things done, I will in the bulk of this book analyze the conditions in which they operate. What is it about African cities — their histories, economies, and positions — that occasion the emergent collaborations as a particularly incisive modality for those experiencing them? I will discuss how the history, macroeconomies, and urban policy and development frameworks related to African cities set the stage for informalizing large portions of everyday life within them, and how residents deal with this informalizing process. Accordingly, I will review the various economic, political, and social dimensions of informality at work in African cities. I will talk about the varying implications of informalization at different scales of operation and the ways in which urban quarters attempt to situate themselves in and mediate these differences of scale.

Again, my objective is to talk about the ways in which African cities are productive. The experiences I discuss here have been complicated, and clear and simple lessons are not easily packaged. The language of description will thus also be complicated at times. It will not always be clear just what is going on, as stories open up to other stories. I have tried to find a form of narration close to the actual processes underway — one that is close to the interweaving of superficially distinct identities and domains. I fully appreciate how difficult everyday life in most African cities has become, and I neither romanticize nor celebrate what is going on. Rather, I believe it is important to emphasize that what is going on has worth and value, and is a crucial aspect of Africa remaking itself.

A Methodological Note: Multiple Engagements as Methodology

It is difficult to carry out sustained and systematic social research in many quarters (that is, division or district) of African cities, especially where the changes seem most pronounced and the social interaction complex. Because the conventional categories for understanding such changes are themselves opened up, "twisted out of shape," and rearranged, it is difficult to be confident that one is working with stable and consistent entities over time. For this reason, I have chosen to concentrate on the provisional itself. In other words, I have chosen not to attempt to conduct systematic social research, but to immerse myself in various settings under whatever conditions and rubrics were possible. Again, I was particularly interested in various ways in which residents were able to collaborate with each other outside of formal associations and institutions. I was interested in instances of disarticulation of quarters from quarters, of quarters from state and municipal government, of social identities from each other, and of formal economies from informal economies. I was interested in how this disarticulation became a resource or a mode of operation for social collaboration aimed at accomplishing a broad use of the city. In other words, I attempt here to add a new dimension to urban analysis by concentrating on particular aspects of individual and collective behavior outside of the conventional contexts of household, institution, and quarter.

I believe that these "outsides" are important domains and considerations for understanding African cities as more than "failed" cities. African cities are more than simply cities in need of better management, more popular participation, more infrastructure, and less poverty. This is not to say that African cities don't need those things. Rather, I believe that we will never really appreciate what an accumulated history of urban Africa has to offer our knowledge about cities in general unless we find a way to get beyond the enormous problems and challenges.

If the limited resources deployed for urban development in Africa are to be effective, it is important to make common cause with the daily efforts of African urban residents. This is a common cause about using the city as a generator of imagination and well-being, of making links with and operating in concert with the larger world. The only way to make such common cause is to amplify the sensibility, creativity, and rationality of everyday practices and behaviors that either are invisible or appear strange. My intent is to open up the ways in which African urban realities are deliberated, policies are made, and programs are implemented. African cities have a lot to offer us in terms of enhancing our understanding about large swaths of social life. It is particularly those dimensions of everyday life "in-between" the categories and designations that have the most incisive opportunity to do this.

This book is based on nearly fifteen years of work in various African cities. Long ago I made a decision to explore the various means of operating in these cities. I have tried to find various ways of spending time in quarters. In some instances, my affiliation with quarters has been as an activist, an NGO or local government advisor, teacher, fellow Muslim, development worker, and/or researcher. For many years, I worked off and on for various African-based Islamic welfare agencies trying to help communities think through different ways of improving living conditions while keeping critical aspects of their Muslim identities intact. I have taught at universities in

Ghana, Sudan, South Africa and Côte d'Ivoire, where I have attempted to bring the expertise of the university closer to the day-to-day realities of specific urban quarters. During the extensive decentralization of urban governance that has taken place over the past decade, I have been a policy analyst and advisor to several municipal governments. I have worked with a regional grouping of urban development NGOs to experiment with different ways of generating knowledge and doing research with the communities in which they work. I mention these different positions in order to acknowledge the diverse means through which the perspectives and analyses within this book have been put together.

Perhaps our knowledge of the issues discussed here could be substantially enhanced through long-term, systematic comparative research interweaving survey and ethnographic methods. Such projects, however, constitute a massive undertaking. There has been limited interest in urban Africa. In part, I have assumed different vantage points and professional positions because a single entry point or professional modality simply is not adequate in order to have access to many critical urban processes. Thus, I have come and gone — city to city, position to position. The frame of positioning undoubtedly has influenced the way I look at the cities talked about here. Such comings and goings are processes not unfamiliar to many urban Africans. Although this method certainly is not the only one in use, it has been adopted by many city dwellers in order to try to come to grips with what is going on.

Because many observers have continuously raised the problematic of exactly what may make cities specifically "African," I want to make clear that my intention is not to establish a geographical specificity or a particularly "African" modality of urbanization. The impact of different precolonial forms of urbanization, colonial logic and administration, and postcolonial development on African cities makes them heterogeneous in character. Yet in the face of global economic restructuring, the particular economic arrangements, cultural inclinations, and forms of external engagement that largely made African cities different from each other are being unraveled.

In addition, specific urban places, separated by marked physical and cultural distance, are being interpenetrated, in large part by the actions of African actors themselves. For example, cities as diverse as Mbuji-Mayi, Port Gentile, Addis Ababa, Arusha, and Nouadibhou are being tied together through the participation of those who make them their base in an increasingly articulated system of countertrades. These countertrades involve connections to Bombay, Dubai, Bangkok, Taipei, Kuala Lumpur, and Jidda. These circuits in turn "spin out" and link themselves to the more conventional migratory paths of West and Central Africans to Europe, and increasingly the United States, and East Africans to North America and the United Kingdom.[28] These circuits are organized around different commodities, yet a common profile has taken hold. Valuable primary commodities, such as minerals in particular, are diverted from "official" national export structures into intricate networks where large volumes of underpriced electronics, weapons, counterfeit currencies, bonds, narcotics, laundered money, and real estate circulate through various "hands."[29]

African cities have also historically found themselves in the same boat when it comes to piecing together a functional sense of coherence and viability from a mostly haphazard collection of aspirations and livelihoods. Many non-African cities may also be in the same boat. However, African cities do share a region and are, thus, the objects of specific policy and program initiatives and administrative functions that are organized along regional lines. These initiatives and functions have a major impact on how cities are governed and developed. What distinct African cities make of this "commonality" is, then, important for what happens to them in the future. Additionally, the identification of some commonality, empirically based or not, may be critical to support the very process of expanding the spaces of operation within which residents of these cities are engaged.

What is key here is that African cities reflect, in different dimensions and power relations, conduits of engagement with various geographical spaces and domains, both material and spiritual. Instead of seeing these cities as predominantly marginal from a larger urbanizing world, the majority of African cities have been platforms of mediation. They have been places where assimilation, integration, and the reworking and consolidation of new, specifically endogenous ways of thinking and doing things could take place simultaneously.[30] These characterizations have been both the strength and vulnerability of the city in Africa. Again, this urban elasticity provides a multiplicity of ways in and out, while, at the same time, leaving cities either excessively fluid or sedentary.

In one respect, judgments about the "degree" of development, capacity, productivity, or marginalization assume a certain sense of connection among African cities. They are primarily viewed as colonial creations, still largely linked to the world through the residues of these colonial relationships. Seeing African cities only in terms of their colonial and postcolonial relationships, however, often makes it difficult to see how "modern," "innovative," and "resourceful" they may actually be. It may also preclude a fuller understanding of the multifaceted ways in which they are engaged with the larger world.

If there is to be an empirical connection among distinct African cities, it is unlikely to be found in simply reiterating their common subjection to some overarching framework called "colonialism." Rather, if colonialism is to be retained as a useful concept in understanding African urban histories, it requires appreciating the different influences that were brought to bear on particular urban spaces. Shaped in different ways, cities could then provide important references for each other. It was easier to do certain things in some cities, and not in others. Through sojourning, migration, and limited amounts of trade, cities did manage to eke out some form of linkage.[31] I will not take up an analysis of these interlinkages in this book, but it is important here to state their existence so as to affirm that distinct spaces of maneuverability that simply have not been used or exploited have existed in African cities for some time.

1

The Informal

The Projet de Ville in

Pikine, Senegal

In the first four chapters of this volume I present a series of case studies that attempt to show how urban actors endeavor to maintain a sense of local cohesion while seeking opportunities — for livelihood, cooperation, and access — at a scale beyond their immediate local environment. While these capacities and practices often appear to be ephemeral, there may be nothing that is ephemeral about what they do. It may be difficult to say for sure that this is what is happening, this is who is doing what, or these are the boundaries between what it is and what it is not. But what I hope to show in these cases is that very concrete assumptions, practices, and arrangements are at work.

Individual actors may not be entirely cognizant of what their own contributions may be to these social formations, and certainly no one is operating in a way where the whole story is clear. Still, local actors find various ways of welding constraint and possibility, convention and extravagance, and the "traditional" and the "modern" into a social mobilization that both unleashes the hidden possibilities of the "tried and true" and, at the same time, "tames" the dangers of the unknown.

The case materials presented here concern sites and processes through which very different urban quarters try to work out a means of maximizing resources and opportunities. At the same time, they try to solve actual or potential conflict situations generated by differences in capacities that often derive from such efforts. These efforts do not emerge autonomously as some free-floating, mobile form of social action that hangs over communities or operates outside established modalities of getting things done. Rather, these responses emerge from a recombination of contingent relationships among bodies, spaces, signs, infrastructure, and other urban materials and provide tentative links between different ways of life and different kinds of actors. They try to propel forward local economic, social, or political action rather than trying to stabilize particular social structures. Yet, at the same time, they often find new arenas for the commonly accepted ways of doing things, and thus lend stability to important values and practices through enabling them to function in different ways. Each case will make use of a loosely drawn conceptual notion as a means of provisionally tying together the various scales, events, locales, and practices that are the elements of each case.

The case, then, does not serve to illustrate a specific conceptual notion. Rather, a specific notion is employed as a means of focusing attention on a process of interconnection in the gaps between clearly designated and defined urban institutions, spaces, and actions. Thus, the notion of the *informal* will highlight the heterogeneity of social collaborations that coincide with a major urban redevelopment project in Pikine, a large suburb of Dakar, Senegal. The *invisible* will be used to outline the diffuse yet forceful mechanisms of collective resistance to the wide-scale introduction of specific rationalities of development in Winterveld, a fringe urban area of Pretoria in South Africa. The *spectral* refers to both the symbolic status of certain showpiece development efforts in Douala, Cameroon, as well as the space of remaking relationships of social power and the lingering sense of incompletion that haunts the way in which the city is visualized or imagined by its residents. *Movement*, as applied to a brief case study of diverse African actors in Jidda, Saudi Arabia, is used to foreground a particular valorization of mobility at work in efforts to respatialize not only livelihood but the salience of long-term urban institutions.

A more comprehensive analysis of the particular scenarios and practices depicted in these cases would, of course, have to consider specific historical antecedents, geographical positions, and political environments. The objective here is simply to provide some indication of the breadth and diversity of efforts that certain African localities make to access or create wider arenas within which to operate. At times, an elaborate game of dissimulation is involved. Seemingly parochial spaces can mask wide-ranging collaborations among diverse actors both within and outside a locality. In other instances, many different networks and positions have to be engaged and manipulated so that a given set of individuals, households, and groups can continue to live together as a "community."

The case materials presented here stem largely from work I did for the African NGO Habitat Caucus. The caucus, made up of urban development NGOs in fifteen major African cities, works collectively to establish context-specific platforms of dialogue between local community associations and municipal governments within a select number of neighborhoods within each city. These platforms serve as a basis in which to negotiate specific partnership arrangements in terms of local planning, administration, and service delivery.

My work in all of these situations was to assess what local community, and broadly developmental, associations were doing, especially those involved in various forms of income generation, urban services, or advocacy. In most cases, these associations were tied to established NGOs, both local and foreign. A major part of this assessment was to examine what participants in these associations understood about local economies. Particularly important points of concentration were how residents actually produced livelihoods, gained access to opportunities, spent income, and organized local production and social support. As part of this process, focus groups were established and both structured interviews and free-floating discussions were done. In addition, specific informants were tracked as they moved around during their daily lives.

All of these caucus-affiliated associations faced significant hurdles. There were problems of funding, managerial capacity, power sharing, and decision making, and most particularly the pulls of participants to other activities. The discussions and deliberations that took place within these associations were spirited and thoughtful. The collaborative experiments in environmental management, housing construction, and microenterprise, for example, were usually innovative and sustainable. Yet, it always seemed that resolving problems, looking for important resources, and, in sum, doing the real work to make something happen, was "referred" somewhere else or took place somewhere else.

These case materials are the result of moving away from these more formally organized community associations in order to identify various instances of where that "somewhere else" actually was. In the process of engaging these associations over an extended period of time, it became clear that there were other, more provisional and ephemeral, forms of association and collective activity that association members also participated in and that seemingly had a greater impact on their life. The case materials are thus firsthand reports of scenarios and events in which I have participated and witnessed.

The narrative on Douala does not so much concern a specific quarter but rather is an example, drawn from the work of a Habitat Caucus affiliate, of the ways in which image making can become an important and highly contested aspect of urban development. The sketch on the reappropriation of Sufi institutions as a means of dealing with conflicts in Jidda comes from my many years of affiliation and work with African-based Islamic welfare associations and the information gained from this participation.

The Projet de Ville

Most standard discussions of urban Africa inevitably point to the predominance of the so-called informal sector. With a history since the 1970s of diminishing formal employment — largely accounted for both by the decline of public sector employment and by the limited industrial base of African cities — informality is a crucial facet of African urban life. What is the nature of this informality, and is it simply a compensation for the glaring inadequacies of African urban economies? In this case study on Pikine, Senegal, I aim to highlight some complex dimensions of informal urban livelihood. I demonstrate not only how informality occupies a space where good institutions and productive economies are purportedly absent, but also where informality uses a proficiency in emergent formal institutions to elaborate new spaces of operation.

The so-called informal sector is a kind of umbrella for a multitude of "stories." After several decades of intense examination, the informal sector has been found to embody a wide variety of motivations, objectives, and trajectories. It involves heterogeneous activities, including, for example, street hawking, the petty production of products such as cooking utensils, and furniture repair. It also includes a broad group of services such as letter typing, transport, urban agriculture, and even the large-scale production and trade that falls outside of the conventional organization and regulation of firms. In addition, there are diverse sets of objectives at work. People may participate in informal sector activities because of ease of entry, labor market flexibility, survival, or simply because it is easier or cheaper to provide certain services informally.[1]

Structural adjustment, globalization, political change, and trade liberalization have come together to extend and intensify unconventional cross-border trade throughout the continent. Substantial amounts of capital and capacity are often deployed to find alternative ways and circuits to move raw materials and process consumables. This trade brings together a melange of characters, including well-off businesspersons, soldiers, militias, middlemen of various nationalities, and petty traders. Unconventional trade is at its greatest in states where chronic political crisis has undermined regulatory systems or where formal institutions function and retain some level of authority primarily through their participation in such unconventional trade.[2]

The informal sector has grown enormously since 1980. As recently as 1990 it absorbed at least half the workforce in many African cities, a figure that is thought to be substantially larger today.[3] In part, this growth reflects the precipitous decline of employment in the public sector and the relative underdevelopment of formalization in the private economy. For example, in Angola public service and state enterprise employment absorbed half of Luanda's working population;[4] while in Kenya, public sector employment increased steadily in the 1980s only to dramatically reverse itself early in the next decade.[5] The internal and external constraints on Africa's capacity to integrate itself into globalized production strategies and financial markets have effectively informalized much of the continent's overall urban economy.[6]

While many informal sector entrants value the relative independence and flexibility incumbent in this sector, increasing numbers of informal sector workers are actually engaged in highly dependent relationships with more formally organized economic operators. Some of these relationships can be consistently lucrative. This is the case primarily for entrepreneurs who have moved earnings from other activities, most often agricultural production, into investments in land, facilities, and machinery used to attain subcontracting orders from the formal sector.[7] Through such subcontracting or equipment leasing relationships, informal sector workers often are caught in highly exploitative relationships. Services are delivered or products produced at prices set by others as a means to access materials and markets otherwise unavailable. The expansion of the informal sector in many African cities has largely been in the area of such subcontracting relationships. For example, women doing piecework at home saves larger firms the costs of maintaining a formal labor force.[8]

The relationships to formality are also varied. Some enterprises simply are not aware of the frequently complex web of regulations applicable to even the most minimal of economic activities. Others try to maximize profit by deliberately avoiding regulations. In many African cities there are specific regulations for where business can be conducted, under what circumstances, and when and how, as well as rules for specific sectors of activity, from transportation to food sales. Regulations are often accompanied by specific financial requirements — for example, licensing fees, taxes, penalties, investments in proper facilities, and compliance standards. One study found that the revenue of microenterprises would be reduced by nearly half if all regulations were adhered to.[9] An informal sector is thus partially elaborated because of the excess and inappropriateness of regulations that persist in the absence of systematic and realistic ways of assessing domestic economies.

The dynamism of the informal sector is of course contingent on macroeconomic considerations. National policies regarding trade liberalization are particularly salient for African cities because they open the way for the supply of cheaper imports. However, these opportunities are constrained in countries that experience repeated devaluation of their national currencies. Policies aimed at attracting foreign direct investment affect interest and taxation rates available to the formal sector, either by providing or attenuating a particular competitive advantage to this sector.

Policies regarding land and infrastructure use, allocation of raw materials, access to markets and production facilities, and costs of capital also affect informal sector capacities. For the most part, these policies are usually tailored to the needs and advantages of formal enterprises. With the formal sector as the primary object of policy interventions, participation in the informal sector usually remains on the survivalist level despite the aspirations of participants. Opportunities and platforms for expanded investment or accelerated rates of return are limited. Without consistent sources of supply to meet increasing demand, or without the ability to reasonably predict how informal firms will operate in shifting policy and economic environments, there are few resources to invest in developing new facilities, product lines, or capacities.[10]

The informal sector is also a by-product of changing social dynamics. Even in societies that have been able to consistently provide primary, secondary, and tertiary education to a larger proportion of their population, there is little intergenerational job mobility. Educated youth struggle simply to maintain the occupational levels of their less educated parents.[11] Large measures of social equity have been attained in many countries in the area of education, but historical privileges and class status still largely dictate access to formal employment.[12] The informal sector thus acts as a repository for those with skills but without opportunity. At times, the skills possessed by certain individuals are not suited to the kinds of livelihoods traditionally possible within the informal sector, because educational systems still are primarily oriented to producing functionaries for public bureaucracies. These skills are then deployed in terms of finding various ways of providing a broad range of formal services informally.[13]

The Interaction of the Informal Economy and Social Identity

The informal sector is also a domain of particular articulations and reciprocity between social identity and economic activity. Economic activity is particularized and secured through the mobilization or reformation of specific social identities. At the same time, economic activities reproduce or change the status and development of specific identities. Such interactions between economic activity and identity take place at the level of households, communities, and ethnic and national collectives.

For example, small-scale entrepreneurial activities in Nairobi have largely been differentiated on the basis of gendered access to land. Women urban traders must generate savings through selling their own produce or that of women who have some form of access to agricultural production. In a survey conducted in Nairobi markets, only 2.5 percent of the 1,018 traders surveyed owned land, and 63.6 percent of them, including a large number of unmarried women, had no access to land.[14] Fragile marriages compound the problem because matrimony is a common method for accessing land. Still, retailing can in some contexts involve women in a "food-enriched" environment. In these environments women are better able to provide adequate nutrition to their children than if they were only involved in subsistence or commercial farming. As one study shows, women commercial farmers in western Cameroon have the tendency to simply sell off higher-value crops, while retaining lower-value ones for family use.[15]

The consolidation of female labor into a proletarian, low-wage sector in the formal economy is often blocked by the ability of male "heads" of non-farm households to keep women out of such labor.[16] Low-level informal sector activities can become a means through which women conduct household struggles to acquire an independent base of income that can be used as a basis to access wage labor.[17] Women escaping from rural coercion have often been detained or expelled from the city. Their few goods were frequently confiscated, and urban women were usually thought to be prostitutes.[18]

Resurgent trends in home work and sweatshops draw largely on female labor under highly exploitative conditions. Given increased competition in sectors where women have been able to access formal wage labor, many firms are subcontracting those aspects of the production process that have been organized around unskilled, factory-scale units. These subcontracting relationships usually fall outside of current regulatory frameworks and workers receive no benefits or protection.

While women may find themselves in the lower end of the informal sector, it is important not to underestimate the substantial economic capacity they have attained in most African cities. Without the varying initiatives and projects of women, cities would have been unable to weather the past twenty-five years of economic crisis. One study's documentation of female entrepreneurship in Dar es Salaam holds true for nearly all African cities, where the majority of women are involved in some form of self-employment or farming.[19] These entrepreneurial activities are heavily embedded in the multiple dimensions of everyday domestic life. In other words, they emanate from, respond to, and incorporate child and family care, fetching fuel and water, house building, health care, community and family celebrations, assisting with childbirth and funerals, and tending animals. Domestic, commercial, and social relations are intertwined, each becoming a resource for the other. In the process, intricate networks of collaboration are formed around various tradeoffs, the shared use of equipment, shared markets, side-by-side selling, and the bulk purchase of supplies. A form of "regulation" also emerges, as does an overarching but highly flexible social umbrella that ties together distinct households and social identities.

But something more daring might be in the works — that is, collaborations among women that attempt to take them further afield and thereby redefine the very notion of domestic life. In this case study of Pikine, the intersection between innovations in emerging formal local governance and women's informal economic activities help respatialize the opportunities available to specific groups of women by constructing a field of collaboration otherwise not possible.

Cooperation across Boundaries

The case of Pikine demonstrates how actions undertaken to facilitate the more effective and stable management of place also give rise to efforts to navigate the creation of new forms of livelihood that transverse local places. I want to examine here the particular by-products of one of Africa's most comprehensive and concerted efforts at developing new forms of participatory governance: the Projet de Ville in Pikine, Senegal. Here, efforts to bring formal governance to the people and to enable urban citizens to feel secure enough to become proficient entrepreneurs and forward looking in their individual and collective initiatives generated certain unanticipated, informal results.

In examining this case I am particularly interested in how such efforts at decentralization provide an unwitting platform for actors from different localities to work together in places away from "home." Specifically, I want to discuss how three groups of women from different quarters or districts come to informally collaborate with each other. Given the contestation over how and by whom livelihood can be legitimately produced, along with the intricate difficulties actors face in operating at translocal levels, such collaboration can be viewed as a significant accomplishment or, at least, an important precursor to new extended forms of economic collaboration.

Most of my discussion of this case centers on trying to cover some of the complexities of the particular city, Pikine, from which the women's collaboration surfaces. Without a basic grasp of the terrain of openings, blockages, and complicities, it is difficult to understand what local actors are up against in terms of "extending their reach." Many African quarters are experiencing heightened degrees of contestation about what is possible to do by whom, who can control what resources and spaces, and who has the authority to demarcate particular zones of influence, boundaries designating particular communities of obligation, and networks of information exchange and social cooperation.

Macrolevel interventions, such as the Projet de Ville, interact with these local dynamics to set up a shifting and often precarious terrain of constraints and possibilities that local actors must carefully navigate. In order to understand the complexities at work in the efforts that specific residents make in trying to operate at larger scales, it is necessary to talk about the interactions of major local political powers — that is, religious and municipal authorities, youth associations, and community groups. It is also important to understand the relative disarticulation that can exist in relations between quarters that are otherwise geographically contiguous and that often are subunits in an overall municipal structure.

On the Need for Coordination

The Pikine Projet de Ville, conducted under the auspices of the United Nations Local Agenda 21 Program, was launched in March 1998 to establish a concrete framework for the governance and development of this large, cosmopolitan suburb of Dakar. The city of Pikine, actually an extension of Dakar, was established in its present territorial configuration in 1996 as part of a sweeping reorganization of Senegalese municipalities. The suburb of nearly two million people stretches across the long, sandy peninsula that links Dakar with the rest of the country. It is a diverse mixture of hurriedly assembled, formal low-cost housing developments, self-constructed multistory apartment blocks and multifamily dwellings, small barracks built of wood planks and other found materials, and small cement-block one-to-two room houses. Hundreds of small stalls, markets, workshops, and garages are also crammed into the circuitous, narrow lanes that dominate the area where, because of the crowding, the physical terrain, and deficiencies in planning and regulation, the service provision for water, sanitation, and electricity is very patchy and poorly configured.

A cross-section of local administrators, leaders, and activists had been convinced for some time that in Dakar a drastic reorganization of municipal government was necessary, because the city was moving down a path that included both unregulated growth and at the same time deepening impoverishment.

Much of the impetus for the national legislation that divided the Greater Dakar area into forty-three municipalities was derived from the Fourth Urban Project of the World Bank and the pilot decentralization project, the Municipal Development Program, funded by French Development Cooperation, Germany's GTZ, and the World Bank. The change in the structure of municipal governance was to be a prerequisite to the eventual establishment of a Municipal Development Agency that would attempt to finance major infrastructure development and rehabilitation projects for the city.

The problem faced by the Senegalese government, which was cognizant both of the woeful ineffectiveness of current local government structures and of pressures from the international community, was how to affect the restructuring in ways that would not further erode the ruling party's already limited support base in Dakar. The way in which decentralization legislation was framed and implemented was a complicated story of political maneuvering. It basically focused on multiplying decentralization in Dakar in a way that would maximize local responsibility and limit local autonomy. Therefore, political dependence on the center would remain while the center could withdraw from the direct administration of many aspects of local life.

The present city of Pikine includes most of the former city of Pikine, in addition to several towns and villages of long historical standing that have undergone rapid population growth in recent years. The original town of

Pikine was established in 1952 when squatters were cleared out of the pericentral neighborhoods of Dakar. It has continued to mushroom under the combined effects of rapid demographic growth (over 3 percent annually) and rural exodus. Faced with the lack of local financial resources, it is becoming increasingly difficult to meet population needs in terms of access to essential urban services.

The city is divided into sixteen wards, each with their own major municipal administration. Mayors are part of an overall executive council at the level of the city of Pikine. Each ward elects representatives to sit in an overall city council, the number proportionate to the population size of the ward. Under the decentralization guidelines established by the state in 1996, each ward is responsible for maintaining the local public infrastructure that falls within its territorial jurisdiction, establishing collection points for solid waste to be retrieved by Pikine City, and regulating land transactions and local markets. The city of Pikine is also part of what is known as the department of Pikine, which also includes parts of the neighboring municipality of Guédiawaye. A prefecture presides over this department. The prefect is essentially a representative of the national presidency, and its powers include approval of the municipal budget.

The city has a young population, with 60 percent of its residents under the age of twenty-one. In the majority of the city's wards, at least 25 percent of the population is between the ages of zero and four. Population growth trends point to a prospective explosion of the urban population and amplify how ill prepared Dakar is to accommodate this growth. Given this social complexion, it is amazing that Pikine City does not have a single public secondary school within its current boundaries. This lack further taxes the energies and incomes of households whose adolescent members must often travel long distances to attend school. Primary schools average eighty pupils in each class. Schools have had to implement split morning and afternoon sessions in order to accommodate the student population.

In some areas of the city, up to 40 percent of children do not attend public schools because they are unable to pay even the minimal fees. They are thus forced into arrangements where child labor is exchanged for tutelage in a network of "informal" schools. Despite existing outside of state supervision, these schools provide an important context of instruction, if only in the rudimentary skills of literacy and mathematics. On the other hand, so-called private Franco-Arab academies accommodate large numbers of students from the wealthier households of the city. There is thus an increasing fragmentation of capacity and human resource development that is "tugging" at the social cohesion of many quarters, opening them up to both heightened insecurity and tensions over rights and access to resources.

Some appreciable actions for development have been taken. These usually involve partnerships between local associations and international donor projects. For the most part, development inputs are usually introduced without proper coordination and remain scattered effects when taken at the level of the municipality as a whole. Despite the efforts by local authorities, occasionally supported by nongovernmental and donor partners as well as the central state, Pikine confronts severe problems of sanitation, unemployment, and a substantial lack of infrastructure and basic services.

Dense population clusters in the older urbanized sections of the municipality have greatly overtaxed existing infrastructure, particularly the supply of water. Rapid population growth on the perimeter of the municipality is taking place in context where bulk infrastructure basically does not exist. Environmental degradation and health problems have ensued. The municipality also contains highly urbanized quarters and sections that largely remain rural villages. Given the need to better articulate the highly disparate complexion of the municipality's components, as well as its scattered development actions, the Projet de Ville was established to set up a strategic framework for consultation and action both at the city and ward level.

As a major cross-sector intervention in municipal restructuring and so-called planning from below, the Projet de Ville is worthy of extensive discussion. It is also important in that it has provided an opportunity to both occasion and witness those small "leaps" through which local actors in poor communities extend the spaces in which they operate. In doing so, they begin to exceed the parochial politics that limits their experience of urban citizenship and opportunity. My discussion here of the Projet de Ville focuses on what it tried to accomplish and how. More important, the project is also used as a backdrop to lend greater visibility to "small" processes through which the city — as a nexus of relationships larger than a collection of discrete quarters — is engaged and used as a resource.

In general terms the Projet de Ville sought to create an ongoing framework of dialogue and negotiation between municipal authorities and other local actors. It sought to strengthen the capacity of local stakeholders so that they could more effectively participate in the management of municipal affairs and design and implement priority action programs for the effective management and development of each ward as well as for Pikine City as a whole. Although officially an initiative of the municipal government of Pikine City, the Projet de Ville was largely carried out by a nongovernmental service organization, the Urban Popular Economy Program of Environmental Action Development in the Third World (ENDA ECOPOP), with whom a protocol agreement was signed. The bulk of the information discussed here is taken from the broad range of documents generated by ENDA's role as the lead agent for this project.

As an advisor to ENDA on this and related projects in the West Africa region, I have had substantial discussions with the various professionals and community participants in the project, and my observations here are based on these interactions. While the analysis has not been enriched by systematic community surveys or formal research, it is based on structured interviews with key participants in the program, including local authorities, members of community associations, and technical partners.

The design and implementation of the Projet de Ville included several types of activities. People's forums and local consulting sessions were conducted in each of the sixteen wards, a technical study and socioeconomic profile was prepared for each ward, and a series of training sessions for local councilors and activists also took place. The city of Pikine and its wards were in charge of the general management of the process. They were to ensure that each component of the project was implemented and that the various planned activities were relevant and coherent. As the project manager ENDA handled the technical coordination of activities planned within the framework. Each activity was to include the full participation of the associations within each ward, as well as any interested resident. These associations included those organized by neighborhood and by profession, as well as those for women and youth, in addition to local development associations and various cooperatives.

Within each ward, the key local stakeholders were identified. These stakeholders usually included members of local associations, craft guilds, trader associations, transport and portage syndicates, and women and youth groups. In the suburbs, young people are particularly active. They usually have lived in the city all of their lives, yet they are in general far removed from any active participation in formal institutions and economies of any kind. They tend to be shut out of local institutional arrangements and networks that either retain some kind of functional linkages to the home regions of their parents or grandparents or control informal economies in the city. Thus, their militancy is perceived to be their only potential resource. As substantially delinked and with few prospects, youth in Dakar have developed a significant history of taking matters into their own hands. Cultivating an indifference to censure and criticism is an important facet of this process.

As an organization ENDA coordinated information retrieval and established basic data sets for each ward, including the number and character of quarters within each ward, population size, public facilities, infrastructure, and basic economic activities. Participatory forums were organized in each ward to identify the main issues at stake in local development. Using this method of local analysis and consultation a Local Action Plan was established for each ward, after which a follow-up committee, chaired by each ward's mayor, was set up to advise municipal authorities on the concrete steps to be taken to meet the objectives of the action plan. Each committee had three commissions, which specialized in local governance, social development and communication, and sports and culture, respectively. The follow-up committees had no independent power to undertake projects but existed solely as a consultative and advisory group to the already-established municipal structures.

At the Pikine City level, specialized committees were established around five strategic issues: habitat and environment; economic and social development and poverty eradication; sociocultural and educational development; local governance; and communication, information, and social mobilization. These committees were charged with coming up with a series of recommendations that were to be incorporated into a City Strategic Development Plan. These commissions have only recently completed the first phase of their work. The sixteen wards largely remain disconnected from each other despite a process that has attempted to forge a heightened sense of articulation among them. In part, this sense of disconnection is attributable to the particular kinds and levels of contestation and conflicting agendas at work in most of the wards.

Pikine West is the most urbanized ward of the city, where barely an inch of space is available to do anything new. Shifting alliances between a technically competent municipality, a militant and highly organized youth group, and new informal groupings of youth entrepreneurs, whose escalating incomes derive from some form of relationship to migration and/or illegal economies of increased scale, fight over what to tear down and rebuild. They fight about whose commercial interests or houses are expendable and whose are not.

Mbaw, at the perimeter of the city, is a ward of highly diverse economic capacities and urban positions. The fight here is over how to use available land. Will it be used for agriculturally oriented local economic development or for "middle-class" housing? Or for the extension of the nearby industrial zone or the rejuvenation of the coastline fishing industry? The fight here is

Street scene in Pikine, a suburb of Dakar, Senegal.

also between the customary interests of Lebu households to whom the area originally belonged and the new urban residents with formal jobs in Dakar. The sense of disconnection also has to do with how residents of Dakar from different walks of life see themselves as already connected to each other. More important, it has to do with the extent to which degrees of connection have to be properly managed in order for persons to "connect" to the "right" positions for themselves, or the right state of being.

While decentralization has brought the reality of public regulation, authority, and responsibility closer to the day-to-day lives of urban residents, it has also amplified the lack of economic viability underpinning the conditions of residence. It also amplifies the arbitrary character of the city's administrative designation and boundaries, as well as the problems incumbent in any city-level systematic planning.

Finding One's Way

The capacity of local communities to engage larger scales of economic operations entails not just adhering to normative prescriptions of good governance and development. Such engagement also entails finding ways of readjusting long-standing orientations to urban life to new conditions and opportunities. Urban residents have their assumptions about what it takes to find their way, improve their lot, and get things done. Lacking suitable infrastructure, employment, and social institutions, households in Pikine must compensate for a highly tenuous link with urban modernity by finding ways to graft "customary" practices and institutions onto this precarious space. Yet, many urban dwellers will come to feel locked in by the frequently overbearing demands of these practices and institutions. The haphazard and disarticulated dimensions of urban life are then engaged to circumvent the constraints and expectations that often appear unsuited to the demands of adapting to city life.

The elaboration of strong Islamic Sufi traditions plays a major role in the Senegalese economy and national identity. This elaboration has been coupled with a long tradition of modern administration and formal democracy, which has provided more space for personal freedoms than is often the case elsewhere on the continent. Dakar also has strong links to the north through the city's status as a key node in the colonial administration of West Africa and, now, as a key site of regional and international meetings.

Despite its pervasive influence, Islamicization in Senegal was by no means an "overriding" of customary arrangements and practices. Islam penetrated the country from different trajectories. It arrived in the general east-to-west sweep characteristic of much of the rest of West Africa, but it also came from the Maghreb, especially with the influence of the Tidiane Sufi order. Religious expression was elaborated differently in urban and rural contexts. The use of these varying expressions to forge different relationships with colonial authority meant that Islam was imbricated in Senegalese society with different intensities.

At the same time, these varying intensities enabled a multiethnic and multireligious region to attain a substantial degree of implicit social consensus and integration. An agglomeration of highly diverse peoples appears as a fairly successful consolidation of national identity. The Senegalese seem to proficiently manifest the conventions of national and urban modernity. Peculiar histories and practices — on the part of the country's main ethnic groups, the Serer, Dyula, Toucouleur, and Wolof — find some strength or protection, if not common ground, in their mutual participation in Senegalese national identity.

The strength of this national identity allows at least the Senegalese elite and middle classes to also take on the trappings of urbanized modern life without necessarily feeling like they are losing something. Whatever their educational and economic background, the Senegalese frequently claim that a dynamic tension exists between two "incorporations": the incorporation of ethnic particularism within an overarching Senegalese identity and the incorporation of that Senegalese identity into urban modernity.

Yet, given such a consensus, the space for independent action can be sometimes perceived as limited. Here, the process of finding one's way through urban life and deliberating the steps to be taken in order to improve livelihood and community are not viewed as emanating from the individual's own imagination or assessments about what needs to be done. Rather, a social equilibrium has to be maintained, as signaled through an ongoing dependence on relations with customary authority. This authority is usually the *marabout*—a position that combines religious leader, sage, and merchant. But, according to popular Dakarois discourse, this social equilibrium is not in itself the means to make life better, but rather protects the opportunity for individuals to eventually improve their lot.

Maraboutic authority can be both a spiritual medium and, in many urban quarters, the actual local political authority. The continued importance of the marabout is not reflected by his embodiment of an intact and cherished set of values and norms. Rather, he is most often valued as a schemer and fixer with whom one consults in order to pursue a project of "self-realization." While the person might be accused or held responsible for consulting a marabout in order to do harm, the person does not "own" the harm. Rather, they are only following the instructions of the marabout, who, after all, is closer to the truth of things than anyone else (except other marabout).

While social solidarity is taken seriously in Dakar, it is not an end in itself. The social order and the strong sense of social homogeneity constructed over a diverse cultural landscape is not the object or locus of a state of well-being. In other words, a state of well-being is not found in this social order. Most Dakarois speak almost fatalistically about how they have to position themselves to be able to enact that future or project that has been "written" for them, as well as make sure that others don't wittingly or unwittingly get in their way. An intact social order is not seen as representing the coherence of the state of well-being that is sought. Rather, the social order must not be alienated or become an enemy, for it would be the most powerful enemy standing in the way of a person trying to attain that state of well-being. Instead, this social order is relied on to cushion the particularly chaotic implications of everyone pursuing individual "projects" whose "final shape" is not seen as contingent on the attitudes, behaviors, or well-being of others.

I refer to these popular assumptions here because a profound sense of both stasis and explosion ensues from them. Certainly in Pikine everyone, from mayors to grassroots activists, complains about how difficult it is to change anything. On the other hand, impulsive, short-lived ruptures also punctuate this stasis. These ruptures are usually expressed in moments of reactive violence. For example, *car rapides*, converted bakery trucks seating (squashing) twenty-four passengers, are the common mode of transportation in the city. Take the not uncommon occurrence of such a vehicle accidentally veering off into a street-side market stall, injuring a child. Seemingly out of nowhere, the driver is killed and the vehicle is burned, all within a matter of moments.

Ruptures can also come in the form of totally unexpected transactions or momentary alignments treated as a necessary bet. Such transactions are a way of creating social space when the stasis becomes overly claustrophobic or risky. In the discussion on Pikine, it is important to keep in mind how this stasis is produced, and how deep it runs in the ways in which many Dakarois think about what it is they must accomplish and how. For this stasis is a fundamental by-product of the pursuit of something totally unknown but recognizable; something totally attainable but perhaps never attained by anyone.

Planning a City: On Power, Quarters, and Development

As mentioned earlier, the Projet de Ville in Pikine involved a series of consultative and strategic planning activities at the level of each of the city's submunicipalities. These submunicipalities, with their presently estimated population size, include:

Dalifort Forail	14,000	Pikine North	58,439
Diammaguen Mbaw	53,475	Pikine West	52,254
Djiddah Tiaroye Kao	130,659	Sicap Mbaw	79,177
Ginaw-Rail North	54,000	Tiaroye Gare	87,650
Ginaw-Rail South	42,120	Tiaroye sur Mer	89,387
Keur Masseur	72,568	Tivauane Daicksao	37,498
Malika	8,137	Yeumbeul North	58,510
Mbaw	23,893	Yeumbeul South	62,050
Pikine East	63,787		

The method of demarcating submunicipalities varied widely. In some instances the demarcation boards took historical towns and villages as the focal points and included the areas that had been built up around them during the past decades. Often the precise dividing lines were based on political considerations. Circuitous lines were drawn so as to ensure that the coherence of distinct quarters in submunicipalities was fragmented. Alternately, efforts were made to ensure that each submunicipality had sufficient numbers of quarters having demonstrated loyalty to the former ruling Socialist Party (Partie Socialiste). At other times, specific quarters were left intact, particularly those with a strong ethnic complexion.

The role of ethnicity is an important consideration is assessing how urban politics works in Pikine. The territory on which Pikine rests historically belonged to a small ethnic group, the Lebu. The Lebu were the original inhabitants of the Cape Vert region that is now Greater Dakar. A large portion of the land in the eastern sections of the municipality — in Malika, Mbaw, Yeumbeul, and Tiaroye sur Mer, particularly — remains under Lebu customary authority. Much land, however, has been alienated from their control over the years.

Pikine as a whole largely reflects the presence of all Senegalese ethnic groups, the predominant of whom are the Wolof, Serer, Dyula, Mandingo, and Peul or Toucouleur. Individual quarters within submunicipalities may favor the predominance of one ethnic group. But this trend reflects the peculiar histories of how land became available to specific opportunities of settlement more than it does any general tendency for distinct ethnic groups to constitute themselves as specific social or political blocs.

Only two-fifths of the city supports regularized habitation with registered plots and formally reticulated infrastructure. This area basically includes the three submunicipalities of the original town of Pikine, and the newer cooperative housing developments for the middle class in Mbaw and Keur Masseur. Most of the rest of the city has been settled through informal tenure, construction, and reticulation of infrastructure and services. Thus, the peculiarities of specific social networks in terms of negotiating and accessing settlement opportunities has played a major role in the ongoing dynamics of how specific quarters operate. These negotiations have reconfirmed the power of customary Lebu authorities in some instances, while fragmenting and dissolving them in others. Opportunities were also opened up to foreign African entrepreneurs, particularly around the important railway center at Tiaroye Gare. These entrepreneurs play a major economic role in the city and make up a critical "floating" piece in an expanding game of political alliances.

While local councils for each submunicipality are elected and serve on the amalgamated Pikine city council, they are first and foremost political appointees. Voters select the party; the party selects the persons who will be councillors and mayors. In most cases, the mayors have no intrinsic connection to the municipalities over which they preside. For Senegal as a whole, over 60 percent of its municipalities have mayors who reside in the capital city. Thus, local authorities usually have exceedingly tentative relationships with local citizens. With the exception of the Pikine West, North, and East wards, very few residents in the remaining thirteen wards have any idea about who these local authorities are or even the fact that a public local authority exists. I had a discussion with a group of youth selling clothes in front of the city hall in Djiddah Tiaroye Kao who had no idea what the building was.

As mentioned above, the "real" authority in most parts of the city remains that of the marabout, or religious authority. The Senegalese context is particularly unique in that two Islamic brotherhoods, the Tidianes and the Mourides, have come to play a major role in the political, cultural, and economic life of the nation. Such a situation is certainly not unprecedented in Africa. However, the meteoric rise of the specifically Senegalese *tariqa* (brotherhood), the Mourides, as a religious and economic force has once again made the marabout a critical political figure in the everyday life of many urban quarters.

Both the Tidiane and Mouride orders rely on hierarchical forms of authority. Leadership roles are inherited and are the purview of specific "saintly" families. Elite Tidiane families have used this position to cultivate access to widely respected professional and political positions in Senegal. The Mourides, on the other hand, have focused on building a commercial empire. Mouride commercial interests extend across national boundaries and often rely on illegal measures and cheap labor. For many years, the Mouride holy city of Touba was essentially off limits to Senegalese law enforcement and customs officials. For years, residents and commercial enterprises paid no secular taxes.

The feature most associated with the Mouride order is its emphasis on hard work as the key to securing a place in paradise. As mentioned earlier, I indicated, in contrast, the limited value that is accorded hard work as a factor in attaining an earthly state of well-being. Nevertheless, the ideology of hard work as a guarantee of a fruitful life after death ensures that large measures of hard work, without the need for substantial remuneration, can take place and can be mobilized for various economic interests.

At the same time, Mourides do not account for the massive growth in economic capacity over the last decade in terms of this mobilization of diligent labor. Rather, the overall success of economic expansion is attributed to the fealty and spiritual power of the chief marabout, the *khalifa general*, and his relatives. Thus, the Mourides constitute a particularly effective mechanism for ensuring the exertion of labor but without having to hold it in account or without having to elevate it or consider it as the primary factor in economic success. For if it did so, then hard work could be appropriated not only by the Mouride economic machine but by any kind of collective effort that might operate for its own interests.

The power of this ideology operates with a specific practice at the neighborhood level. Whatever social cohesion persists within the quarter is usually viewed as the accomplishment of the marabout. Most youth do not believe that the authority of the marabout stems from some kind of special wisdom or morality. In fact, many youth speak disparagingly about the intellectual and moral capacities of these religious figures. Any respect accorded to them is, rather, based on their status as "fixers" — that is, on the fact that they can fix things. The marabout is capable of such fixing because he usually is part of an overarching network of political and economic connections that have great reach. Increasingly, the youth are concerned about these networks because many of them anticipate that they will eventually need to migrate elsewhere. Marabout are able to fix visas, place migrants in niche activities, and mobilize other kinds of support. In recent years, the purported involvement of some major marabout families in the international narcotics trade has only added to their mystique as "fixers."

Even at a local level, the authority of the marabout is reproduced through their ability to put together support networks. Take, for example, the context of a single mosque. A young man has been attending prayers and other activities for many years. He has completed his schooling, but like most men his age he remains unemployed with no prospect of a formal job. He approaches the marabout with a request for advice and support. If the marabout deems the young man sufficiently worthy, he will "suggest" to the other male members of the local *umma* (religious community) that they contribute some money to help the young man start a trade. Often the marabout will be in contact with marabout in other quarters faced with similar situations. They will often connect youth from different quarters in some small commercial venture; alternately, they will find some small position for the youth in the enterprise of someone in another quarter affiliated with another mosque.

This latter practice enables an individual marabout to demonstrate his capacity to reach beyond the confines of the quarter in order to bring about a specific turn of events. Just as important, it excuses the marabout from having to get too bogged down calculating which among his local constituents should be provided assistance using local resources. For the marabout certainly cannot ask the male members of the local religious community over which he presides to absorb all the surplus labor of youth that exists within the quarter. Within most quarters of Pikine, the economic capacity of male members of any given mosque is usually quite low.

If the marabout is to enter this game of trying to facilitate economic opportunities, he must ensure that on at least some occasions his "fixing" really works. He must ensure that when his efforts don't work, he at least made the relevant connections to other marabout with their own commercial networks, and that it was their responsibility that things didn't work out. In this way, the marabout avoids fostering conflict within the quarter about who gets to work and who doesn't.

In these quarters, most young people are, in the end, not working, although they have small opportunities now and then. They continue to believe that getting a job is a matter of securing a proper affiliation. So that even when things haven't worked in their previous consultations with the marabout, they are sufficiently convinced of his power to keep trying. The commercial interests of marabout have long depended on this conviction. Youth work for long hours as fare collectors on the private transport systems controlled by Mouride and Tidiane interests, as well as in their machine repair yards. Increasingly, the Mourides have taken over major commercial markets, and jobs are opened up for porters, hawkers, stall keepers, and cleaners. A portion of wages is always turned over to the marabout, and a portion of this portion is remitted to the khalifa general in Touba.

Youth are willing to work for almost nothing. They do this not only because there are few other opportunities but also because they are repeatedly told that they are working for the opportunity to be in line for some other opportunity. Most possible employment opportunities will end at low-skill, barely remunerative service jobs. Still, marabout are able to convincingly demonstrate, for the most part, that they are sufficiently powerful to make other opportunities happen as well. The critical factors necessary for accessing these opportunities are loyalty and devotion to the marabout, as well as a willingness to work for his interests.

Thus, this system of local politics and resource provision tends to center capacity and power in a few hands. Control over the quarter is exercised primarily by dominating the mechanisms through which individuals residing in the quarter can access opportunities and information beyond it. Limited public service provision and lack of development largely work in favor of the marabout's interests. For example, in one quarter of Yeumbeul South, the only local water tap was located in the yard of a marabout's house. When the activists within the quarter attempted to build the technical and financial partnerships necessary to expand the number of water taps in the quarter, the marabout put up vociferous opposition.

While the authority of the marabout still dominates the management of everyday affairs in most quarters of Pikine, it is certainly not the sole manifestation of associational life. Each submunicipality has multiple women's interest groups, usually falling under the larger umbrella of Les Groupements de Promotion Femínine. There are youth groups established by the state and run autonomously by local chapters, Les Associations Sportives and Culturelles Youth. Les Associations de Parents d'Elèves are associations of parents who supplement the resources available for primary education in local schools. Groupements d'Intérêt Economique are local development associations that are sanctioned vehicles for undertaking economic-oriented projects. Additionally, there are various local development associations, occupational groupings, and syndicates of transporters.

Each kind of association has historically been concerned with issues specific to the nature of their constituents or activities. Women's groups have primarily served as *tontines* — savings and microcredit associations. They have constituted an important nexus of local redistribution and resource sharing that has become well institutionalized over the years, even if they have shied away from overt involvement in political and development issues.

Today, in spite of sectoral concentration, more associations believe that they have a legitimate and necessary role to play in the development of local communities, regardless of their capacity. In part, this stems from their recognition that national and international donor institutions and service agencies require local partners to engage in development planning and project management. Thus, involvement in development activities is seen by local associations as a means to capture resources. Demonstrating an ability to access such resources enables the association to be seen as an invaluable resource to the community.

Localities have also witnessed how other quarters have become sites for various pilot projects — water provisioning, electrification, sanitation, waste collection, and new public facilities. Naturally, they seek out possible partners for improvements in their own quarters. In most instances, this "seeking out" is restricted to activities of self-promotion and publicity, because associations believe that if they make enough "noise" money will come.

In addition to the various formally constituted youth associations — either those attempting to advance a militant secularism or those closely affiliated with the religious *turuq* (the various Sufi brotherhoods) — is a thriving local hip hop culture. Pikine hosts perhaps the largest number of hip hop groups in Africa. In many ways, this local hip hop "social machine" is a turbulent one. It tries to piece together the aspirations of youth to be part of a larger world and serve as a means of connecting youth across Pikine's different quarters and wards. In part, teachers and activists use hip hop as a "hook" through which to conduct drug education and other social concerns, and it is thus an important way of drawing youth into the orbit of specific youth programs.

Hip hop is also a means of "moving through" Dakar, as particular venues, clubs, and cultural events become associated with the hip hop scene. Perhaps most important, hip hop offers a "content" to a particular way of mobilizing networks and affiliations among youth that is more than recreation or sport. Instead of drawing attention to how bad social conditions are or trying to organize communities to make things look better, hip hop is, in some ways, an already packaged, coherent universe of social performance that emphasizes both individual skill and creativity. At the same time, that skill and creativity is incorporated within a larger "community" capable of valorizing such expression.

Perhaps the most well-organized collective effort in the city concerns its various commercial markets. The large Zinc Market in Pikine North and Tiaroye Gare Market are the major commercial centers of the city. The Tiaroye Gare Market consists of some six thousand formal canteens. Entrepreneurs pay CFA120 per day for a single canteen (US\$1=CFA640), 150 for a double, 75 for a stall, and 60 to sell goods on foot within the formal market. An additional ten thousand traders of various sorts set up either informal stalls or work as ambulatory hawkers around the market by the rail tracks where trains linking Pikine and Dakar pass roughly thirteen times per day. The overall scene in the market can convey an impression of near chaos, but in reality a local market committee exerts strict control. Entrepreneurs of largely foreign origin dominate the committee, most of whom are from Mali, Niger, Mauritania, and, more recently, from Liberia, Ghana, and Nigeria. The francophone Africans have operated in this market since its inception.

These foreign entrepreneurs have historically controlled a large percentage of bulk supply to the market. They also play an important role in ensuring that fees are collected and that the market is kept clean. In order to mitigate the encroaching power of local Mouride interests, they have cultivated networks of children and youth who circulate the outskirts of the market with various goods for sale and to whom they offer protection. These entrepreneurs literally extend their commercial ventures into the surrounding areas, capturing potential customers as they travel by car rapide and train or simply as they move in or out of the market area. In doing so, they generate additional income that allows them to defuse occasional attempts by other entrepreneurial groupings to disrupt their control by withholding the payment of market fees. Inside and outside the major markets, foreign Africans — whose interests also extend to running bakeries, clothing shops and tailors, general stores in the quarters, and pharmacies — diligently pay all taxes and fees.

Because of this diligence, new local authorities depend on these commercial interests and offer whatever protection is within their authority to avail. Collecting taxes from businesses run by marabout is often difficult. If marabout were to pay taxes to the local government, it would signify their recognition of the local government as the preeminent authority in the community. There is great debate within Mouride circles over whether the state should be accorded this recognition. So far, this Mouride uncertainty, reflected in sporadic withholding of taxes owed to local municipalities, has strengthened the position of foreign African entrepreneurs.

In some areas, this alliance is being subjected to new strains. For example, it was announced in early 1998 that Camp Tiaroye, the historical military outpost that was the reception and command center for West African participation in the two world wars, will be closed. The closure will free up the only large tract of land that remains available in the center of the city. Already, various interests are organizing to influence the disposition of this land. Part of it will be designated for public use — new sports and cultural facilities. The remainder will be available for commercial development, and, as such, there is a concerted effort to keep foreign African entrepreneurs out.

An intensifying contestation over the control of commercial interests in particular areas is creating pockets of insecurity, particularly in the areas around Tiaroye Gare. The local authority has not been able to insert itself as an effective complement to market management in the area. The role of economic liberalization in expanding the sources and quality of imported goods is also intensifying the competition among merchants who can no longer rely on a stable set of customers or suppliers. The effect of efforts to launder larger sums of money derived from various illegal trades is also filtering down to the level of municipal markets as certain commercial interests are willing to take some losses by underpricing goods in order to cover up large amounts of disposable cash.

At the same time, entrepreneurs with a growing capacity to operate at larger scales face various blockages. The bulk of Pikine's economy centers on a vast range of informal enterprises. In Tiaroye, for example, these enterprises largely involve the repair of tires, clothing, machine parts, engines, and various equipment. Certainly, repair occurs more than does production. The more an object is repaired, the more likely it is to "break down" again, thus leading to more repairs. Repair activities are relied on to absorb at least a small proportion of the large numbers of youth who have no work and no prospects for it. It is from this large pool of youth that a new generation of *talibe* (loyal followers) must be created. If, for example, it were possible to establish a network of medium-size firms specializing in producing inputs for the private transport industry — engines, tires, machine parts — the vast majority of repair operations would be put out of business. In other words, the labor requirements for producing long-lasting inputs for transportation are significantly less than what presently exists for repair-centered activities.

This situation doesn't mean that the economic activities of the Mourides and Tidianes won't eventually include an increased emphasis on production. So far, however, their economic activities have almost exclusively centered on commercial activities. They block efforts that threaten their dominance over them; these "threats" come in the form of direct competition or in the development of enterprises that would produce locally the goods these religious networks dominate by controlling much of Senegal's import business.

An effort to wear down the power and role of the religious brotherhoods in governance and economic development has sometimes created a dynamic space of accommodation among interests that otherwise might not work together. Even this accommodation can operate against the objective of broadening participation and coordination in urban development processes.

For example, the Pikine West ward is the most highly urbanized submunicipality in the city. There the settlement patterns and the system of service provision is the most regularized, with the exception of the new housing estates in Mbaw. Pikine West has the highest concentration of formal economic and commercial activities and the strongest tax base. At the time of my research in 1998, the mayor, N'deye Ami Sow, was a woman with extensive training in economics and public administration, a unique situation among the submunicipalities. Pikine West is also the seat of the city's most militant and competent youth association, Association Wakhinane.

The Association Wakhinane was largely built around antidrug program work. Drug consumption among suburban youth has been a problem for some time. The need to raise money to buy drugs — from marijuana to various sedatives and amphetamines — has increased levels of crime in Pikine over the years. In attempting to develop a more holistic approach to solving the drug problem, the association has tried to address a wide range of developmental issues, and it has been particularly vocal in criticizing customary and marabout authority, most notably in the latter's lack of effort in trying to improve social and living conditions in the city.

The association has been especially adept at international networking. It has brought its issues and organization to the attention of various donor and multilateral institutions, and even solicited the visit of President Jacques Chirac of France, who officially opened up the association's new facilities. The association has been good at making Pikine's social dynamics visible, and then using this capacity to secure important relationships with international organizations. These organizations have proved willing not only to support the association but to provide important training opportunities for its members. Again, here is a source of power that derives largely from an ability to navigate external networks and relationships.

The relationship between the submunicipality of Pikine West and the Association Wakhinane has been a complex and varied one in the few years since the ward was established. For the association, the mayor and her technical staff brought a new set of competencies to the community, along with the public authority to ensure new levels of development planning and service provision. For the mayor and her staff, the association provided a critical voice willing to stand up to vested power interests, particularly the religious brotherhoods, which could interfere significantly in the development-based actions that the ward sees as necessary in order to solidify its position as the predominant player within Pikine city politics as a whole. On the other hand, the mayor also belonged to the "wrong" political party; a party that Association Wakhinane tended to view as the primary source of "evil." Interestingly enough, however, the dynamics between the municipality, Association Wakhinane, and various emerging community associations within Pikine have not changed appreciably since the opposition party, the Parti Démocratique Sénégalais, came to power in 2000, and whose stronghold was always Pikine.

The mayor tried to establish new local politics within the ward. She tried to make decentralization work by promoting greater local accountability. She also tried to link the ward more closely to national political dynamics that would then bring additional resources and opportunities. Other mayors had been given their positions based on their political affiliations and as reward for past loyalty. At the same time, they were expected not to be very active in terms of actually doing anything in their wards. In contrast, Pikine West has been very assertive in trying to secure a particular niche within an overall hierarchy of municipal positions and political maneuvering.

As such, the mayor went head-to-head with the association on various occasions. In the process, she accrued significant political capital simply in her willingness to stand up to an association seen as powerful, even if many don't necessarily agree with its views. At the same time, despite the party affiliation of the mayor and ward structures, the association believed that, unlike the situation that prevails in the other submunicipalities, there were real prospects for actually getting things done and that they had to affiliate with the municipal administration in some way.

This complicity, however, ends up downplaying the process that the Projet de Ville has attempted to open up. That is, it downplays a broad-based consultation and strategic planning process. This process is suppose to use the aspirations of many different associations to get involved in development activities and to assist the municipal structures in the overall governance of their communities. In part, the ward structures of Pikine West and the Association Wakhinane were wary of this opening up of municipal-level politics and local initiative, even though they publicly supported it. The capacities of these other associations were nowhere near as developed as either those of the mayor or the Association Wakhinane. Consequently, the broader involvement of a plurality of associations in governance issues potentially threatens to dilute or divert the process of consolidating a municipal power base sufficient enough to tackle the power of the marabout.

Both the ward administration and the association believed that this consultation process could hinder their efforts to ensure that Dakar pays special attention to Pikine West and that this attention translates into higher levels of investment. Such investment would enable them to hold off trends that threaten to marginalize the overcrowded and dilapidated Pikine West ward in terms of the overall politics of Pikine City. Neither the mayor nor the association wanted to get too bogged down negotiating major development maneuvers with the often narrowly drawn, parochial agendas of an increasing number of interest groups and quarter-based development committees. After all, investment and capacity was moving eastward to the newer developments of Mbaw and Keur Masseur where there is an influx of middle- and lower-middle-class residents. The activism of these residents threatens to dominate the future trajectories of development within Pikine City as a whole.

In fact, the greatest broad-based participation in the Projet de Ville's consultative community forums came from Mbaw and Keur Masseur. It came primarily from residents who had not lived in these wards for very long, and who worked in formal occupations in Dakar. Mbaw is perhaps the most disarticulated submunicipality in the city. It is the site of some fifty thousand parcels of land that will be developed over the next decade under a state-administered land production program (Zone d'Aménagement Concertée de Mbaw Gare).

The state is supposed to undertake development of all parcels before their release to private developers and cooperatives. Many of the plots, however, have already been dealt in highly questionable circumstances to developers before the requisite infrastructure has been supplied. In the process, the state relinquishes the ability to ensure effective land use planning, and feeds into an already intense dispute over the future of the ward.

The submunicipality of Mbaw abuts the last significant remaining undeveloped forest land on the Cape Vert. The ward also encompasses significant tracts of agriculture land used for chicken farming and market gardening. While supplying Pikine City with important seasonal fruits and vegetables, food production in the ward is undercapitalized and generates low yields. There are serious questions as to whether food production of significant scale really could or should take place in this area. The ward also abuts La Zone Franche Industrielle, conceived as a duty-free enterprise zone, with a large refinery, tanneries, a chemical plant, and several other small factories. The zone has not fulfilled even a fraction of its expected promise. There is also debate as to whether to make additional investments in order to attract more industry or to confine efforts to upgrading and extending the capacities of oil refinement. The industrial zone has also greatly depleted the local fishing industry, which increasingly is moving away from the coastal areas of Pikine to the Gambia.

Because of substantial questions concerning the industrial, agricultural, or coastal economies of this area, it is much easier to target it as a site for the construction of large-scale housing estates for residents with formal employment. One entire ward, Diammaguen Mbaw, exists primarily because of housing developments built by Senegal's largest developer, Société Immobiliére du Cap Vert (SICAP), and the large irregular settlements that have grown up around it. Similarly, in Keur Masseur, a large irregular community has grown around Cité Aïnoumady, a middle-class estate developed by cooperatives of workers employed by some of the largest Senegalese parastatals — for example, Sotrac, Sotiba, Séneléc, and MTOA.

While these smaller communities of relative wealth provide some economic capacity to the submunicipalities, they are essentially self-contained dormitory communities. The active involvement of Mbaw residents in the Projet de Ville indicates their growing willingness to become involved in wardwide and citywide issues. This participation, however, is focused primarily on securing the safety of their investments and ensuring a decent living environment. How this participation connects to the economic aspirations of the large majority of poor residents of these wards remains to be seen. The Projet de Ville in Mbaw has already broken down over a conflict between the mayor and the project follow-up committee. The dispute involved the mayor's approval of the extension of a private housing development on land that the committee had intended to use in order to expand a successful market gardening project.

Throughout the city, even widely acknowledged crises such as those that concern sanitation and flooding are subject to intricate political negotiations. Sonèes, the national public water concessionaire, has been largely unwilling to operate in the "irregular" settlements of the city. In these settlements, the built environment is so crowded that systematic waste collection is nearly impossible. For years, residents have simply buried both liquid and solid waste in the narrow lanes that run between buildings. This practice has severely reduced the absorptive capacity of the largely alkaline soil, resulting in a situation where stagnant water pools are permanent fixtures in many of the city's quarters. In the quarters that line the national road or that are situated between this road and the southern stretch of the peninsula, the small tributaries that have provided a natural run-off have largely been clogged with garbage, resulting in periodic flooding.

Within the terms of decentralization legislation, wards are responsible for collecting solid waste and for transferring it to a series of collection points accessible to the trucks that are managed by Pikine City. In Pikine North, households pay CFA1,000 per month to have their garbage collected by a horsedrawn *charette*. The charette then takes it to the collection points where bulk garbage is removed three times a week. In many other wards, there is simply no organized solid waste collection.

In Santhiaba, a quarter of Tiaroye sur Mer, an activist youth organization, GIE Goorgoorlu, pressed the local authorities to introduce a system of waste collection. The quarter is organized around a traditional Lebu village, and Lebu customary authority has reorganized itself in the form of traditional councils known as *frey*. These councils are a direct response to the heightened urbanization of the area, as well as to decentralized public administration. The frey concern themselves especially with the regulation of borders — in other words, what enters and leaves the area, whether it be investment, residents, bulk supplies, and even garbage. As the collection of solid waste within the quarter was eventually to be retrieved at a collection point at the border of the quarter, the frey insisted that its removal fell within its jurisdiction. As an exclusively male organization, it also questioned who, exactly, would handle this collection. In their eyes, the "handling" of such waste was primarily the responsibility of women. The women's groups within the quarter, working with a technical team from ENDA Tiers Monde, in turn insisted that they had to manage the administration of the project, including its finances, if they were going to work in it.

Such administration was considered a major political activity in the life of the community. Because it didn't simply affect women's interests per se, major negotiations were necessary in order for women to manage this service without it appearing to be a substantial advance in their political capacity. This was done by giving the frey the role of coordinating the terms of pick-up procedures at the collection points with the municipal authority of Tiaroye sur Mer.

In other situations, customary authorities have been kept at bay in such processes. In Tivauane Diacksao, the mayor, who can neither read nor write, was chosen on the basis of his close links to local marabout and his long service to the Socialist Party. He was a widely respected local figure, and the Socialist Party was concerned about the strength of the opposition, the Democratic Socialist Party, in the community. Acting against expectation, the mayor gave his full support to the Projet de Ville. In effect, he turned over nearly the entire management of the ward to the follow-up committee, acknowledging that he and his councilors lacked the capacity to deal with the critical problems faced by the ward.

This scenario contrasts with the situation in Yeumbeul South. There the mayor had attempted to dominate every facet of life and development within the ward, in part by trying to play off different associations against each other. He had neither supported the process of community mobilization and development nor entered the scene with specific proposals and practices of his own. Instead, the mayor used his position as a means of distorting the dynamic, yet contested and volatile, process of community restructuring underway. In this case municipal "authority" is being constituted almost by default, as the mayor plays on the convergence of opportunity and vulnerability that characterizes a community in transition.

The shortage of potable water in Yeumbeul South had been particularly acute, and sanitation problems had reached crisis proportions. A partnership composed of UNESCO's Managing Social Transformations Program (MOST), ENDA Tiers Monde, and several grassroots organizations Association des Jeunes de Yeumbeul pour la Promotion Sociale, Association des Jeunes pour l'Education et le Développement, Union des Frères de Yeumbeul, and Association pour le Bien Etre de la Population undertook to increase the supply of potable water in the two wards, as well as improve sanitation. The first phase of this effort, which began in 1996, provided five communal water taps and seventy-five ventilated pit latrines, as well as a system of solid waste collection via horse-drawn charette.

As these inputs were to be locally managed, a capacity building program was implemented to train local residents in maintaining the infrastructure, as well as in administering the financial aspects of the service delivery system. A community management committee and a technical committee for maintenance and repair were established. This initiative introduced needed infrastructure and improved waste collection and sanitation. Important local administrative structures were instituted in order to improve environmental management and the management of extralocal services and political relations. The project also amplified challenges that are widespread throughout Pikine, as well as in other cities.

As resources are limited, the initial phases of such a project are able to introduce only limited improvements in infrastructure capacity. If only a limited number of water taps can be provided, then an important question is where to locate them and who will have access to them. Certainly, an important consideration in locating such taps, depending on whether they are reticulated to natural wells or to the bulk supply system, is the ease of construction and costs entailed. Given the costs and technical complexities, certain locations are more viable than others in engineering terms. How do these locations correspond with the most viable "social" locations within a community? How does the process guarantee that the diverse interests and capacities of the community have access, not only to the resource but also to the possibilities of deliberating the disposition of that resource? These were considerations subject to intense debate in the Yeumbeul South project.

The associations of Yeumbeul South also reflected varying points of view, capacities, and interests. They range from the representatives of traditional authorities to more politically militant youth groups. How can often widely divergent orientations to everyday community life — with their own visions about well-being and the future — collaborate over important decisions such as the distribution of essential resources within the community? Associations are implicitly strengthened by virtue of their capacity to deliver needed services to the community. Therefore, the disposition of development products becomes a locus of competition among associations.

Resources such as water and electricity, and services such as waste collection and environment cleansing, cannot always be provided on a house-to-house basis. Accordingly, how are they most judiciously targeted in such a way that will promote efficient use and social cooperation? If grassroots management processes are the best means of ensuring a judicious public character to resource provision and use, what are the most appropriate structures to ensure efficient management?

Efforts were made in Yeumbeul South to ensure broad representation on these local management structures. Much time, however, was also wasted negotiating who was to be responsible for particular facets of the project. In management, decisions often have to be made quickly and decisively. Tariffs must be collected for the use of the resource in order for it to be maintained. Too many hands involved in the management process subjects it to excessive political considerations. Therefore, much effort was spent in Yeumbeul South trying to figure out what specific actors could do best. Potential lines of equivalence among discrete tasks were drawn. If, for example, representatives of the traditional Lebu authorities were not involved in managing the construction of latrines or financing the charette pick-up systems, then their roles as chairpersons of irregular meetings with the public water agency could be widely viewed as a task having equivalent importance or prestige.

Development inputs and their management change the character of a community. They change the nature of what residents have to consider in order to gain access to water or lighting. Successful access not only concerns appropriate social considerations but technical ones as well. These technical considerations require specific levels of education, and traditional authorities, many of whom cannot even read or write, frequently lack the education to understand many of them. They are frequently threatened when critical features of community life seem to pass from their competence and control. Those local actors with sufficient education can then use their more proficient understanding of technical matters to shape the community in ways that exceed the once relied on social norms and hierarchies.

At the same time that new modalities of resource and service provision can alter these social hierarchies, they also must be respected in order to prevent subterfuge. In addition, working through customary practices may be effective in convincing people to change their behaviors in ways better suited to the service provided. Improved service also means that people must pay for it, and consumers must therefore be persuaded that the benefits of improved service outweigh the sacrifices entailed in mobilizing scarce resources for maintaining it. In localities where improvements in living conditions tend to center around various locally initiated projects and the mobilization of local funds, a saturation point is frequently reached where the costs involved in attempting to sustain these initiatives are seen as too high.

At the same time, the more "modern" associations are concerned that it may take some time before the new patterns of social behavior and cooperation establish themselves. These new patterns of behavior are necessary in order to make the most beneficial use of new levels of service provision and access to resources. In the interim, the lingering power of customary authorities could be mobilized around these new development inputs to reiterate and entrench inequitable patterns of access and use. These inequities could be particularly unfavorable to the women and youth whose activism and role in environmental management has been most critical. In these circumstances, it is important to establish some mechanisms of financial autonomy.

In Yeumbeul South, an investment fund was started in order to generate income that would ensure an available pool of money to maintain these services. In order to establish such a fund, a series of income-generating opportunities was set in motion. These opportunities were particularly targeted at those whose economic circumstances would not in the foreseeable future permit even the most minimal financial contributions to service use. The poor need to access independent incomes in order to contribute to enhanced levels of service delivery and development in their communities. As a result, they also become less available to the patronage or manipulation of more powerful interests within the locality.

The role of ENDA, the service NGO helping to facilitate the development process, centered on maximizing points of contact and negotiation

54   *For the City Yet to Come*

among actively and/or potentially discordant interests within the community. Once these intersections are more thoroughly entrenched in the life of the community, the direct role played by such an NGO can diminish. During the first phase of the Yeumbeul South project, associations remained quite weak and vulnerable. This was the case even for those organizations that had been in existence for some time. Their willingness to deal with each other was also largely predicated on their sense that they had little choice but to deal with each other, given their relative isolation and lack of access to broader institutional networks. Associations have been strengthened through this development process, and increasingly become sites for conflict themselves. There are now more opportunities for individual groups to establish alliances with other institutions and associations outside the locality in order to consolidate their internal strength.

The peculiarities of how development dynamics are negotiated in each submunicipality, and how these peculiarities amplify the overall disarticulation of wards within the city, in part reflect the absence of strong leadership at the city level. Quite simply, Pikine's mayor had no sense of political obligation to the city. He was a party functionary who spent the bulk of his time trying to diffuse a growing bloc of opposition from several wards. While the Socialist Party controlled all but two of the ward-level administrations — Pikine North and Tiaroye sur Mer — the opposition Democratic Socialist Party swept all but one of the seats in Pikine in the 1998 parliamentary elections. The Socialist Party was despised in much of the city, which further detracted from the efforts of new local governments to acquire legitimacy.

There is also a major problem of local government finance. The annual budget for the largest submunicipality, Djiddah Tiaroye Kao, with its population of over 130,000, is roughly only US$150,000 per annum, of which only 32 percent is actually met. In all of the wards, only 20 percent to 40 percent of funds earmarked for their annual budgets is actually received. Each ward is supposed to be accorded a fixed amount of money from the national budget and a share of the overall municipal and national revenues based on population size and overall contribution to the budget. In addition, submunicipalities are to draw money from market fees and land taxes. However, in areas where markets are small, where traders rarely pay, where residents fulfill almost none of their financial obligations for service fees, where there is systematic evasion of taxes, and where fiscal transfers simply never arrive, budgetary shortfalls are enormous.

In many wards, the water and electricity in schools have long been suspended because of nonpayment. Many public facilities, including local clinics, are without supplies, and the staff, paid for by national ministries, is limited and unable to do much. Dense and narrow streets in many quarters are exceedingly dangerous after nightfall, and wards are unable to afford either the provision or maintenance of public lighting. In Pikine North, the lack of maintenance of the water supply network has resulted in massive damage to many pipes, leading local residents to advocate for the reestablishment of communal taps.

Given the shortage of finance, there is marked competition among wards to access external partnerships that might provide funding for development projects. The consultation processes initiated by the Projet de Ville lent great visibility to the needs of submunicipalities because they provided a framework for different sectors of the community to come together to identify critical needs, recommendations, and solutions.

As mentioned earlier, the ensuing follow-up committees and subcommissions have no authority to take independent action but are to defer to the leadership of the submunicipal structures—the local councillors and mayors. These structures barely function: without significant progress in the strategic and local economic development planning processes at the municipal level, it is difficult for ward follow-up committees to do much, although they do press haphazardly for any improvements that might be possible, for example, seeking donor money for a few additional water taps, for local waste collection, or for supplemental tutoring programs. In the eastern regions of the city, where critical decisions have to be made about where to place economic emphasis and investment, development actions largely proceed according to what donor programs are willing to fund.

Real local political power largely rests with those who participate in or engineer networks of relations that cut across wards, municipalities, and other larger boundaries. Yet for Pikine City as a whole there is little systematic mobilization of these capacities for generating some kind of overview, let alone systematic planning and a coordinated administration of development inputs. This does not mean that cross-cutting collaboration does not take place. It does, but it has to be managed in very delicate ways and through small actions.

For example, if a group of residents, youth, or women in a particular quarter want to start some kind of a project, they must always consider very carefully with whom they speak to about it or go to for advice. Any such initiative must take into consideration who the actors are who dominate access to outside political influence, to connections with NGOs, to local public authorities, or to traditional authorities. If such a group secures links to an outside Senegalese NGO, it has to think about what other links might be disrupted by virtue of such a partnership.

In sum, any such initiative has to make something happen without alienating people or stirring up blockages. The configuration of authority and politics inside quarters and wards usually means that any initiative is likely to stir up blockages from somewhere. Exactly what these blockages may be or where they come from cannot always be anticipated in advance, no matter how carefully preparations have been made.

Like an individual who consults a marabout, groups who attempt to initiate some project must often consult an outside force or institution. These outsiders must either have sufficient power, influence, know-how, or resources to mediate the intensified contestation over who has the right to do the activity that the initiative involves. If some kind of investment is going to be made in securing external collaboration, how does a group come to trust actors operating outside of the established mechanisms through which trust is usually accomplished within local contexts?

The local dynamics of development initiatives in the Santhiaba area of Pikine provide a useful example of the complexities to be negotiated. Activist youth in the quarter wanted to use the Projet de Ville to express their frustration. After all, they lived in a highly ghettoized section of the city with few amenities and opportunities. The local frey, wielding substantial influence, were very reluctant to give the youth any significant role in planning the future of the quarter. In response, the youth simply concentrated on cultivating their own constituency.

Elementary school pupils only have one-half day of tutelage, and thus increasingly are less well trained. A group of Santhiaba youth, under the auspices of GIE Goorgoorlu, began to systematically organize sports activities for children and then provide supplementary instruction during the early evening hours. Equipped with nothing but their own dedication, and an education not significantly more advanced than that of the children they worked with, the youth nevertheless created a context where they could mobilize the children of the community. This was done in a way not dissimilar to the practice employed by marabout to provide the Quranic training that almost all Senegalese Muslim children receive.

By the mid-1990s, women's groups in the quarter had come to implicitly support these efforts by the youth. In part, they did so because it meant that the frey would become preoccupied with countering the growing influence of this youth group and, as such, would pay less attention to what the women were doing. In the process of organizing sports events, one of the youth leaders managed to make an appeal on a local radio station for uniforms. This appeal was picked up by the local representative of a Brussels-based NGO, who agreed to provide uniforms and sports equipment. It was also heard by the daughter of the owner of a major transport company, who volunteered to ship uniforms and equipment for no charge. Demonstrating their capacity to cement external allies, the youth group approached several local marabout and convinced them that the Internet could be used as an effective tool of mystical power. The youth group used the subsequent support of the marabout to connect a computer to a local telecenter so that they could broaden their visibility through the use of the Internet.

At the same time, women, who are in actuality the economic lifeblood of the community, were expanding their fish drying and retailing activities under the umbrella of the Union des Opératrices de la Pêche Artisanale de la Grand Côte. Within this framework, women who bought, dried, and sold fish to various markets in Dakar sought to increase their bulk purchases, storage facilities, and retail outlets. What had been the more individualized commercial pursuits of local women became increasingly a corporate effort. This was a process that did not go unnoticed by men in the community. While not doing anything concrete to block the efforts of the youth, the women found ways to "give voice" to the importance of the frey. After all, the frey could embody and do the work of ensuring a sense of coherence in the community — something that the women wouldn't have to be bothered with. If their increased economic position were to overtly displace the male-dominated local authority structures, those structures might then attempt to intrude on their economic affairs and demand a closer accounting of women's resources.

Nevertheless, at key moments, women did publicly raise the issue that their increased economic power could in the future make it possible for them to assume a more direct political role in the management of community affairs. For now, they would continue to defer to male authority. In some way, the women were reluctant to take their chances in this political field. Also, they believed that real influence rested in expanding their commercial power. They circumvented direct confrontations through finding ways to indirectly support the youth groups willing to take on the frey.

By 1997 women began to recognize that a proportion of the increases in their incomes from fish retailing should be invested in other activities. If some small investments were made in activities outside the direct scrutiny of the local political structures, small opportunities might be provided to enlarge their autonomy within the local community. The question was where such investments might take place. This was not only about securing sufficient distance from the surveillance of local actors, but also the possibility of ensuring some minimal level of trust because the actual use of such investments would be largely outside of their hands. Through their connection to the Projet de Ville follow-up committee of Tiaroye sur Mer, a subgroup of Santhiaba women involved in the fishing union learned of the difficulties faced by a youth association in Mbaw in extending a pilot market gardening project. These women also were very active participants in Projet de Ville activities in Mbaw. Their urban agriculture project supplied various small markets across Dakar with onions, eggplants, and carrots. The youth association wanted to expand their activities but was being blocked by the local authorities that wanted to acquire more land for real estate development.

The young women came from families who had lived in Mbaw for a long time. Many were selling their land to middle-class families from Dakar and then living off the profits on smaller, more peripheral plots with provisional housing. At the same time, these families discouraged their youth from mixing with the new residents from the "big city," fearing they would compromise traditional values. But these local youth were already trying to find new forms of expression for them, primarily through the suburban (Pikine, Guédiawaye) obsession with hip hop styles. Many conflicts within families who were long-term residents of Mbaw centered on the feelings of youth that the older generation had sold out, not only their land but also their solidarity. Hip hop provided some new form of solidarity as well as a means of deflecting the recriminations to which the young women were subjected as the cause of family problems. Hip hop emphasized the need to be tough, depend on oneself, and do everything possible to show up men, who tended to dominate money and opportunity.

The older generation was losing the economic capacity to enforce their authority. As such, more of these youth, both men and women, began making their own decisions, feeling free to manage their own time, knowing that the appearance of household unity meant that their parents largely had to accept where they went and what they did. The youth's aspiration to find a "middle way" was expressed in a willingness to consider relationships — not necessarily with their new middle-class neighbors — but with youth from other quarters, at times neither Muslim nor speaking the same language.

One of the markets the youth of Mbaw supplied was in Grand Yoff, a large settlement southwest of Pikine. One group of customers at this market was composed of women from southeastern Senegal, who ran a small zone of *clandos*, nonlicensed restaurants that also usually sold locally brewed alcohol and mainly had clients from Casamance. These clandos were quite popular, especially because the prices for cooked food were very cheap, and the women had established a large outdoor cooking area. There had been, however, some controversy over the fact that they also cooked pork, and there was a general uproar in Dakar about this. Even though there was nothing illegal about cooking pork itself, the women were harassed for operating without licenses and they often had to pay off the police.

Working completely outside any established associations, women from Santhiaba started meeting with female youth working in the market gardening projects in Mbaw at the end of 1997. These relationships were largely driven by the frustration experienced by many women entrepreneurs in Santhiaba in their dealings with the male youth in their community. For even as these youth were fighting against the entrenched power of the frey, they frequently did so by trying to assume a more authentic moral and religious voice. Many felt that the only way they would be able to succeed was to act as "real" Muslims. In doing so, many women, both young and old, began to feel sidelined once again. The more secular voices of the Mbaw women, to which those from Santhiaba were exposed in various associations affiliated with the Projet de Ville became more appealing.

The two groups came to discuss the possibilities of selling prepared food in some of the new upper-income settlements, such as Sacre Cour III Annex and Keur Daniel, that were being developed along the major road linking the central city to the airport. The Mbaw group knew that the women running the clandos in Grand Yoff were in contact with other women from the border of Senegal and Guinea-Bissau who would work for very favorable wages. The frequent payoffs to the police were eating into the restaurateurs' profits. The youth from Mbaw were willing to discount the produce the southern Senegalese women used in their clandos in return for the women setting up informal cooking facilities within the new housing estates and providing low-cost labor that would prepare appropriate Islamic foods.

Women in Santhiaba would buy a proportion of the fish they retailed at cost and turn it over to the prepared food venture. They also volunteered some of their older daughters to supervise the operation. While youth from Mbaw and women from Santhiaba would take the bulk of the profits, the women running the clandos were assured a steady and discounted supply of produce and fish. Increased possibilities for obtaining prepared food were thus provided for the mushrooming housing estates that had few stores and commercial facilities.

In such a venture issues of trust about whether prices were really the lowest possible, about who handled money, and about who would take what profits can prove complex, especially when there are so many different actors involved and there are no written agreements. Certainly this venture had its share of growing pains, especially as the partners of Santhiaba felt compelled to keep their participation as invisible as possible. As the estates along the VDM road mushroomed in size, there were pressures on this partnership to increase the volume of their activities and to ward off potential competitors.

In part, this collaboration worked out its difficulties through identifying other, even more precarious, ways of extending their complementarity into new domains farther afield. The confluence of Guinea, Guinea-Bissau, and Senegal has been a particularly murky frontier, where national borders are criss-crossed constantly through a variety of informal and illegal trading circuits. The area is also a frontier of highly diverse population groups with different religious and economic orientations. Especially along the border of Senegal and Guinea-Bissau, the religious orientations of towns change quickly. The area has also been a highly dangerous and criminalized frontier of separatist groups, renegade soldiers, and trade mafias. Although women from Guinea-Bissau and Casamance have long navigated this frontier by moving various agricultural products, small coteries of urban women from Conakry and Dakar have started to enter this mix, trading everything ranging from small amounts of gold, electronics, marijuana, and dried fish.

Surrounded by young males doing everything possible to raise the money to emigrate out of Senegal, young women from suburban Dakar have also in recent years begun to take increased risks to find ways of improving their economic situations. While women traders from Dakar have been moving goods across permeable borders between Senegal and Gambia for years, these overtraded circuits force younger novices to take greater chances and move farther afield. Having had many conversations with the young women from Casamance and Bissau who served up the food in the VDM estates, several of the young women from Mbaw put together some of their savings and bought a variety of cosmetic products. These were sold on an exploratory trip in 1999 across some of the towns from which their young cooks had originated. Several excursions were completed along a circuit of towns that included Dakar, Banjul, Georgetown, Vélingara, Kolda, Farim, Mansôa, Bafatá, Gabú, Koundara, Kédougou, and Tambacounda.

These initial excursions were undertaken mostly out of curiosity, adventure, and the somewhat exaggerated tales circulating Dakar of money to be made. Some of the youth returned home as soon as they reached Gambia, others kept on going from town to town, observing what was going on, inquiring as to what local youth needed to buy, and sometimes being guided into small opportunities by their partners who came from these towns. Even though many of the borders were weakly controlled in the years before Senegal's intervention into the Guinea-Bissau conflict of the late 1990s, traders were often harassed and subject to shakedowns. Yet, the border patrols did not know what to make of these youth from Dakar, and often out of their own curiosity allowed them to move more easily than some of the older men who had worked the territory for a long time.

After a year, these small teams of young Muslim and Christian women, Balante, Mandika, Wolof, and Peul, were confident enough to buy and sell as they went along. This enabled quick purchases of dangerous goods — such as *yamba* (marijuana), gold, and gems — that could be exchanged quickly at various points along the border without risking long hauls back to Dakar. They learned to get away with exchanging identities, standing in for each other, and pretending to be from each other's ethnic and religious group. They were able to walk days in the bush, coax rides from important officials, outwit customs patrols, promote jealousies among criminal bands, and be the most devout followers of the religious leaders most popular in a particular locale at a given time. Although the women claimed that these treks to the frontier made them little money, they did indicate that the forays went a long way in cementing tight working relationships back in Dakar.

In this small way, groups from very different neighborhoods and situations made the leap outside of their narrow confines and found tentative and modest ways of collaborating together. I do not hold up this collaboration as some kind of major development; rather I cite it simply to demonstrate that in the interstices of complex urban politics, new trajectories of urban mobility and mobilization are taking place. Distinct groups and capacities are provisionally assembled into surprising, yet often dynamic, intersections outside of any formal opportunity the city presents for the interaction of diverse identities and situations.

2

The Invisible

Winterveld, South Africa

In the following discussion on Winterveld, a fringe urban area outside of Pretoria, South Africa, I take up the invisible as a political force within community life. A seemingly well-organized and well-known civic association is revealed to be a rather murky and highly mobile assemblage of interests and activities whose composition is always changing. The civic association acts as an invisible presence in a highly diverse community that has failed to use this diversity as a resource. It is a presence always reminding the community not only of what it missed becoming, but also what it must not become in light of all the development plans and projects that attempt to steer Winterveld in particular directions. In a community that largely must exist by masking the more insidious aspects of activities taking place in neighboring communities, this assemblage attempts to amplify the hidden resourcefulness in such an apparently marginal position. Even if residents cannot now take full advantage of such resourcefulness, it is reiterated as something intrinsically part of the lifeblood of the community, always on the hunt for new areas in which it can display itself and be used.

But I will start here not by addressing South Africa, but rather a place seemingly far removed — Benin. I do so because Benin is where I witnessed an event at around noon one day in November 1988; an event that seems to summarize quickly what I mean here by the invisible. On that day, a crowd emerged from the central market in Cotonou carrying a naked, dead body of a young woman. The woman, reputedly a witch, had died the night before in a violent thunderstorm. Mathieu Kerekou, then head of state, had recently tried to discourage the nation from its preoccupation with witchcraft. Yet, it was unclear whether this rather angry celebration of the witch's death was only about the witch herself.

As the marchers proceeded the police were put on alert. Just as the police were to break up the crowd, the marchers displayed pictures of President Kerekou. The police could not then attack the crowd or it would appear as if they were against the president. But the pictures of Kerekou were in a style reserved for those made for a funeral procession. As it turned out, the witch's initials were the same as the president's. The march proceeded and more people joined in, even some friends of the woman whose body was being defiled.

The real story may have been back at the market. Many sellers and customers alike had seemed spontaneously to be carried away by the proceedings. When the procession had left the market, several other young women remained behind, stripped themselves and ran through the market screaming, "Finally, we have become alive." Tables were overturned and there was a general uproar, lasting barely a minute, as the naked "witches" disappeared from the market. According to a rumor that spread wildly throughout the city during the next several days, US$75 million in small denominations left the market during this time. Where the money had come from in the first place and why; who it belonged to, how it was taken out, and where it eventually went were issues that were hotly debated in the course of the following weeks. During this time, the president was also forced to resign.

Of course, the market is a place where fortunes are won and lost. In the Yoruba pantheon of deities, Eshu is both trickster and god of the marketplace. The Yoruba say that Eshu can turn shit into treasure, but he just as often turns treasure into shit. Eshu turns life and death into themselves. The Yoruba are both terrorized and amused by the sheer extravagance of attempting to bring together things that don't belong. For with Eshu, what you see is not what you get; or what appears to be going on is not what is going on.

In most African cities, a complicated interrelationship between the visible and invisible sometimes seems to dominate the concerns of urban residents. In some ways it is very clear what is happening in the city — that is, people are doing whatever they can to survive. Because there are not a whole lot of different kinds of opportunities to do this, whatever people usually end up doing doesn't seem to be anything out of the ordinary. Moreover, because there are many unemployed people and those without something to consume the bulk of their time, it also appears that many residents simply wait. They wait for something to happen or are on the lookout for something to happen. They stay put — in front of their compounds, in front of the local stores, in front of the major intersections near their homes — to see what comes to the neighborhood and what comes to them. They see what new products or persons arrive and who visits whom. On the other hand, livelihoods are also made and opportunities accessed by virtue of always being on the "go" — for example, transporting goods or messages, going to offices and markets, or canvassing the city for the best prices or opportunities.

In combining these acts of waiting and moving, whatever takes place in the city, at a certain level, is highly visible and knowable. Seemingly little can occur without someone knowing about it; secrets are few and far between. This heightened sense of visibility has helped regimes control the city, even when they have little legitimacy and few concrete tools of repression. If spaces and opportunities for acting outside intense scrutiny are to be created, the act of making things visible itself must be manipulated. If you don't want people to know about something or to wonder about whether or not something is taking place, that something must, in many instances, be performed right under their noses.

Because life is hard, the city has become a place where there is a tendency for kin, friends, neighbors, and other associates to find ways of "joining in" whenever a person accesses some kind of opportunity. This possibility of joining in plays a big role in enabling people to make it in the city, but it also can make it difficult for individuals to consolidate those opportunities and use them as a basis for independent action. They end up being overly encumbered with too many responsibilities and links to the activities and situations of others. In cities, people must often "try on things for size." They must experiment with different ways of being and doing things. These efforts are often best done outside the scrutiny of a large number of other people, because individuals shouldn't be made to feel overly self-conscious about their "try-outs." At a different level, resources of some volume and or value must be shifted around, redeployed, and applied to various objectives without it being too well known exactly what is going on. Things must be said, money must be generated, resistance must be expressed, and antagonists must talk to each other. All of these aspects often rely on large amounts of invisibility to do something effective and useful.

Therefore, the politics of what is visible and invisible is an important one in African cities. This politics does not simply concern identifying the forces and people responsible for the specific reality that any given individual, household, or group might face. It is also about how the city is used to generate resources, desires, and opportunities. At times, households, associations, and governments must be made to look as if all is well even when it is not. At different times it is also useful to make it appear as if things are not all right even when they may be, for successfully managing impressions can avail one of opportunities or excuse one from certain obligations.

At times this manipulation of visibility has been problematic. In Abidjan, Côte d'Ivoire, for example, large numbers of young people have died of HIV-related diseases. Most have silently disappeared. Until recently, quarters in Abidjan have acted as if nothing is going on. It is a community with an extensive history of people coming in to stay and people leaving to go elsewhere, and death is simply imbricated into this already accelerated and extensive ebb and flow. There are so many residents who are "away," that the state of being "away" can seem to encompass and deal with a broad range of issues — even if HIV is consuming the insides of many quarters.

On the other hand, the visibility of the naked in Cotonou introduces a disturbing turn of events that "takes over" talk in the city for several weeks. Clearly, most residents have their own ways of articulating money, sorcery, political power, and commerce. In most residents' minds, these dimensions are clearly linked, and they behave accordingly. This highly visible event, however, disrupts quick and easy explanations. New, albeit precarious, horizons of action are opened. While certain measures of caution are reinforced, people also recognize that a trick has been played on their fears and their ways of handling them. For their caution has allowed a strange, daring feat to occur. Something very visible happened. Within it or behind it, something invisible is being rearranged. Something new is brought to life, even though those usually responsible for conjuring (i.e., the witch) is dead.

What I aim to show in the discussion about Winterveld is not that invisibility, as a practice or modality of urban operations, reflects some intrinsic cultural predilection or capacity. Rather, invisibility can act as a political construction — that is, a means of both configuring and managing particular resources and the medium through which specific instantiations of the political are deployed.

It must be remembered that the many years of colonialism did not simply attempt to turn Africans into good individuals. It also heightened the visibility and crystallization of their "traditional" selves and social formations so that they could be the objective and concretized targets of remaking.[1] A key method of constructing such visibility was the resistance registered to the remaking itself, that is, the various ways in which bodies and groups refused to cooperate or assimilate with one or more aspects of the colonial enterprise. Colonial cities did operate as arenas for the consolidation of a wide range of local practices, initiatives, and identities. But for the most part they did so only under conditions in which this consolidation was to be inextricably linked to its dissolution and remaking.[2] To refuse the consolidation of endogenous capacities meant that in many ways they could not be drawn on or referred to as self-conscious incentives to pursue specific collective aims in face of European power. To unreservedly submit to the remaking process meant that there was no basis on which to get power to at least make gestures toward "showing its cards." This is why the urban practices I refer to here attempt to do two very different but related things at once: on the one hand, politics becomes a matter of constituting a generic identity without privilege and without any specific terms other than itself. It is thus one capable of putting together distinct actors and spaces into a collective collaboration, but one that maintains their distinction. On the other hand, such tactics aim to make the specificity of identity just that: untranslatable, nonexchangeable, highly local, and unable to be "hooked up" or "phased in" to a larger agenda of comparisons and normalization.

Winterveld as Place

Winterveld is a fringe urban area located some 40 kilometers northwest of Pretoria. While replete with singular characteristics, the community's fringe urban status provides it with features that are familiar elsewhere. These characteristics include oscillating tensions among urban and rural identifications; competition for land and jobs between agricultural and nonagricultural uses; and a large pool of low-cost labor available for agricultural production (but that in reality is not readily available given that most residents are trying to enter the world of urban work and thus prefer to do agricultural work only on a short-term or ad hoc bases). They also include the progressive incorporation of the area within an urban orbit — regardless of levels of inflow and outflow — if for no other reason than the nature of the aspirations of residents to become increasingly urbanized; and the marked social conflict over the nature of development inputs. At the time of this writing the population estimates for the area ranged from 170,000 to 240,000 people. There is uncertainty about more precise numbers because substantial demographic shifts take place within the municipality.[3]

For the most part, Winterveld is an area in decline. The social diversity, the conflation of urban dynamism with rural values, and the collective ingenuity to make things happen — which characterized the community for much of its history — are largely gone. The highly murky character of recent local politics has lessened popular interest in civic matters, and one is hard pressed to identify what could be done to restore the vitality once held by the community.

Winterveld is a sprawling community spread over 120 square kilometers running some 20 kilometers north to south, and varying from 3 to 8 kilometers east to west. With a few marked exceptions where population density is quite high, most of the locality consists of large plots each containing several households built off of the main arteries along overgrown dirt roads largely hidden from anyone's view. Large parts of the community retain a rural feel, although as a whole it is tied into an urban economy. Objective measures of poverty may make Winterveld no more poor than many other South African rural communities, yet the fact that it is so linked to the urban economies of Greater Pretoria escalates the costs of living, diminishes the viability and value of practicing a more rural-oriented livelihood, and thus increases the experiential intensity of poverty.

The impoverishment is compounded by the community's history. Abundant signs of pride remain, reflected in the care that households have taken in the construction and maintenance of many shelters and compounds. This is especially the case in the areas that constitute some interface between the densely populated zones of Beirut, Vilakazi, Pinkies, Makgatoh and the heavily rural areas of Vuma and Vuka farther north. In this interface livelihoods and dwellings convey a resourcefulness inherent in having one foot in the rural and another in the urban.

Interestingly, it is in these interface areas, occupied by a large percentage of the landowners residing in Winterveld, where resistance to change is most adamant. This is in part because of a strong conviction and commitment to a particular way of life. These areas are close to an array of urban amenities and opportunities, yet distant enough to have "room to breathe" and avoid the social complications and tensions that come from dense quarters. An immanent sense of loss becomes the driving motivation to undermine any appropriation of this interface as an important linkage between the distinct worlds making up the larger community.

Winterveld is situated within a large urban conglomeration of four contiguous municipalities. The administrative divides between municipalities stem from a combination of singular histories, artificial legislative boundaries, and a burgeoning emphasis on local democracy. In this setting, diversities in social composition, activity, and relationship to outside worlds constitute an important resource of survival and social coherence. Yet, these same diversities have become threats to the consolidation of effective local political power. Attempts to put together common developmental and political objectives have frequently resulted in violent conflict between different community groups and power interests.

Winterveld assumes great symbolic importance in the South African imagination. It was the district that then President Thabo Mbeki chose to represent when each parliamentarian became obligated to take responsibility for a particular South African community. It is symbolically important because it embodied a particular extreme of apartheid and yet was one of the few places in South Africa where blacks could continue to own land under apartheid. The singularity of Winterveld rests in its historic availability to a wide range of diverse peoples who came to own land there and availed that land to the tenancy of an even more diverse group of people. Because of this diversity, the community was eventually relegated to systematic underdevelopment and a structurally tenuous juridical and political status.

Winterveld's peculiar history is a double-edge sword. Being an important symbol of apartheid injustice opens up possibilities for action and access to resources. Such attention also implicitly imposes a series of pressures, motivations, stakes, solutions, and frameworks for seeing and interpreting the community. These pressures often constrain the parameters for local action, introduce untenable levels of contestation, and over-politicize developmental processes. While Winterveld is presently far from being paralyzed by these vulnerabilities, they are nevertheless at work in various ways, and a rough exposition of such manifestations forms an important part of my discussion here.

A politics of "contested visibility" is quite marked in Winterveld: in other words, what can be shown or seen; what is considered relevant to the community's development and what is not; what can be said about what is going on; who can speak for whom; what are "real" social dynamics or momentary figments of the imaginations of specific actors trying to protect themselves. All elements are subject to intricate political maneuvering, which ends up multiplying differences between segments of the community where none may have really existed. Certain stakeholders are marginalized for the sake of apparent community cohesiveness. People may be homogenized into common groupings where substantial differences may exist in their interests and actions.

Competing representations—the by-products of an intense politics of what can be legitimately made visible or what cannot—are an integral aspect of Winterveld. They not only serve as attempts to negotiate a complex series of internal political and social dynamics, but also are the means through which such negotiations are linked to how Winterveld's position as a national symbol can be used.

History as Twilight Zone

Winterveld originated with the demarcation of 1,658 plots of between four to 12 morgen (a five-morgen plot equals an area of 310 by 600 square meters) sold to individual black purchasers over a twenty-year period, beginning with the Released Areas clause of the 1936 Land Act. Two major farms, Klippan and Winterveld, were subdivided for this purpose, encompassing an area of some 10,386 hectares.[4] Most of the fertile land was in the western section of Winterveld, which was marketed in the largest parcels during the early 1940s. By the 1950s smaller plots were parceled, usually on soil more tenuous to consistent yields.[5]

The area was parceled according to three distinct zones with plots of varying size: what were known as ten morgen areas in the north, such as Vuma and Vuka; five morgen areas in the middle belt, such as Kromkuil, Vilakulu, and Marivati; and the smaller plots in the Klippan areas that eventually were designated Klippan North and Klippan South. The increasing population was initially absorbed by the Klippan areas, which remain the most densely populated with an average of fifty-two persons per hectare.[6] By 1981, the ratio of plot owners to tenants averaged 1 to 1,237, with 1 to 6,166 in Klippan South and 1 to 163 in ten morgen.[7] During the early 1980s population growth in the northern ten morgen area was increasing by 11.2 percent per annum, while Klippan South was stabilizing at 0.9 percent.[8]

The initial landowners were looking for secure investments in physical assets. They included a highly diverse grouping of ethnic identities, social positions, and motivations. Southern African migrants who had worked the mines sought some haven for their earnings and an instrument of security in South Africa. There were also stakeholders in freehold areas; traders and shop owners in urban areas all acquired multiple plots on the larger offerings. In addition, there were civil servants, petty producers, and small traders, and thus, a mix of subsistence production and semicapitalist farming ensued.

Although the community was set in a region where Tswana people were historically in the majority, 84.5 percent of the initial 1,142 plot owners were from non-Tswana ethnic groupings.[9] By 1989, roughly 70 percent of the population had lived in Winterveld for longer than ten years; 33 percent for longer than 20 years, and in the most dense area of Klippan, 60 percent had been in residence for longer than twelve years. Perhaps most important, 78 percent of the landowners had owned their land for more than twenty years.[10]

The urbanization of the area commenced in the early 1960s when black residents were displaced from urban and periurban areas in the immediate vicinity of Greater Pretoria and shifted to Ga-Rankuwa (established in 1961) and Mabopane. Mabopane is an area contiguous to the southern borders of Winterveld and where building was initiated in 1969 to absorb displaced black residents.[11] The initial intention was to anchor Winterveld as a key nexus in what was to be known as the Odi-Moretele metropolitan area.[12] The spatial configuration of Winterveld, Ga-Rankuwa, Mabopane, and Temba, in fact, is increasingly identified as the salient parameters for the eventual construction of a single urban municipality. In 1977, this area was to become officially part of the "independent" Republic of Bophuthatswana.

In the early 1980s, the Bophuthatswana government constructed a fully serviced township within the far southwest region of Winterveld, known as Beirut. Several years later, the private development of Lebanon was added farther to the south. This area consists primarily of Tswana-speaking households and has been considered the "urban" area of Winterveld, especially in light of the recently developed housing project known as Slovoville, which runs contiguous to the Beirut section. This project has provided roughly two thousand additional units of housing. Lebanon and Beirut consolidated a more "middle-income" grouping within Winterveld, and their interests have largely dominated local politics within recent years.

The shift of Winterveld to the administrative ambit of Bophuthatswana was a major turning point in the life of the community. As an area of ethnically diverse black landowners renting to an equally mixed population, Winterveld posed potential problems of political control. The South African government was eager to shift juridical responsibility to the Bophuthatswana government, but the latter was equally reluctant to include Winterveld within its territories because the majority of both tenants and landowners were not Tswana. The negotiations around the terms of its incorporation into the newly formed Bophuthatswana state were framed within a series of larger geopolitical considerations. These basically forced the administrative shift of the settlement to the Bantustan government. The South African government agreed to transfer some R200 million for the purported objective of developing the community (at the time, US$1 = approximately R2).[13]

In terms of the 1977 Bophuthatswana independence agreement, the negotiation of a commitment to develop Winterveld and its formalization as a discrete municipality were to precede any and all rationalization of citizenship status on the part of its residents within the Bophuthatswana state. Registration with Bophuthatswana was required, usually in terms of application for temporary residence permits. The implicit agreement, however, was that people could continue to live in Winterveld for an unspecified interim period without having to adopt Bophuthatswana citizenship. Residents, however, had to decide whether they would apply for Bophuthatswana citizenship or permanent residence within five years.[14] Additionally, the South African government resettled those residents who did not wish to stay in Bophuthatswana. This resettlement took place mostly "next door" in the township development of Soshanguve, which was to remain in South African territory.[15]

In terms of the independence agreement, landowners had the option of developing plots on an agricultural basis; selling their land on the open market, exclusively to Tswanas; seeking reimbursement from the Republic of South Africa for agricultural holdings, which would then be transferred to the Bophuthatswana government; or exchanging their current plot holdings for those deemed within the orbit of a newly established urban development zone. The latter option was often accompanied by offers to plot owners to participate in urban upgrading and serviced plot schemes in Mabopane. Non-Tswana tenants were encouraged to participate in rental or home-owning schemes in the Mabopane extension or, alternatively, participate in Bophuthatswana government-sponsored upgrading schemes on rezoned land.[16]

These prescribed land and tenancy scenarios were not, for the most part, enforced. An important exception was that only Tswana could acquire land from this point onward. Despite other ambiguities and loopholes, residents were insecure and reluctant to invest resources and energy in land improvement and development products. In 1978, eviction orders were served on groups of non-Tswanas for squatting or for not having proper permits. Thirty thousand people were moved to another homeland, Kwa-Ndebele.

In response, the Winterveld Action Committee (WAC) was formed, made up primarily of local church and community activists and falling under the umbrella of the Pretoria Council of Churches. For the next fifteen years, WAC constituted the most important institutionalized site of resistance to the impositions of the Bophuthatswana government. It also provided a small complement of development services.[17]

An Inter-Government Management Committee was established in October 1979 to coordinate the implementation of what was to be referred to as the "umbrella agreement." This agreement was to govern the dispersal of development finance; the provision of feasible alternatives to individual preferences and requirements as to the final destination of residents; land disposition; stabilization and legalization of tenancy; and standards for the delivery and servicing of infrastructure. The agreement also was suppose to come up with a strategy for regional development. Ten surveys and research projects were undertaken to formalize upgrading and development strategies. A Winterveld Development Foundation was to be established in order to manage, control, and coordinate the overall planning and execution of development and improvement of the area.

The umbrella agreement, however, was never formally ratified.[18] The absence of ratification further institutionalized a climate of ambiguity for Winterveld landowners and tenants. Residents were able to maintain some semblance of a status quo but were also subjected to various forms of harassment. For example, eighteen state-aided community schools were established in the area but with Tswana as the exclusive language of instruction. The majority of students eventually were forced to attend schools in Soshanguve or in locally initiated independent schools. The operation of these schools became a major source of income for some landowners.

Despite the fact that Bophuthatswana President Lucas Mangope had indicated that "illegal" residents would no longer be allowed in Winterveld, the so-called illegal population continued to grow. Some landowners implicitly encouraged this growth as a "hedge" against the government-sponsored manipulation that sought to direct population flows of Tswanas into the area.[19] Because the umbrella agreement was never formally ratified, other piece-meal agreements provided a five-year development allocation for Winterveld, the creation of a local authority, and definitions for who could formally consider themselves a Winterveld resident. By 1987, approximately R122 million of the development allocation had been spent. Approximately R47 million was spent in the construction of 548 houses in the Mabopane West housing scheme, 1,800 serviced sites on the Nooitge-dacht Farm immediately west of Winterveld, and additional self-built struc-tures on 800 stands, including residential infrastructure for roughly 2,100 stands.

Although the development was officially intended to relieve overcrowd-ing in the Klippan area — particularly the sections known as Vilakazi and Makgatoh — most of these residents could not afford the prevailing rents. In addition, all "temporary residents" were not eligible to own property.[20] By 1987, six additional school facilities were built to add to the eighteen existing community schools. The bulk of expenditure was concentrated in a limited geographical area and had the concrete result of institutionalizing a divide between a hastily assembled "urban" section of Winterveld and a more "rural" section. In actuality, this was a spurious dichotomy because the density levels of parts of Klippan South are some of the highest in South Africa.[21]

According to official explanations, housing was concentrated in the nearby Mabopane areas because the sunk costs were already largely pro-vided. It also clearly was the intent of the Mangope government to "com-promise" the special characteristics of the Winterveld area through a pro-cess of concentrated "colonization." By targeting new residential oppor-tunities and development products to the southwest region of the commu-nity, which was closest to Mabopane, links with Mabopane would be in-tensified. A more mobile economic sector of residents would be cultivated whose interests would be closer to the surrounding urban township struc-tures than to the social realities prevalent throughout most of Winterveld.

Average household income for Winterveld in 1989 was R594 per month. In Beirut, 50 percent of households earned over R800 per month, while in Klippan only 19 percent managed to achieve such earnings. In Beirut, households spent 14 percent of their disposable income on housing costs, while in the rest of Winterveld the figure averaged 1.8 percent.[22] Such a control strategy of favoring urban values may have been limited due to the fact that many of the most militant African National Congress activists came from the Beirut and Lebanon areas. Yet, residual elements of this approach continue to operate as these areas remain a center of political and economic activity.

The Development Bank of Southern Africa assumed responsibility for the development facets of the original independence pact as defined in the Winterveld Development Program of 1984. Concrete movement on this development program only got underway in 1987. The contents included a ten-point program targeting rural development, the building of social institutions, education, physical infrastructure, health care, small business development, financial support systems, housing, local management, and institutional development and urban planning.

These funds were tied in highly insidious ways to a complex web of complicity between the Bophuthatswana and South African governments. The Development Bank of Southern Africa managed funds originally allocated by the Department of Foreign Affairs. As a result, most residents suspected that the development framework also masked military and intelligence activities. The Winterveld Development Authority (wDA), charged with implementing the ten-point program, only got off the ground in 1993. At this point, roughly 70 percent of the original development allocation had been spent, with approximately R45 million still remaining.

The wDA, however, also became a vehicle for an increasingly bitter fight over who would eventually constitute the democratic local authority. After the establishment of new provincial governments, the official role of the Department Bank of Southern Africa fell away. The community was effectively divided in two, with the northern part administered by the wDA and Klippan by the Department of Local Government and Housing. This arrangement lasted until local government elections in 1995. At present, the Northwest Housing Corporation holds the remaining development funds in trust for the Department of Local Government and Housing. Given that this agency has been under investigation for widespread fraud, it is quite likely that no money is left.

Social Economies

There have been few systematic assessments of socioeconomic dynamics in Winterveld. The most recent survey conducted several years ago under the auspices of the African Medical and Research Foundation in large part reconfirms the major study undertaken by the Bophuthatswana government in 1989.[23] A major conclusion of the latter study points to the significant depopulation trends underway. Households that were in an economic position to move were doing so. This left a more impoverished population base in most of the community.

In a focused interview survey in 1997 roughly 40 percent of the respondents disliked the area and felt that their house was poorly located. Most respondents who wanted to move preferred relocating to a nearby urban area, in part because Winterveld is one of the most poorly serviced "displaced" urban areas. Within the survey, only one-fourth of the respondents had access to on-site water and only 2 percent to water-borne sewage. In fact, anecdotal information indicates that most of the Winterveld residents able to leave have chosen Soshanguve, Mabopane, and other areas close to Pretoria. Employed workers spend an average of 30 percent of their income per month in transportation costs and average over three hours a day in round-trip commuting. This does not include the frequently long journeys required just to get to available taxis or buses.[24] In 1989 nearly 50 percent of all households had incomes less than R500 per month,[25] and anecdotal evidence suggests that over 80 percent of the residents are unemployed.

On average, landowners paid R7,630 for properties of an average plot size of two thousand square meters, valued in 1997 at an average of R18,370.[26] Some landlords ask up to R30,000 — a price that far exceeds the average in most of South Africa's urban informal settlements. The vast majority of housing structures are now cement and brick, with an average size of four and one-half rooms.

Nearly two-thirds of the population are not economically active. Of those who are, nearly 50 percent are engaged in informal sector activities. The bulk of activities include car repair and body work, burglar gate construction, shoe repair, and coffin building. Roughly one-quarter of informal sector employment takes place outside the Winterveld area.[27] The distribution of groceries and soft drinks is now largely the purview of the informal sector as well. Of those engaged in formal wage labor, roughly one-quarter work in the manufacturing sector; two-thirds of employed women work as domestics; and one-fifth of formal wage earners work in the construction sector, primarily in Greater Pretoria.[28] Formal business in Winterveld has been in decline for some years: one need only to drive around the various wards to see the remnants of workshops that are no longer operative.

Almost half of all durable goods are purchased in Pretoria, with another third purchased in Mabopane, usually at the large city center shopping complex that is contiguous to the Mabopane train station. This complex constitutes a town center for the surrounding municipalities, although households spend nearly one-third of their total expenditure for goods in Winterveld itself. *Spaza* shops (small in-home shops selling basic supplies) and other informal trading modes that give ordinary people access to credit are, along with bartering, important components of trade. According to some residents, the noncash economy is growing, as in-kind services of various types are being exchanged in order to access consumer goods.[29]

Like many highly informalized economies, regulation takes place by reputation, extortion, mobilization of household labor, and repeated transactions through tightly organized networks institutionalized through induction, legacy, or apprenticeship. The interface between the local state and the predominantly informalized local economy — with its concomitant networks and corporate groupings — becomes the crucial site of intervention for a wide range of players.[30] Whoever controls the symbols of development, let alone the actual developmental products and the regulation and delivery mechanisms of development, can access a wide range of accumulation opportunities that do not necessitate, in the words of Jean-Phillipe Plattean, "massive corruption."[31]

Development has increasingly become the locus through which a coalition of powerful interests is shaped. No player can actually get rich, but they come to dominate local political economies in which the engineering of actual or potential inequalities becomes the basis of consolidation among players. In such a scheme, regulations and legality become instruments for extortion and threats that freeze local social conflicts and modalities of social organization that were more fluid and interactive.

Many tenants remain in Winterveld because they have been there a long time. They have evolved relationships with landowners and/or neighbors that reduce the costs of living and promote the sharing of resources. An unknown number of residents from Zimbabwe, Mozambique, and Zambia make up an artificial demographic group of "foreign" African immigrants who probably now constitute the majority of Winterveld residents. Designations and numbers are highly uncertain, as Mozambicans are largely integrated into the South African Shangaan-speaking community and the Zimbabweans into the Ndebele one. Despite the fact that most recent arrivals to South Africa go to the Johannesburg inner city and to squatter camps closer to Johannesburg, many of these "foreigners" have turned Winterveld into a convenient and viable base of operation for a wide range of unconventional activities.[32]

The early Mozambican and Zimbabwean settlers primarily worked in the mines. While many such migrant workers returned home, sizable numbers remained in South Africa, where they sought physical assets as well as a location from which they could parlay their experience in the mines into some other form of economic activity. Indeed, many of these former mineworkers who settled in Winterveld channel goods, provided to them "under the table" by current mineworkers, to buyers of all kinds. These goods come from their countries of origin or from the networks of other mineworkers with whom they once worked. On the other hand, goods acquired from compatriots and other various networks are sold to mineworkers throughout the country; individual entrepreneurs thus ply large territories. The trade continuously changes and ranges from the smuggling of diamonds, precious metals, rhino horns, and guns to more conventional consumer goods such as electronics and packaged foodstuffs.

Some of this illegal activity is elaborately syndicated. Winterveld entrepreneurs constitute a nodal point in links between mineworkers, buyers, and workers at the Maputo port in Mozambique. Most of these activities seem to be loosely organized; cooperation does exist, but on a deal-by-deal basis. In part, these arrangements act as a mechanism of protection because threats from more "endowed" syndicates and other competitors can be quite intense. Perhaps more to the point, loose cooperation provides a mechanism for the individual entrepreneur to access a more diverse and wider range of opportunities. For the most part, specific deals or activities are rarely repeated in the exact form in which they have already taken place, and they rarely take place more than a few times in the same location or with the same composition of "collaborators."[33] At the same time, some consistency must be brought to the playing field. If the structures of deals and the composition of deal makers are too fluid, things might get out of hand. Competition may be debilitating, even violent. While traders don't want to be locked into overly fixed structures, there also must be mechanisms to socialize trading practices and behaviors. There must be means of ensuring some consistency and predictability.

The churches that sprung up in Winterveld during the 1990s are an important factor in these socializing tasks. Some churches play a major role as points of reference for temporary "business coalitions" or syndicates that are formed among members of different congregations. There are scores of small independent churches scattered within the predominantly Mozambican and/or Shangaan-speaking wards. The individual memberships are quite close, given the quantity of time individuals spend together fulfilling religious obligations and attending prayer meetings.

Information that participants in these loose-knit syndicates generate and exchange among themselves is important. But this exchange is not the most important means through which deals are put together. Collaborations tend to take place on a deal-by-deal basis. Participants for a "team" are recruited from various churches: information about the trustworthiness and capacity of potential participants and the possible roles they might play in the deal are largely based on the roles participants in these deals play in their respective churches. Churches provide a context that implicitly vouches for the behavior and reliability of particular individuals. At the same time, those who put together deals don't want to recruit others from their own churches in the event that things go wrong.

The church may implicitly recognize the existence of such unconventional activities. By leaving it to other more "invisible" or provisional networks to carry out deals, the congregations avoid the risk of being identified with them, and they are not committed or dependent on their success or failure. In other words, whatever happens does not come back as a piece of information or feedback relevant to the maintenance of social ties within any individual church.

These trading networks are simply one aspect of how Winterveld remakes itself into a relatively formally unregulated territory. This status is reinforced by the face that the Winterveld economy does not operate in isolation. Winterveld is frequently used as a territory to recruit labor, mask operations, and conceal goods derived from activities initiated in neighboring Soshanguve and Mabopane. In these highly urbanized areas, a large portion of local economy centers on various rent-seeking activities in a charged atmosphere where turf is strictly divided and intensely contested. A broad range of local government officials whom I interviewed indicate that extralegal determinations, made through the use of formal political and public administrative positions, have completely subsumed the functioning of local government. These include areas concerning who can trade where, who can travel where, who can live where, and who can have access to what licenses and what economic opportunities.

Violent conflicts have frequently arisen between taxi drivers. These conflicts are largely about which taxis can ply what routes, but they also concern the secondary trades engaged in by taxi owners and drivers, such as prostitution, liquor distribution, and the distribution of various construction materials used in informal housing. Some former Winterveld residents now living in Soshanguve use their connections to Winterveld as a means of entry into illicit local economies. More important, they use Winterveld as a site through which to undermine their fellow competitors in Soshanguve without visibly appearing to do so.

For example, a large amount of liquor provided to *shebeens* (informal bars) is stolen from various warehouses. Depending on the amount of stolen liquor on the market, there is a great deal of eagerness to "dump" the goods quickly and take whatever profits one can. Over the years the trade has become highly organized, with substantial efforts made to stabilize prices, customers, and payoffs. In most Soshanguve wards there is an implicit agreement among renegade liquor suppliers about the number of shebeens they can supply. Some of these suppliers, however, connect local shebeen owners being supplied by a rival group to "hit and run" distributors in Winterveld. Winterveld distributors undercut prices and pay the competing Soshanguve distributor a finder fee. Needless to say, these Winterveld distributors seldom remain organized for more than a few deals.

When cheap liquor is unexpectedly being made available to shebeens for prices lower than the prevailing one, the different distributors then find a reason to get together to try to keep out what appear to be outside competitors. This practice of "silently" stirring up trouble allows apparent competitors to collaborate on a temporary basis without altering the uneasy divisions of territory that prevail in Soshanguve. This practice is especially the case in the narcotics trade and in the theft and distribution of bulk lots of various consumer goods.

On other, more rare, occasions, the situation can acquire the complexity of high corporate dealings. I have talked with several South African "agents" of Congolese living and working in a small fabric shop in the Mabopane shopping center. The shop is used as a relay point for stolen cell phones acquired from Malaysia, where it was the task of the Congolese to hand out free lots of the phones to recent Mozambican immigrants in Winterveld. The immigrants in turn take short-term gains by spreading the word that they are responsible for the apparent influx of very cheap phones, and they make money by assuming the risk of being associated with undercutting the established price. These claims satisfy the person working in the Soshanguve local authority finance office who reputedly tries to control the market. The consolidation of niche positions in Soshanguve thus is derived in no small part from the maintenance of a large measure of fluidity in Winterveld.

While such a complex framework of unregulated activity secures great flexibility for local entrepreneurs in Winterveld, it also leaves them vulnerable to various forms of extortion and harassment, especially from local police. For years, police have collected various "levies" from so-called foreign immigrants. For Zimbabwean residents, who dominate the retailing of foodstuffs, this has often meant the destruction of spaza shops or the theft of their goods.

Most efforts underway to bring development to Winterveld, accompanied by steps to regularize the status of both long-term and short-term "foreign" residents, may make the community more secure. The skills deployed in unconventional economic activity can be converted to more formal and regulated enterprises. There is strong resistance to these efforts, which comes not from well-defined organizations that fight off each and every effort at development but rather is affected in large part because critical actors seem to be constantly changing sides. Key actors may support specific initiatives in their capacity as members of a civic organization, and then more silently arrange for those same initiatives to be actively opposed by the church to which they belong.

Some fear that new local policies and programs will introduce greater scrutiny and surveillance. For others, official institutional development means the imposition of norms and structures that might potentially disrupt the social relationships honed over long periods of time. Some of the poorest residents worry that any development process that alters the prevailing forms of tenancy and social obligations might jeopardize their subsistence levels.

Local Politics and a Ghostly Presence

Winterveld's town council is largely staffed by individuals seconded from and accountable to the Northwest Provincial Government. Current local government legislation gives elected local authorities only limited powers over their administrative staffs, and thus highly ambivalent relationships often ensue. In the case of Winterveld, administrative staff members frequently refuse to implement resolutions taken by the council because of its disregard for budgetary constraints and the appropriateness of expenditures. Councillors complain that civil servants are often disrespectful and oblivious to their deliberations. According to councillors, these workers are more concerned with using their positions to engage in various business activities and cultivate patron-client relationships based on their role in tendering contracts, issuing licenses, and approving land use plans.

The local council has yet to establish much credibility with the community. The older, trusted political activitists who led Winterveld through the 1980s were largely sidelined prior to the first local government election. The intensity of political competition then was so great that at one point there were three "versions" of the African National Congress vying for predominance, which they did largely through the notorious WDA. The WDA managed the residual funds that were earmarked for the community's development from the former transfer of Winterveld to Bophuthatswana control.[34] The WDA thus became an important political instrument through which a younger breed of activists gained predominance. According to some residents, it also acted as a platform of extortion, bribery, and even sexual manipulation.

The subsequent actions of many councillors have not helped to establish credibility. The lack of councillors with professional backgrounds does not inherently constitute an absence of political ability, yet some councillors have criminal backgrounds and almost no formal education. After winning positions on the council, some who at one time couldn't pay minimal school fees for their children were driving luxury cars. Allegations of bribery and corruption abound. For example, when security companies were formed to guard building materials for the Slovoville project, relatives of councillors were hired, insurance was taken out, and still materials disappeared. Luxury hotels catered town council functions, which consumed nearly three-quarters of the annual budget.

Collectively, councillors and line staff operate in tandem in terms of implicitly consolidating political power in the Beirut, Lebanon, and Slovoville sections of Winterveld — again, what is often referred to as the "urbanized" part of the community. As a result, the highly dense sections of Klippan South, which are frequently identified as the key sources of political volatility in the area, are excluded. The Klippan South neighborhoods are identified by some councilors as the strongholds of the Winterveld Crisis Committee (WCC), a renegade civic organization that has assumed almost legendary status in the community. It is alternately viewed as that which will save or destroy Winterveld. What the WCC actually is, however, depends on whom you talk to. In my discussions with nearly one hundred people from different walks of life in Winterveld, there was never any consistent definition of the organization.

At one moment, the WCC is the operating vehicle for activists who were excluded from the African National Congress party lists during the first local government elections, or who volitionally chose to exclude themselves. At other moments, the WCC is cited as the work of spaza shop owners who fear a loss of customers if Slovoville continues to grow in the western part of the community. At still other moments, the WCC is defined as a renegade group of youth aligned to criminal elements extorting loyalty from the poorer and more rural residents of Winterveld, and sometimes "covering" themselves with proclaimed affiliations to the Pan-African Congress. Still others cite the WCC as the front organization of a secret cabal of landowners. Elements from the WCC are also accused of encouraging the nonpayment of rent and of providing important materials, such as standpipes, to circumvent local government regulations.

When community meetings are held, people will identify themselves as representing the WCC, but the cast of characters that represent the organization varies widely according to issue, setting, and time. Few can discern any obvious patterns in these variations, although speculation is rife. Attempted assassinations were carried out on the organization's two top designated leaders, who have since rarely appeared in public, claiming the need for a long period of rehabilitation. Many disaffected affiliates have left the organization, but their subsequent stories don't gel sufficiently to get a clear sense of how the WCC actually works. On top of these confusions, councillors cite subterfuge by the WCC as an easy explanation for their inability to get anything done. However, the relative invisibility of the council as a proactive political force in the community is complicit with the administrative staffs' interest in maintaining some control, especially in terms of fiduciary matters.

In addition, activists in the council implicitly "steer" large numbers of residents to support the WCC. This activist element within the council believes that the consolidation of new policy directives within the "urbanized" area of Winterveld constitutes a basis for extending wide-scale development throughout the other parts of the community. These activists are piloting specific land acquisition deals with specific landowners and using available development finance to build more houses where bulk infrastructure already exists. In doing so, these activist elements are trying to make the power dynamics taking place elsewhere in Winterveld less relevant to the overall political control of the area.

The idea behind this strategy is to break the back of a cohesive group of landowners. These landowners are seen to be the power that manipulates the murky politics that prevail in much of Winterveld. Because the demand for further development is likely to be strongest in the most "urbanized" sections of the community, it is there where a precedent could be set for the public acquisition of land from current landowners. Once landowners start to sell, the unity among landowning interests will begin to dissipate. Some councillors believe that this fragmentation will prompt the most recalcitrant owners to take overly drastic measures and thus further erode their available sources of support. If the council has the chance to prove it can speed up development, it is more likely to extend its authority and influence to larger swathes of the community.

On the other hand, intensifying development and investment within the "urbanized" areas of Winterveld further widens the sense of a divide between Beirut, Slovoville, Lebanon and the other areas of the community.

This is a move that risks amplifying the perception that the local authority is acting only in the interest of a limited segment of the community. It prompts other areas to invest in more "renegade" forms of resistance, including not only support for the WCC but also ad hoc service provision measures that show that the local authority need not be the only player in town in order for development to occur.

The concentration of efforts to speed up development within the "urbanized" quarters is strengthening the hand of more narrowly defined local interest groups, such as the Beirut Residents Association and the Lebanon Residents Association. The former group maintains a rent boycott for tenants of "town houses" now nearly uninhabitable because they were hastily built by the Bophuthatswana government. These groups are attempting to focus that attention of the council exclusively on their concerns and are actively trying to stop any effort to further increase the density of the area through new land acquisition.

For most councillors, underdeveloped areas are viewed as a political liability. They consider much too complicated the task of achieving some consensus as to what can be done with limited resources.[35] For other councillors, a great deal of manipulation purportedly took place at the time of local government elections. Foreign immigrants were rewarded for their support with promises of the provision of formal identity documents and the regularization of their status; these areas, of course, are outside the authority of local councillors.

Different factions expend inordinate energy keeping each other in check, and the implementation of even short-term development objectives is largely diluted. Even with such differentiation, the municipal government is perceived by large parts of the community as a homogenous political caste, and thus the process of political contestation within the local government does not advance because the networks of particular factions across specific communities and territories within Winterveld are themselves limited.

The complexities of local politics are not made easier by the severe financial crisis faced by the local authority. Subsidies to the local authority were to be progressively cut by 50 percent at annual increments over a five-year period. These subsidies were to help defray the costs of basic service provision, including the creation and maintenance of roads, sewers, refuse collection and dump sites, parks, and cemeteries. The Northwest Province, via the Department of Local Government, Housing, Planning and Development, presently covers roughly 80 percent of the costs for services. The local authority is unwilling to adjust the budget to deal with the annual 20 percent decrease in the amount of subsidy the provincial government provides to Winterveld, and thus it has attempted to save by cutting costs of contractors. As to be expected, this has resulted in contractual disputes with most service providers.[36]

Similar difficulties have been experienced with the overall budget of approximately R14 million for recurrent expenditure and maintenance. A flat monthly service rate of R10 was charged to each household despite the status of land ownership and tenancy. The bulk of these tariffs, however, were not being collected. At the outset, a flat rate of R2 was charged, with only 24 percent recuperation. As of the end of 1998, not a single ward meeting had been conducted by councillors concerning tariff payments.

The local authority claims that recovery is difficult given the dissatisfaction of the residents. Across the board, there are major construction faults with the majority of houses in Beirut and Lebanon. Local resident associations attempted to force the Bophuthatswana Building Society, the financing agent for these developments, to make either repairs or restitution. When the building society was dissolved, responsibility was transferred to the Northwest Housing Corporation, which in turn claimed that its authority extended only to the management of escrow accounts. Because residents feel that they cannot abandon these houses, there is an unwillingness to pay for services or any other payments. Therefore, the only local authority income seems to be derived from the newer sections of Slovoville.

The Winterveld local authority is entitled to almost R1 million of intergovernmental transfers for the fiscal year — approximately one-fourteenth of its total budget. Property charges are supposed to be R20 per month per household, but given the fact that there are no reliable households figures on which to formulate viable budgets, probable income is highly speculative. Budgetary designations indicate an expected income of nearly R2 million based on R20 charges per household, which would implicitly calculate the number of households in Winterveld at some 8,114. The local authority estimates that it has the capacity to draw revenue from a base of 2,500 formal and 1,500 informal households, but because it remains unclear just what is meant by informal households and what their capacities are, it is likely that revenue could be derived only from a base of 2,500 formal households. If that were the case, roughly R433 per household would be required for the local authority to meet its budget.

The Winterveld Presidential Lead Project for the provision of water is an important aspect of how Winterveld relates to the wider region, and it provides another example of the workings of the WCC. A private company, Rand Water, was the implementing agent of the R79 million nationally funded project. The objective of the project was to provide twenty-five liters of water per person per day, accessible at no more than two hundred meters from the site of residence. At the time, 54 percent of households had to walk farther than five hundred meters to collect water, with 32 percent walking more than one kilometer.[37]

The community requested that water should be piped to individual plots in order to minimize the distance necessary to retrieve water, given the large plot sizes. All standpipes function on a prepaid meter system using tokens, and the water retailer leases the land on which the standpipe is installed. Accordingly, in some instances, these standpipes were to be placed outside of plots in order to ensure water access for tenants in situations where landowners are either resistant to having their properties serviced or where there is illicit manipulation of water provisioning.

For example, there are numerous instances of illegal house and yard connections established to the main reticulation system. These connections permit either unpaid access to water for the consumption of individual households or access used for sale to other households within the immediate vicinity. The intention of the project was to provide higher levels of service to those willing to pay, and to institute a community-monitoring system to reframe unconventional access to water as the misappropriation of a community and user resource.

Higher levels of service were offered in the form of a tank system with fixed quantity provisions of two hundred liters for yard connections. In this arrangement, households were expected to cover 50 percent of the capital costs up front. Access to financing was facilitated by the project. In all levels of service, a sales administrator acted as the water vendor. A water retailer sells credits to this salesperson, usually a community resident with business experience. The salesperson works from local police stations equipped with computers operated by both salesperson and the system administrator at the water retailer. The salesperson then loads credits for individual consumers at fixed consumption rates, and final water pricing includes a small overhead for the salesperson. In addition, water bailiffs are hired to ensure that there are no illegal connections and to report faults.

The introduction of water in a place that for the most part did not have it, and that relied on various informal systems of provisioning, had substantial implications beyond simply connecting the community to water. Connections to sources of bulk supply were often unconventional and sophisticated. Local social economies regulated who got water under what circumstances, and who could use it for what purpose. The manipulation of water provisioning at various points was an important source of income for some. Sixty percent of the 445 households interviewed in 1994 obtained their water from vendors, spending anywhere from R22 to R75 per month.[38] Because most vendors have been landowners, connection to reticulated water is not an attractive outcome for many of them.

The project has implemented a community management and local employment generation approach. Provision is made for the specific consumption requirements of user groups. The community will eventually own the infrastructure and system of service provision. Local labor is used, and the project has attempted to use construction work to support small local contractors. Project management consisted of four working committees — financial, technical, tendering, and community relations, with a project steering committee providing coordination and oversight. The thirteen wards of Winterveld were allowed to select five representatives per ward for this committee, for a total of sixty-five participants, each of whom is paid R75 per meeting. Eight individuals were selected by the steering committee to receive extended training to act as social consultants. These consultants, known as the "Group of 8," were to ensure that community perspectives are adequately channeled into project implementation and to disseminate information to communities.

The Project Steering Committee (PSC) was designated the primary client, with the Department of Water Affairs as the secondary client. The PSC contracted the services of design and training consultants, as community participants have undergone a training process in distinct areas of specialization for which they will be responsible. In addition, there was a construction manager and materials manager for the project.

Tenders were submitted for five levels of construction inputs. These were organized according to financial scale and capacity, and corresponded to individual facilities and actions, tertiary segments, secondary/collector levels, and trunk levels of the provision hierarchy. For example, a contract "A" would entail two or three employees on work of less than R10,000 all the way up to a contract "E" tendered to conventional contractors. Seventy-five contracts were issued, and fifty-five were completed as of the beginning of 1999. The intention was to facilitate the upscaling of contracts for local contractors; however, given the size of the project this objective proved to be unrealistic.

The project drew on the participation of between six hundred to eight hundred local laborers at any given time. The approach was to compensate for limited wages with training. Limited wages have meant that the majority of laborers are Zimbabwean and Mozambican, who often calculate their earnings and opportunities with a different set of references. The ethnic composition of the labor force has caused some problems for the project: police harassed Mozambican laborers on behalf of those interests opposed to the project, including, at various times, landowners and the local authority.

Despite the efforts made to manage the project through broad-based community participation, various levels of resistance were encountered. There were those whose didn't want to pay for services. There were landowners who were currently not receiving any form of remuneration from tenants and used the project to enforce a punitive stance against them. Unsurprisingly, the WCC was cited as the embodiment of various forms of resistance. At the same time, however, it acted as the umbrella under which those "foreigners" working as laborers in the project sought to protect their interests. The project repeatedly told the local authority that it would be forced to deal with the WCC if they were not more cooperative with the project.

Again, the WCC emerges as a kind of free-for-all organization, allowing different actors and sectors to shift positions or assume highly ambivalent ones. Thus, for example, community interests in Vilakazi might play along with the project in terms of using it as a way to secure work for small-scale local contractors that would then lend them credibility as they sought opportunities outside the quarter. At the same time, informal water retailing has been major business in this quarter, and the WCC was used as a vehicle with which to try to preserve this aspect of the local social economy. On the other hand, the WCC was used by groups of residents in the Magatoh section as a way of trying to break the hold of a Mafia-like water retailing system.

The PSC preceded the establishment of the present local authority. The local authority was designated as the de jure water authority in terms regulating service provision, but it had little capacity to manage this role effectively. In 1999, negotiations were underway to establish a nonprofit company to manage the retailing of water, with present members of the PSC eligible to apply for managerial positions within the new company.

One of the intentions of the Presidential Lead Project was to give rise to a new generation of community organizations. There is no doubt that a sense of community participation in this project was real. Yet the lack of coherent community organizations prior to project implementation and the overarching need to put in place relatively standardized infrastructure meant that any collaborative approach would be fraught with problems. In spite of its social aspirations, the project was primarily one of physical engineering. Although the project used the provision of infrastructure for water as a tool to address a variety of social objectives, these were clearly secondary and were always adapted to the timetables, practices, and agendas of delivering a large infrastructure project.

In a project of this magnitude, with all the complexities it raises, complications are certainly to be expected. Political pressures for such a project to be successful are enormous. Considerable effort has been made to institutionalize capacities and consultative processes that can be used to further the overall development of the area. Yet, the complications raise critical issues.

For example, in the Lekgama area, a small contractor made several mistakes in laying part of the secondary network — a situation that was compounded by the reneging of the contractor on wage agreements made with workers. In the process, electrical cables were damaged and the key institution in the area, the Lekgama Community Center, with its wide array of local economic development and service programs, was forced to halt operations. Several employees of the center were officially part of the project steering committee. Still, they had little knowledge about what was going on except that they had previously been told that the area was supposed to form a water committee. They had little idea of whom to contact to deal with the situation. Additionally, the landowner who had donated part of his holding to the center had attempted to inform the contractor of his fears that the procedures being employed were excessively careless. Both informed the project that they were turning over the issue to the WCC, which in this instance simply meant that they were going to ensure that no one in Lekgama had any further dealings with the project. The project made a concerted effort to bring them back on board, but this time as "official" representatives of the WCC.

The project contained important elements of a community-based management approach to infrastructure delivery. Nevertheless, the overall framework of project design was the responsibility of external institutions. If community resourcefulness is to be comprehensively mobilized in the future, there must be some balance between community participation in government-managed processes and government participation in community-initiated and community-based development. Whatever the WCC actually is, its existence in large part is based on consistently "reminding" different scales of government action that various sectors of the community have their own interpretations and practices as to what constitutes viable development.

Winterveld has a particularly singular history and configuration as far as communities go. Many of the challenges it faces derive directly from the singularity of this history, which combines great pride, the legacy of continuous black land ownership, and the social diversity that ensued from this status.

The community's approach to its own diversity also played a role in its present difficulties. People of substantially different backgrounds and walks of life, and with access to different social networks and opportunities, lived with one another as a community. According to a community worker I spoke with who has lived in Winterveld all her life, the result of this diversity was that daily existence could be more easily improvised and rearranged. If one arrangement or relationship didn't work or became problematic, there were others that could be turned to or explored. Eventually, interest in long-term commitments to neighborhood improvement waned. So did investments in the continuity of stable social formations, networks, and practices. This development was especially important because the capacity to improvise requires a "stable" set of formations and arrangements to work on and with. Increasingly insignificant as a haven from apartheid control and removed from where the "action" was, the Winterveld population found itself with less opportunities to use its diversity as a resource to operate across wider territories and spheres of action.

Now, various sectors of the community try to protect the limited ways in which they have access to the wider world. Many fear that conventional development will cut off those opportunities. As a result, certain groups get involved in development projects as a way to crystallize new coalitions and intersecting networks that then try to fight off development. They use their resistance against development as a means of exploring alternative outward-looking opportunities. Powerful parochial interests also use resistance to slow down necessary change. Different aspirations and capacities often are in cahoots. What is clear is that tactics seeking to crystallize and consolidate development in one territory or sector of the community as a platform on which to spread development throughout that community often stir up a hornet's nest of unanticipated reactions. These trajectories of development end up becoming the "host culture" through which more informal, murky, and sometimes insidious forms of economic pursuit and social influence are activated.

3

The Spectral

Assembling Douala,

Cameroon

Although the notion of the spectral is close to that of the invisible used in the discussion of Winterveld in chapter 2, it is not the same thing. I use the notion of the spectral here to refer to a series of refractions among real life, artifice, imagination, and action whereby residents hedge their bets as to what events, relationships, resources, and opportunities actually mean to their everyday navigation of the city.[1] For in a city such as Douala in Cameroon, the subject of the following case study, it is increasingly difficult for any one sector or arrangement of sectors to consolidate systems of representation, consensus, and social contracts capable of regulating the relationships that residents have with each other.

Instead, practices come to fore through which diverse populations and interests insinuate themselves into each other's lives and circulate through each other's perspectives and meanings. This is a practice of keeping things open and possible in situations where the definitions of power are not readily apparent or are arbitrary. At the same time, this engineered openness is experienced as a kind of haunting. It is a sense that there is much more taking place than meets the eye, and that everyday life is a force field of resurgent traces from some past, something not yet laid to rest. At the same time, this haunting is experienced as a kind of beckoning from some future that appears increasingly vague as residents have increasing difficulties getting a handle on the present—a difficulty that they are in part responsible for.

Many residents of Douala make it clear in their everyday conversations that they believe their city is haunted. They believe that there is something beyond the bad politics, inadequate infrastructure, and sometimes feverish sense of entrepreneurship that drives their everyday urban lives. It is something not said because there is no language to say it, something not remembered because memory is viewed as dangerous.

Urban residents in Douala live their lives trying to maintain a sense of stability in social ties, places to live, and economic niches to occupy. Household ties remain the critical locus of stability. A sense of solidarity must be achieved when there is sometimes simply not enough resources to go around. At the same time, the challenge for individuals is how to sufficiently extricate themselves from household responsibilities, perspectives, and norms so as to keep themselves open to new alliances, sources of information, and opportunities. For the possibility of household reproduction depends on acting with a certain indifference to it, especially in cities where it is increasingly unclear just what steps can be taken to ensure some predictability of outcomes. In the end, this is a matter not only of individuals navigating complex social ties and precarious economies but also of efforts to make the very meanings and values attributed to notions such as social solidarity, livelihood, and efficacy circulate through wider, seemingly contradictory, versions and displays.

Not only do individual residents circulate among each other, but the very meanings of their various points of anchorage — household, networks, and livelihoods — must perform a kind of circulation as well. In a context where it is often unclear just who has the right and ability to do what, and where once-relied-on forms of authority are increasingly unable to put their stamps on how daily life is to be enacted and understood, there is a pervasive anxiety on the part of urban residents as to who they can live and work with, who they can talk to, and what kind of collective future they can anticipate. In such conditions there is a tendency to retreat into specific particularisms — of ethnopolitical groupings, reinvented traditions, or heavily defended local territories. But as cities like Douala continue to grow and continue to be shared by residents from different walks of life, the challenge is how residents keep each other in some kind of consideration and keep open the possibilities of some kind of common future. In part this occurs through a circulation of meanings, styles, vantage points, experiences, and ways of talking — tried on and discarded, and perhaps tried again. These elements thus come to belong to no one, even though particular groups may make strong claims on them at any given time. This performance of circulation — which produces an incessant sense of incompleteness and haunting in whatever arrangements are momentarily put together by diverse residents trying to figure each other out and live together — is what I refer to here as the spectral.[2]

In addition, the regime that has ruled Cameroon for the last two decades increasingly recognizes that it need no longer substantially invest in the definitional aspects of rule — that is, to deliberate clearly defined jurisdictions, zones, policies, and sectors. This allows unregulated practices of accumulation to unravel centers of social gravity once relied on, with the state intervening primarily to depict certain actors and spaces as threats demanding that the state take extraordinary and emergency actions. Given the everyday tactics of residents trying to make ends meet and a regime trying almost anything to extend its rule, it is no wonder that residents of Douala often complain about their inability to really know what is going on or to know what the real causes are behind how the city functions or is unable to function. At the same time, a prevailing unease exists about making things too clear or too set, because one does not know the likely implications such clarity might have on what people are able to do next.

In part, this opacity is about the residual affects of an urban colonial history in which what was attained by Africans in terms of their engagement with cities — particularly in the areas of social cognition and social practice — could never be fully instantiated within the city. Even when substantial rearrangements in cultural life and social economy were precipitated by an urban presence, the potential interconnections among emerging networks of social practice, economic specialization, and cultural reformation were constrained. Clear vehicles of institutionalization were usually foreclosed, largely by the dearth of available public spheres that were not heavily scrutinized or repressed by existing regimes.

These urban attainments therefore were usually dispersed outside of the city, invested in transitional populations situated in-between the distinct forms of rural and urban rule or moving back and forth among them.[3] The city became a site of deferral where locally honed aspirations, emergent institutions, and economies capable of extending and deepening African uses of urban space were, for the most part, readapted toward deflecting the impositions and segregation of colonial rule. Simultaneously, they were also applied to maximizing the potentials of underregulated spaces of operation at the peripheries of cities, but without the urban topological and social complexion necessary to really incubate and develop these nascent urban orientations and practices.

At the same time, colonial rule was always partial and heterogeneous;

always rearranged or distorted through the ways in which it was implemented.[4] As a result, urban Africans incessantly looked for openings to actively "partialize" and distort imposed rule, to make it work for self-conceived agendas. This was a process that often meant large measures of dissimulation, of enacting what on the surface may have looked to be highly traditional or parochial practices as covers for incipient urban styles.

If urban modernity had connoted a sense of completion — completion in terms of self-sufficiency or the termination point of a development trajectory and state of realization whose basic terms had no need to be exceeded — then there is also an attitude in Douala of speeding up such completion. What urban residents then experience in everyday life is itself a spectral image of something already over and done with. As one of the city's major artists, Malam, states:

> We in New Bell always seem to imagine ourselves as somewhere else. While we don't necessarily want to leave this place, we act as if we have already left . . . and this attitude works in several ways. On the one hand, those who are neighbors, who share this street, for example, sometimes act as if they don't see what is going on . . . the life around them doesn't bother them because they are not really here, they are living their dream, and so people are more free to do what they want to do. On the other hand, because so many people are in so many other places in their minds, this can be their only common point of view, and so they can't really ask each other for anything, can't rely on each other because no one has a sense of what they are really experiencing. Also it means that things are speeded up; the children have already left the house and gone somewhere else; the father is already old, the mother is already old; the normal rhythm of growing up, of dying, of leaving and coming is all collapsed into a single note that everyone sings, and as such, can't hear each other, can't hear each other being criticized, being scrutinized, being liked or disliked, being told to stop what they are doing or do something different . . . it is a way of living everywhere and nowhere at the same time.[5]

The Art of Life

Part of my discussion here on Douala concerns a large sculpture assembled with bits and pieces of objects found throughout the city and then erected, with much fanfare and dispute, in one of the most important public circles in the city. The construction and presence of this sculpture was one of the most significant events in Douala during the 1990s. Its importance lies in the fact that it embodies much of what everyday citizens think about their city and the way in which it was constructed. In other words, the sculpted assemblage of junk was in part able to generate so much passion in the city because so much of the city was and is a kind of assemblage of junk. In this discussion, I want to point out some of the dynamics of settlement, urban growth, and community governance at work in Douala. I emphasize particularly the logic at work in assembling communities that tend to deter an easy fit with the prevailing conceptions of urban development and urban modernity, but in a city that, at least in its exaggerated professions, truly takes modernity to heart.

In regard to the recent history of development in Douala's largest suburb, Zone Nylon, I want to discuss how specific aspects of such development intended to enable local communities to operate at larger domains can backfire when development interventions fail to appreciate the assemblagelike character of local urban settlement. In the case of Zone Nylon, the construction of a small "modern downtown" sought to lead the surrounding quarters into a more cosmopolitan and proficiently modern engagement with the city and beyond. But a failure to appreciate how the city was actually made seemed to widen the distance between the quarters and these aspirations. In a cogent metaphor, this divergence is highlighted in the disputes surrounding the appearance of the sculpture in the public circle. The case of *La Nouvelle Liberté*, as the sculpture is called, reveals some of the complicated dynamics involved in making the work of assemblages visible and acknowledging their importance in making the city.

In this chapter I also include two other stories. First, I discuss how efforts on the part of government authorities to erase particular troubling aspects of urban life leave a range of spectral residues whose engagement reorders the conventional hierarchies of urban identity and capacity so as to valorize the weakest and most marginal of the city's inhabitants. Second, I discuss how the spectral itself becomes an object of attention and guidance for a small gang of urban youths.

Into a New Millennium

Douala is a sprawling, ramshackle city of 3.5 million, named after the original inhabitants of the area. From its inception, the city has reflected an intricate contestation as to what it is to itself and to the larger world. In other words, the unfolding and construction of the city has contained multiple levels of argument about suitable images. What is the image of the city that works? What should a city be, and how?

Contemporary Douala emerged from the relations among federated but autonomous towns that were settled along the Wouri River, opening onto the bight of Biafra. The first settlement was Bell (now Bonanjo), with Akwa and Deido soon to follow. Like today, settlements reflected the convergence of peoples coming from elsewhere, either to look for more land or to escape disputes.

The early 1960s perilously congested the "inner" city areas of New Bell, Lagos, and Congo. As in rapidly growing cities throughout the world, this period saw substantial movement to the periphery. Because Douala is situated in a riverine terrain punctuated by the various tributaries that run off from the Wouri River, such peripheral settlements were amassed in the flatland regions running southeast of the urban center in an area that was to be known as Zone Nylon. The area took this name in reference to the poor absorptive capacity of the land and the seemingly endless way this spontaneous settlement stretched across a largely inhospitable terrain. Because the expanding settlement fell outside the interrelationships among the historic quarters that had defined much of the city's dynamics since its inception, authorities responsible for the municipality and the region mostly ignored it. Without basic services, schools, markets, and infrastructure, Zone Nylon was also perceived as a hotbed of insurgency. There also was a seemingly incessant realignment of settlement patterns as new subzones were formed with their own peculiar characters and authority structures.

During the late 1970s, the local Catholic archdiocese lobbied strenuously for government intervention in addressing the escalating problems of flooding, sanitation, health, and joblessness. The national government established the Mission d'Aménagement et Equipement Terrains Urbains and Ruraux in an effort to address the widespread growth of irregular settlements throughout the country. The Agence de Restructuration et d'Aménagement de Nylon (ARAN) was established in 1982 specifically to manage the "urbanization" of the Zone Nylon. Initially, ARAN was to concentrate on implementing a clear layout and land use policy, so as to provide the infrastructure for water, roads, and drainage.

Scores of local associations emerged over the years to lend some stability and governance to local quarters. They argued that various social and economic development programs should accompany the provision of infrastructure. Although the government had initially promised a wide range of social services, it was clear at the inception of the restructuring activities that infrastructure provision had the primary objective of enabling more effective management of the area by the municipality.

Because restructuring necessitated reducing the density of the Zone Nylon by resettling nearly 20 percent of its residents to other parts of the metropolitan region, the process was rife with conflict. Some residents had substantial family and social investments within specific quarters. After all, it was largely through individual initiatives — the building of informal "feeder" roads, the clearing of land for settlement, and the filling in of land to open up new settlement possibilities — that new quarters were founded. Other residents, enticed by the promise of new land that could eventually be sold informally as a means of acquiring investment income, were anxious to be selected as candidates for resettlement.

To resolve the issue of who would stay or go, and under what circumstances, an area development committee was formed with broad representation from the Zone Nylon's quarters. While many in the committee attempted to implement a fair and rational approach to these decisions, the committee quickly became known for underhanded deals among various local authorities. Local "chiefs" used the process to work out different internal disputes within their quarters, and some used the process as a way to engineer greater ethnic homogeneity in the composition of a specific quarter.

Faced with an intensifying politicization of development decisions and an overt lack of commitment to the project's social development objectives, bands of youths destroyed much of the early infrastructure inputs and the machinery that had been brought to the Zone Nylon. Later, the presiding leader of the area development committee was killed. As the police randomly rounded up youths in the Zone for severe beatings, the long-term control of youth behavior in relation to the project became an important vehicle for consolidating the power of specific community leaders. Faced with the prospect of substantial financial losses, a concerted effort was made to refocus the project on social development. The early stages of the project revealed the extent to which youths were capable of acting autonomously from established local authority structures. In response, key members of the area development committee intentionally cultivated a large clientele of youths to expand their influence across the zone.

A highly ambitious restructuring program was launched with funds from the World Bank and the development cooperation ministry of the Swiss government. The centerpiece of the program was to be a "modern downtown" with a main road linking the area directly to Douala's central admin-

The view from the suburb Zone Nylon of the horizon of Douala, Cameroon.

istrative and commercial districts. Elaborate plans were made to build a central hospital and network of schools and to create an economic development zone for microenterprise, known as the Coopèrative des Artisans de Nylon.

Substantial changes to the Zone were made over the duration of the project, from 1982 to 1991. A large market was built in the Madagascar quarter, which anchors small economic activities spread across the Zone. Essential urban and human services are now provided. Still, looking at the Zone today, one gets the impression that in many respects the conditions that defined the past before the project's implementation have returned. Much of the road construction was poorly done, and most routes are now barely passable. The reticulation system had a limited reach, so the areas around the built-up infrastructure have once again reached high density. As the Madagascar market was built in part to rationalize commercial activities, like many such markets the combination of limited size limitations and the cost of canteens results in a vast spillage of trade across the area, generating tensions between "formal" and "informal" traders.

An impressive half mile of ten-story buildings establishes a "downtown" for the Zone. This area is crossed by the one road that remains largely undamaged. An array of tax abatements and low-interest loans enticed mostly Bamileke entrepreneurs to construct buildings along this avenue. Even though the street-level section of every building contains a shop (or a space intended for a shop), there is a dearth of commercial vitality. In some respects, this half mile is the "showpiece" of the urbanization process, a small "glimpse" of what a city is supposed to look like in the middle of a vast suburb of nearly a half million people. For years, even this half mile has exuded a sense of being incomplete. While relatively inexpensive middle-class housing is provided in some neatly appointed apartment blocks, many buildings are largely unoccupied.

Past managers of the project have been aware of the potential problems entailed in building such a "downtown" when more apparently pressing needs remain. They argue that investing in such an area was also an incentive for contiguous quarters to see an image of an emergent cosmopolitanism in their midst. In other words, the downtown was to be a space of convergence, where people from different quarters could meet. Different quarters would then figure out ways to link their characters and capacities to the elaboration of such a downtown and, by doing so, extend some of its capacities into the operations of each quarter.

Such a process has obviously not taken place. In the areas immediately contiguous to this stretch of "modern" urbanization remain quarters of largely improvised and provisional housing clinging precariously to the sides of gullies, without even the semblance of proper sanitation. Part of the glaring disarticulation brought about by the project is attributable to a lack of funds and the enormous resources needed to make such a restructuring project really work.

Part of the inability to find ways of using the "developed" part of the Zone as a means of anchoring both further improvements within discrete quarters and elaborating greater linkages among them has much to do with local dynamics; that is, the interactions between how quarters are settled and managed and how notions of development are locally understood and acted on. Much of the Zone exudes a kind of imperative for individuals to both mix and be something specific. In examining the ways in which quarters were formed and extended over the years, from Tergal to Madagascar to Bilongue to Soboum to Oyack, it is clear that intricate economies of compensation are at work. In other words, in quarters of largely spontaneous settlement, the advantages of spontaneity — in action, decisions, and livelihood — are often uneasily balanced with constraints on that same spontaneity.

The initially open-ended Zone encouraged a kind of *mètissage* (mixing) of social relations. Households could organize around actors whom they perceived to be key figures — actors with sufficient resources or reach to ensure some protection. If certain individuals or households couldn't abide by emerging patterns of local "governance," they could go elsewhere. Still, no matter where anyone eventually found themselves, for most people who dwell in Douala there remains a strong sense of commitment to one's village of origin. So, in a residual sense, new settlers in the periurban area, to a more limited extent, retained some sense of connection to their former urban areas of residence, and thus in the midst of a particular quarter were affiliations and commitments not just to that specific place itself. Instead, multiple commitments to other places inform how particular households act, and various associations emerged to express those commitments. Much of this facet of associational life remains ethnically defined, but not exclusively.

An important aspect of ethnic identification entails how money is to be handled. Because urban life institutionalizes a process of moving — one quarter to another — and because this urban life requires the pooling of money in order for individuals to attain amounts sufficient to acquire either goods to sell or other valued commodities, how money is handled is a critical issue. Even if an individual has little actual connection to their village of origin, it remains a place of origin; it is a place that cannot be altered. As a place of eventual or at least symbolic return after death, it is a place that can continue to exert a persuasive influence over the behavior of individuals. In the city, individuals can move from one place to another, avoiding relations and responsibilities. This is partly why the formation of many savings associations, or tontines, remains ethnically based.

While ethnic identification does not preclude intermarriage and effective cooperation at the level of the quarter, attentiveness to balances is still required. Internal life in the quarter can be significantly disrupted if it is perceived that one particular ethnic group and their respective commitments and affiliations to other places are predominant. Intermarriage among ethnic groups is one way that implicitly attenuates the potentials of such conflicts. At the same time, the lack of economic capacity and the general precariousness of life are great in these quarters. They draw a substantial limit to the extent to which individuals and households can derive the bulk of their social support and livelihood opportunities by depending on relations within the confines of the quarter in which they live. Thus, offspring are encouraged to move to other quarters and to establish connections there that can potentially be parlayed into opportunities for the entire family.

Such moves to the outside can also be reinforced by the dynamics of local ethnic or associational politics. The intensity of ethnic identification has increased substantially in Cameroon during recent years. A common assessment is that while urban residents always had their ethnic identity as something important to define them, they cannot remember a time when it meant as much as it does today. In part, this is due to the ethnic politics pursued by the ruling regime. For the past decade, ethnic politics has been the means through which the ruling regime has maintained power in spite of stolen elections and substantial demands for change. A self-conscious strategy of distributing resources and power along ethnic lines, combined with a prolonged period of economic crisis, breaks down former modalities of solidarity. As such, it is difficult for persons to avoid assessing their possibilities and responsibilities along the apparent "clarity" of ethnic reference.

As I indicated above, however, a process of mètissage has been an important aspect of substantiating the dynamism of economically fragile urban quarters. The interplay of these dynamics — that is, the need to mix and to be something specific — then generates a certain circulation and extension of households across the Zone. For if the offspring of interethnic marriage are still under pressure to be something specific in terms of ethnic identity, how will they choose? To avoid the implications of a "wrong" or contentious choice, as well as too much investment placed in trying to recruit such offspring to specific ethnic associations within a quarter, these offspring will often move to another quarter. There, the implication of whatever choice they make will usually turn out to be less severe.

As levels of hardship and their concomitant social tensions grow within quarters, families increasingly must find ways to turn to each other under conditions that also wear away the strength of family solidarity. Within such conditions, the dispersal of family ties also has implications; after all, households are, in part, seeking to send their offspring to new quarters. Without territorial proximity available to exert strong socializing effects, family networks are often subject to more underhanded and debilitating means of enforcing different kinds of cooperation. Critical family affairs and life events, such as funerals, baptisms, and weddings, are increasingly subject to various tensions.

These affairs are often taken over by attempts at extortion. For example, in response to an event one side of the family might have to come up with a precise amount of a specific commodity in order to deter the other side from initiating some kind of ominous influence over the affair. Mutual demands and threats, and their resultant economies of compensation, introduce the need for a precise accounting of equivalence, which, in turn, reinforces an obsession with the need for balance. Opportunities to exceed these calculations must increasingly be carried out with heightened invisibility, at the same time as that invisibility reinforces the very fears and anxieties that largely motivate such economies of compensation in the first place.

With these dynamics of family and quarter management in mind, it is no wonder that the formal attempts engaged in by quarters to collaborate on development issues are so often belabored. Having met with a variety of development committees in various quarters of Zone Nylon, the concern with the fragility of local coherence often influences the local community's perceptions of its own capacities. Even in those few quarters where local chiefs are well informed and well intentioned, and where a concerted effort has been made to ensure both comprehensive local representation and the external partnerships necessary to introduce needed development resources, a wariness remains at each step of how to proceed.

In an urban environment long subject to the discourses of participatory planning, it becomes generally evident that forming an association is the key way to bring specific actors to a table of some kind. Quarters also do have their "genuine" activists, and their activism remains crucial to sustaining the viability of many quarters. Moreover, sports teams, saving clubs, and small businesses are organized; roads, paths, and bridges are built; and trenches are cleaned and events are staged. Yet, there is often an ambiguous line between associations that are formed as a way to attempt to solve individual economic problems and those that are informed by a general sense of "community spirit."

Attention to the processes of forging consensus is necessary in order to avoid internal disputes and to mobilize popular support for development initiatives. On the other hand, a prolonged period of stasis occurs when the search for consensus supersedes any other consideration. More important, the very dynamics through which quarters have opened up opportunities, through complementing diverse actions on the part of different identities with different networks and footholds outside the quarter, is disadvantageously underplayed.

To illustrate some of these dynamics, let me briefly digress with a story from one of Zone Nylon's many quarters. One rainy morning in July 2001, I saw scores of people in their best clothes carefully navigating their way in and out of one of the few well-constructed homes in the section of the Zone known as CCM-Oyok, a dense and rambling quarter built along a series of ravines. The porch of the house was crowded with families. I had just come from a meeting in a neighboring quarter where the Swiss cooperation ministry had spent many years attempting to provide well-planned streets and public spaces, clinics, libraries, and social centers. Indeed, the initial impression was of a very hospitable living environment, yet all the public spaces were starkly empty. And so this animated gathering of social life in Oyok came as something of a surprise.

The home with all of the traffic was that of a local healer and clearly the center of community life. The overbearing rainy season brought with it a host of maladies and frustrations; those waiting in line for consultations were quick to complain about the mudslides, flooded homes, and the lanes and roads that were barely navigable. Still, the ambiance at this "clinic" was clearly festive, as if through mutual illness or misfortune at least some recognition of a sense of common belonging was able to persist.

Immediately in front of the "clinic" was the main water tap for the area, set in 8 ft. x 8 ft. x 3 ft. basin intended to prevent runoffs from either frequent use or leakage. But in this weather, diverted streams branching out across the ravine flooded the basin with dirty water, in which the tap was submerged. The fresh water could only be obtained by dipping a bucket into the dirty water — a problem that easily could have been resolved by fixing a rubber extension to the nozzle so as to elevate the flow. The relationship between the crowds at the local healer and the compromised water tap, on the surface, seemed obvious. Although the quarter was rife with many other difficulties, at least here it appeared as if a simple solution was possible.

A large notice board near the water collection area contained an urgent call for all of the youth to gather the next day at 6:00 P.M. to dig trenches along the sides of the basin so as to prevent the collection of dirty water around the tap. The message on the board was signed "the chief." The appearance of this signature, apparently fresh that very morning, was of greater interest to the crowds gathered at the local healer than was the situation of the water tap itself. The healer's assistants were clearly upset that this designation had not yet been effaced. As it turned out, the message did not come from the actual chief of the quarter because he always signed his messages with his name. He was also known as someone who believes that if residents of the quarter try to make any improvements themselves he will not have any basis to make his frequent trips to the municipality to complain about conditions and subsequently be placated with appointments to numerous commissions.

Inquiries were made of the local youth organization, whose head, Guy, was clearly supportive of the effort but denied signing in the name of the chief, with whom he is clearly an antagonist because he believes that the youth should take all local matters into their hands. He further believes that it is precisely people like the local healer who don't want connections made between the state of the water tap and health, because as a consequence he will stop being taken seriously. Nevertheless, Guy is wary of attacking the healer directly, not so much because he is afraid of the healer's powers of sorcery but rather of the enigmatic power of a community that actually believes that the healer has true healing power. Thus Guy must go door to door the night before a community youth meeting to make sure that sufficient numbers of youths attend. He is constantly bewildered to see nearly all of his neighbors voluntarily gathered on the porch of the healer.

The local representative, Emmanuel, of the party holding local municipal power, also knows nothing about the message or the signature. Although he is not adverse to the efforts of local youth to ameliorate the water tap situation, he worries about the need for greater technical expertise. The overall placement of the central water collection point was poorly planned, and a continued improvised effort to divert local flooding, not only at the tap but across the quarter, has tended to exacerbate the overall vulnerability of the quarter to flooding during successive rainy seasons. As I am accompanied on this visit by the coordinator of a recently formed citywide advocacy organization, Emmanuel urges him to contact technicians at the national government's delegation to the city to address the water problem. After all, the local municipality, which the opposition controls, has no money to do anything to actually correct the situation.

Some youths do not want to wait until the next day—they feel that it is useless to commence such work after sunset because once again people are simply going to talk about what needs to be done. Overall, there is little coordination to the efforts of those trying to fix the tap: some attempt to scoop the dirty water out of the basin, but it really has nowhere to go; others get shovels to create drainage areas, but end up blocking some of the existing runoff streams with the mud. Most of the crowd at the healer's place, young and old, plan to show up for the effort on the next day. They know, of course, that any local authority they can identify has not sanctioned the call for their assistance; nonetheless, "the chief" has asked them to come, and their enthusiasm seems to grow as it becomes more evident to them that this "chief" doesn't come from within or without.

Given the vast needs of the quarters in Zone Nylon, and in almost all of the quarters of Douala and African cities in general, progressive improvements in local urban environments will require a multiplicity of engagements with potential external partners. These partners can be foreign donors, government officials, entrepreneurs and even associations from other quarters. No single relationship with the "outside" will ever be sufficient in order for the development needs of a quarter to be fulfilled. It is often this very multiplicity of engagement that local development committees find so difficult to initiate.

This reluctance feeds into the tendency of many local and external development NGOs and programs of development cooperation ministries to "own" particular quarters as their turf. Even though individualized, and often diffuse, initiatives were at the heart of the origin of many quarters, the scope for such initiative as a means of negotiating relationships between the quarter and the external world often remains limited. This is the case even when individual residents in their daily lives are extending their reach into wider domains; for, the fear is that as soon as a diversity of such engagements is initiated, the apparent balance of interests among associations, attained through their collective focus on a single external relationship, will be made vulnerable to a debilitating competition for resources and influence. Again, the calculus of balances must be maintained, even if it prolongs the levels of underdevelopment that everyone desperately wishes to get beyond.

As I have shown, quarters often have effective and largely informal ways of negotiating the world outside their confines. Yet, the behavior of formal collaborative structures seems to treat the outside world largely as an extension of the image of the quarter itself. Thus in the end it remains difficult for quarters to extend themselves into the image of the cosmopolitan imposed by ARAN as the anchoring "downtown" of Zone Nylon. This place of supposed convergence remains, if not unreachable, then fundamentally disconnected from the practices of collective local survival employed by the surrounding quarters. There is no useful image about how this particular sign of urbanization can be potentially important to the quarters that it was supposed to anchor and converge.

Instead, it stands as detached and abstract as the concept of the *feyman*, as one resident of Tergal described it. The choice of this description is particularly interesting, as much of the understanding about what contemporary Douala is, as well as the aspirations of much of its youth, are wrapped up in the notion of feyman. It is an identity without precise definitions. Instead, it refers to an ability to not only acquire money without working, but to get others to conclude that they have no choice but to give you money. It is widely known that those who have acquired great wealth through a variety of confidence games populate the wealthy residential areas of Denver and Dallas — named after popular television shows involving the Carringtons and Ewings.

The confidence games range in size, scope, and believability. For example, a man starts going regularly to a vendor in the market and becomes a loyal customer. After a time, the vendor feels free to casually converse about his or her difficulties and aspirations to make the business grow. The "customer" then begins to lend small amounts of money, and the business does begin to grow. Then, after a while, the customer talks about various opportunities in which the money attainable is big, and shows various documents to support his case. He asks the vendor for a large sum of money to invest. The customer had been very helpful in the past; the chance of bigger profits is difficult to pass up. But, in the end the customer takes the money and is never seen again.

Other stories are much more intricate. Some involve highly organized Cameroonian syndicates who manage to take over large sections of the staff at exclusive hotels in Europe. Through the use of magic, they steal exceedingly valuable jewels from hotel safes, replacing them with exact replicas. What is visible, and what feymen make a point about being visible, is that there are those with little who in the course of several months display vast amounts of wealth. What is not visible, but based on official calculation, is that some $250 million is smuggled out of Cameroon every year into foreign bank accounts.

Thus downtown Zone Nylon appears as a feyman: something that emerges out of nothing, perhaps aspired to but without a clear and visible path with which to reach it. It is something that seems magically intact and whole, without being able to account for its process of construction and the elements from which it is made — even though those who lived near it were able to observe it being built over the years.

What Do They See?

Bessengue Akwa represents one of Douala's quarters where the struggle for remaking urban life has been most marked and often confusing. It is a highly dense quarter built within a recess between two of north-central Douala's main north-south thoroughfares and south of the lateral road that connects them. On the southern boundary runs a large swampy creek. Most households are quite literally living on top of each other, with bad sanitation and barely navigable narrow thoroughfares. Needless to say, there are major problems with security, waste collection, and clean water.

Because the area set back from the lateral road used to be an area of dense bush, the initial settlers—relatively well-off households able to construct two- to three-story compounds—encouraged informal settlements down from the compounds in order to provide security. But within two decades, the area became a sea of contiguous makeshift tin roofs organized in highly ethnically parochial domains. Largely out of general view, the quarter is well known as a cheap refuge close to the city's center.

The quarter's chief is a dynamic and towering young man with a quiet demeanor and with the political skills and the persistence to corral a motley assortment of the quarter's residents into an effective development committee. This committee has wrangled commitments from the municipality to substantially restructure the quarter, including plans to install electricity, build passable roads, clean up the creek, and provide clean bulk water supplies. That the provision of these services means that many of the present residents will have to be moved has not so far proved to be a major obstacle to mobilizing community support, as the prospect often does for many such communities. In part, this is attributable to efforts on the part of the chief and several activists to make the development committee as inclusive as possible, even though the chief plays no direct role in coordinating its functioning.

An important part of the development effort in terms of service provision has been the activists' conviction that the effort provides an opportunity to inculcate a sense of "moral partnership" among residents otherwise overstretched with having to manage delicate territorial relationships. In other words, it is perceived as an exercise in getting residents to take responsibility for each other in ways that exceed their immediate household and local ethnic ties. It thus takes a chance on a variety of local personalities, without clear institutional status, to try out various ways to mobilize local youth, for example, or organize women's support groups. This reframing has, in turn, encouraged patience with the protracted pace of negotiations with the municipality.

Despite these efforts, even the more activist residents seem to remain largely passive observers waiting for the change that must come and hoping that the deteriorating environmental and social conditions will not overwhelm them. It is understandable that any external assistance would be eagerly taken up, and great efforts are made to be hospitable to an array of potential "external partners." But this accommodation also signals the extent to which members of the development committee can't see what resides and operates within Bessengue as potential resources. There is a sustained feeling that residents must behave differently with each other, not so much in order to activate greater local potentials or skills, but to deactivate something insidious that has been released in the prolonged neglect of the quarter.

Just down from the northwest entrance to the quarter stands the tallest and best built structure in the area. It is a structure that from all appearances stands empty and indeed is not being used, which is somewhat ironic given the efforts of the development committee to raise money to create a youth center by renovating the shell of an overgrown, abandoned house elsewhere in town. The currently empty building here was intended as a kind of *auberge* — a guesthouse for stays of various length, with some facilities for meetings and even performance. A former Bessengue resident, Bernard, who had made a little money after migrating to Europe, initiated the construction of the auberge as an investment in the quarter, a signal of the viability of its urban future. But as soon as the building was finished, Bernard disappeared. Apparently his departure was not a matter of the lack of proper permits, land deeds or, continued funding, but rather the common assumption was that powerful forces in the quarter did not want the business to succeed. The possibility of a success — which was good given the quality of the construction and its discrete yet highly central location — would bring in a flow of outsiders, back and forth, and perhaps open up this section of the quarter to more scrutiny from the outside. Whatever the reason, everyone talked about how the owner had been scared off.

In trying to find out a little more about the story of the auberge I was told to talk to a dancer, Francis, who worked at a strip club in the center of the city. She had reputedly gone out with the owner over a several-month period during the time the auberge was being built. She also happened to rent a room in the second tallest building in the quarter — a five-story shell of an apartment building approximately one hundred meters from the auberge. Francis had come to Douala two years ago from the outskirts of Yaounde in order to pursue a singing career. Earning less than $100 a month, she pursued what is called the "usual supplementation" — that is, occasional sex for money. Although she wouldn't or couldn't say where Bernard was, she did indicate that he frequently called her late in the night on her cell phone, usually with cryptic instructions to pay close attention to certain spots behind the shuttered windows of the auberge. The next time he called she was to report back whatever she saw, but more important she was to phone a variety of "associates" and tell them what she witnessed. What she did see, however, was almost always impossible for her to put

A view of Bessengue, a quarter in the central zone of Douala, Cameroon.

into words. So she took to simply inviting those whom she was instructed to report over to her room at least twice a week before sunrise, and together they made their attempts to peer behind the building's opaque visage.

Sometimes some of the guests took notes and passed them around, although Francis says that she couldn't make any sense of them. They would then have coffee and make idle conversation, although the guests would also inquire whether or not the others had completed certain tasks, whether they had made sure to send certain express packages, fetch people from the airport, or wait in the lobbies of certain big hotels. Francis kept saying that it was never clear to her what they were really up to; rather, they seemed to relish each other's assignments and recommendations, and that somehow by simply assuming different positions in different sites that things were made to happen, that they made each other happen. Although Francis was reluctant to have me simply drop by at these appointed times, I was told it might interest me on certain mornings to stand quietly down by the auberge to watch the determined, even joyful, way her guests fanned out from Bessengue at sunrise.

What is insidious in the neglect of Bessengue largely concerns an acceptance of marginality and a blindness of how the quarter fits into or could fit into the larger city. But as the chairperson of the local youth committee told me, what was really troubling to most residents was that the place was

A second view of Bessengue.

being used by unseen others in ways that they could not control, and so inactively became, by default, a means of such control. The anecdote about the auberge, an aphorism really, is about this blindness and the way it is constructed. But it also concerns how others, whose identities and purposes are not really known, come to operate in such a field, and do so in invisible ways we sometimes can't know or anticipate. Perhaps in the near future, local development will require ways of imagining how better to go with the flows.

La Nouvelle Liberté

The following discussion forms the heart of this case study of Douala. Here I briefly outline the story of *La Nouvelle Liberté*, a forty-foot sculpture that stands in one of the main roundabouts in Douala. The story is also implicitly about Marilyn Douala-Bell and her husband, Didier Schaub, who together run an "arts for urban development" center, Doual'art, founded in 1991. Doual'art combines exhibition space with a program of assisting local communities in various development actions. Marilyn Douala-Bell is a direct descendant of the renowned Bell chiefs, a genealogy that has consistently attempted to posit a forward-looking image for the city. Shortly after the founding of Doual'art, an exhibition was planned for the controversial

Cameroonian artist, Joseph Francis Sumegné, whose installations had been received with great renown abroad but were, as yet, little known in his own country. Not formally trained as an artist, Sumegné had apprenticed as a car fabricator, tailor, metal worker, and house painter. His work reflected this background in its use of a wide variety of materials assembled in ways that amplified the particularity of constituent elements, while at the same time produced coherent images.

Following the exhibition in October 1993, Schaub had the idea for Sumegné to construct a public monument somewhere in the city. The extremely vivid way in which the artist was capable of constructing an integrated image from the amplification of the recycled parts that he used in his installations was thought to embody important ideas about the life of the city. Various sites across the city were canvassed, and the traffic circle in Deido was finally selected. This site was significant for several reasons. First, Deido is perhaps the most important node in the circulation of traffic across the city. It is located at the foot of the city's most significant bridge over the Wouri River, and it stands at the crossroads between the city's distinct administrative and commercial centers. It is the main commuting axis for those civil servants in the municipal administration who largely live in a "bedroom" community known as Cité de Droits. After Bell and Akwa, Deido is the third historic village in Douala, and the one most known for its adamant protection of local culture — its residents are commonly known as the *têtes bruleés* (hot heads) of Douala. Finally, the traffic circle was an important site of "illegal" petty commerce, with scores of youths selling secondhand clothes and repeatedly engaging in a "cat and mouse" game with the police.

A long period of preparation commenced after the selection of the site. The municipality had to concede the land and agree to function as the regulator. The wife of the Deido mayor was recruited as the patron of the project, thus adding significant legitimacy and clout to the endeavor. A private company was formed to raise funds and to solicit the contribution of materials for the sculpture and in-kind services, a major example of which was the donation of a warehouse at the nearby port where the sculpture was constructed over the course of two years, as well as a house in Deido that was donated to the artist and his assistant. Further, because the road around the circle was dilapidated, a major effort was launched to rehabilitate the urban site, although this effort was not to be realized until after the sculpture had been installed.

Extensive community consultations were done during the course of one year. In general, there was widespread support for the project: the community was shown sketches, and there was a dearth of critical comments. Some community members insisted that because the Douala were river people, the sculpture should be mounted on a large pirogue. However, they did not persist with this demand after it was explained to be an engineering impossibility. In general, like many purported initiatives the community had been promised, the common assumption was that the project would never materialize. Later on, when the sculpture was finally installed on the site, the residents of Deido saw the mere completion of the project as an important triumph, no matter what aesthetic reservations might be had by elements of the local population.

Three months prior to the anticipated date of installation, the municipal administration was changed. The new mayor indeed attempted to change everything, including the locks on all the office doors, the furnishings in the office, and so on. He also indicated to Doual'art that his cooperation would be predicated on the replacement of the former mayor's wife with his own wife as patron of the project; although in the end, the project proceeded with a compromise that removed the position altogether.

Without fanfare or public announcement, a giant crane carried *La Nouvelle Liberté* to its installation on July 21, 1996. A giant human figure, holding up a sphere and lifting one leg, suddenly towered over the site. Within an hour, seemingly all of Deido and more had gathered at the traffic circle, where police struggled to hold back the crowds. The secondhand clothes sellers, who had persistently resisted being chased off the site, said in a collective announcement, "The work is like us . . . therefore we are always here . . . now we can go." The affirmative excitement, however, was not universal. Because the sculpture was installed on a Sunday while the mayor was attending a church located right at the site, he was heard to say on leaving the service, "What can we do with this now?"

The following day, the installation was front-page news to general acclaim in all the newspapers, although the headline of one newspaper, *El Limbi*, screamed "A Monument in Shit" — referring not to the sculpture but to the advanced state of disrepair in which the road and site were to be found. By early September, crews were sent to repair the roads as quickly as possible — so quickly, in fact, that the job had to be redone three times. Throughout the city, the monument was a constant topic of discussion; indeed, probably no household was without some comment or reflection. The most common remarks were expressions of gratitude: that the sculpture was an affirmation of a way of urban life that people had been reluc-

La Nouvelle Liberté, at the Deido roundabout in Douala, Cameroon.

tant, even embarrassed, to affirm; that recycled and secondhand materials can indeed make up a good life. Throughout the city, people talked about how they had finally discovered that the city was something in which to take pride. Douala was not a failed imitation of "real" cities but rather an example of a particular and valued way of making a city.

The more this affirmative point of view was expressed, the more a countervailing sentiment also was articulated. When the mayor asked, "What can we do with this now?" he reflected an attitude of the elite, who could not understand the monument as "real" art. By exposing car parts, discarded tires, scrap metals, and other various debris, many resident elites felt that the dregs of the city they worked so hard to avoid were being given a kind of hypervisibility, implicating them as part of a way of life they felt they had successfully circumvented.

It was not an accident that such elite sentiments grew louder at the end of 1996 as the electoral campaign, with the country's first municipal elections, drew closer. *El Limbi*, the newspaper that had provoked the municipality into finally completing the necessary repairs at the site, reversed itself and launched a series of articles condemning the sculpture for not being a thing of beauty or being made with precious materials as were public monuments in European cities. Requesting the right to respond, Marilyn Douala-Bell wrote a letter to the newspaper saying that the sculpture represented a way of living in contemporary Cameroon. The efforts of the majority of the urban population to make a functional livelihood from what the rest of the world might otherwise discard was an important means of "breathing life" into a neglected continent.

In response to this letter *El Limbi* shifted the orientation of its criticism, and indicated that the main problem was that the artist, Sumegné, was a Bamileke and that the sculpture was an explicit testimonial to the Bamileke economic domination of the city. In general terms, the Bamileke are viewed as the most skilled and wealthy entrepreneurs in the country. A long history of land shortages and a history of highly structured social relations have propelled them into a highly skilled proficiency in using urban areas as a platform for substantial accumulation and investment. This proficiency goes so far as to result in the self-serving claim of many Cameroonians that non-Bamileke are forced into corruption because they have little opportunity otherwise to economically compete.

As the Bamileke originate from the northwest, historically anglophone, part of Cameroon — which also is the seat of the major opposition political party — the invocation of the artist's ethnic origins at a time of major elections was, in part, clearly a political ploy. It was also an easy way for the elite, who chose not to "discover" themselves or their city in *La Nouvelle Liberté*, to attempt to control the popular interpretations of what the monument represented. After all, even months after the installation, discussions across the city about the sculpture were relentless.

Major artists and musicians entered the fray, with one of the most popular musical groups quoted in a headline in the paper *Mutaçion*, "What can be done if we had made a mistake?," referring to the widespread initial support given to the project by the country's arts communities. Even after the opposition party won control of all five major districts in Douala following the city's first municipal elections at the end of 1996, the attacks on *La Nouvelle Liberté* escalated. Again, the orientation of the criticism shifted. During the first quarter of 1997, Marilyn Douala-Bell and Didier Schaub were singled out for vociferous personal attacks. While one newspaper, *El Limbi*, was largely responsible for leading these attacks, other papers stood by in silence and could not be persuaded to come to anyone's support. Douala-Bell was labeled a "pseudo-princess" and accused of renewing the treachery carried out by her forebears, who had supposedly betrayed their people in treaties with the Germans and the French. Schaub was accused of establishing a radar station for French espionage activities under the guise of the sculpture. Rumors spread that financing for the project entailed various thefts of public funds earmarked for other development projects.

In response to the financial accusations, Doual'art published the total costs of the project and detailed how the money was raised. The total cost of the project was CFA40 million (roughly US$80,000), with a quarter of the funds donated by Doual'art, another quarter from the French government, and the rest raised through a substantial number of small contributions from people from all walks of life across the city. Unfortunately, this disclosure in the interest of transparency backfired in part. A nearly successful attempted kidnapping of the couple's youngest son was believed to have been motivated by the assumption that if Doual'art could contribute $20,000 to a sculpture, it would be willing to pay much more for the return of a son. Over the course of the next several months, the police refused to investigate either the repeated death threats or the attempted kidnapping, and they placed all kinds of obstacles in the way of several independent investigations.

Despite intimidation and a tirade of attacks on the project, *La Nouvelle Liberté* continued to invigorate popular discussion and imagination. Everyday, scores of individuals and families came to the monument to have their pictures taken, and a thriving informal photo sector took hold in the surrounding area. The mayor of Deido, who had initially wanted to remove the project after six months and was relieved by the criticism launched against it in the press, nevertheless made no overt moves against it. It is speculated that the main reason for his reluctance was that his ten-year-old daughter won first prize in a school essay contest, where she described how much the sculpture meant to her. At one point unknown persons draped garlands of electric Christmas lights around the sculpture, and now at holiday times *La Nouvelle Liberté* is illuminated at night.

As Doual'art is a technical advisor to many different development projects across the city, local civic groups repeatedly wanted to speak about the sculpture. More than anything else, they wanted to speak about the materials and how the artist was able to get these particular materials to work so well together. Everyone had interpretations, but rather than being fixed to them people wanted to know if their interpretations made sense and whether or not it was somehow valid for them to think in particular ways about the sculpture. In this way, the sculpture was a popular provocation.

In the end, it is difficult to assess what projects like *La Nouvelle Liberté* really means to a city like Douala. Still, without doubt, the project got residents to talk about the city in ways that were probably unprecedented. Whatever popular opinion was, as opposed to that of certain sectors of the elite, the sculpture is cherished as something that "got done." As one ninety-year-old man remarked at the sculpture's installation, it is as if Africa had finally produced its own Joan of Arc—its own vision of urban life from which it could now do battle. Whatever it accomplishes, *La Nouvelle Liberté* reveals a capacity in the city to recognize its own resourcefulness, even if it means that only something like the singularity and monumentality of a *La Nouvelle Liberté* is capable of bringing such recognition to the fore. Of course, such recognition is precarious; images that can counter prevailing norms don't rest easy. Until this day, *La Nouvelle Liberté* remains uncompleted: there is still work to finish on the leg that is held up in the air.

4

Movement

The Zawiyyah

as the City

In previous chapters I have described cases taking place within specific localities in Africa. But African urban life also crosses local borders. In this chapter I want to emphasize how a protracted and substantial history of movement has opened up new domains and circuits through which urban actors operate, and how the sense of the local is reconfigured across geographical distances and divides.

In this case study about Africans operating in Jidda, Saudi Arabia, my interest is in how a historical Sufi Muslim institution is appropriated and reshaped as an instrument facilitating the collaboration of diverse groups of actors in a place away from home but in many ways operating as home. My objective here is to point out the ways in which particular modalities of organization, long rooted in different African histories, are resuscitated for new objectives and with new resiliency.

Movement as Its Own End

Africa is a space of intensified movement, of movement in a very broad sense that encompasses migration, displacement, and accelerated social mobility. But this movement is not totally subsumed by these categories; rather it has been appropriated as a multifaceted strategy of urban survival—accumulation but also control. It reflects the increasing material unavailablity of specific urban territories as platforms on which to constitute the semblance of stable and coherent social existence. It also reflects the use of movement as an increasingly "normalized" social practice deployed to constitute an experience of stability linked to the capacity of individual and social actors to continuously orient themselves to shifting terrain of economic activity and political disposition.[1] Movement is also a process without foreseeable end. When rural populations come to the city they are deemed migrants, but an ongoing career of sometimes incessant shifts in places of residence and work within the city can be viewed analytically as separate from migration.

Movement also has little sense if it is not set against a process of staying still. Who migrates and who doesn't remains a tricky difference, even when both parties face common economic and cultural situations. Simply raising this issue introduces a necessary complexity in how we characterize particular local fields, forcing us to recognize the intricate interweaving of access to social networks, gender, age, physical location, asset holdings, and political voice in migration decisions.[2] As migration for better livelihood also proves to be more of a gamble, the abundance of stories concerning increased hardship and poverty as a result of migration induces potential migrants to reassess their plans. Equally important in this assessment is the extent to which either structurally or experientially people have a specific place to go. Whether or not people have a specific destination in mind depends on the extent to which particular places are linked through various flows and networks to a highly differentiated "larger world" — in terms of their relative inclusion in a broad topography of interconnections. It also depends on the exclusion that people experience in their present locations.[3]

The entrance of relatively new actors is also shaping these considerations. For example, there has been an increase in the number of women migrants in recent years.[4] This trend has varied consequences, ranging from the reformation of transnational trading syndicates to the substantial expansion of sex trafficking. Women are being used to blaze new navigational paths into countries and regions previously difficult to penetrate, and they are carving out new niches in heavily gendered markets such as service sectors in Europe — often reversing conventional domestic roles of child care and household production in the process.[5]

Migration has also conventionally tended to connote relocating a sense of belonging. Here, the migrants either attempted to incorporate their new positionality within a preexisting space of belonging or sought to act on their new domain of operation in ways capable of incorporating the place from which they came. These ways might include either accommodating additional members of their social network or their customary social practices. A less common analysis is to see the process of movement as a means of effacing specific constraints posited by both environments. In other words, as a particular means of continuously remaking spaces of operation by setting distinct environments together through their embodiment by the migrant, and doing so in ways that owe no specific allegiance to the conventions of either.

Movement in this sense indeed reflects a kind of "dispossession," but it is one in which the migrant seeks to configure a certain capacity for improvisation so as to best capitalize on economic and social opportunities opened up by the very inability of the city to fully incorporate — house, employ, and service — all those who make demands on it. In other words, where migration may have been compelled by the long-term inability of many rural environments to provide for even subsistence needs or the livelihood opportunities concentrated in cities, the proliferation of movement comes close to constituting its own enlarging and self-reproducing logic.[6]

This is not quite movement for movement's sake but approaches a situation where the focus of investment, in time, money, and human resources, is directed toward ongoing movement despite whatever efficacy is derived from a particular destination at a particular time. The very ability to accrue the earnings from one's labor to the progressive development of a specific territorial position is increasingly doubted and held in suspicion.[7] The notion is that limited savings must be directed toward ensuring a capacity to act flexibly in the face of uncertain social, economic, and political conditions. This results in a burgeoning anticipation that everything that will be possible to do in the future is necessarily provisional. This provisionality in turn threatens to undermine all gains if actors are compelled to defend their positions in given territories rather than to acquire an increased ability to adapt to a wide range of territories. With both increased affiliation and affinity with movement, a highly mobile collective subject is configured.[8] The identity of this subject, although unstable and not thoroughly consolidated, resonates with long and multiple African traditions of locality.[9]

Structuring Movement

There are, of course, constraints on movement, which are structured according to specific geographic and political locations. The aspiration for emigration out of many southern nations exceeds the capability to move, and as such accounts for the fact that a larger volume of migration does not occur.[10] The nature of local resources capable of being deployed for emigration, and the various national and regional policy frameworks and regulatory instruments applied to controlling migratory movements, combine to elaborate specific modalities of migration. Here, movement is enabled under specific auspices, each with its own associated requirements, risks, and costs, including labor permits, family reunification, political asylum, illegal status, and overstaying tourist visas.[11]

This interaction of individual or local capacity and external regulation in turn structures specific practices of "enrolling" external, nonlocal territories as important facets of the project of life making and entails particular meanings about the places that individuals call "home" or about where they are presently "located." In assessing specific individual and regional orientations to movement, how particular meanings are ascribed to emigration must be considered.[12] The very aspiration to migrate itself may be largely a culturally defined notion of proactivity, and as such it carries with it a series of embedded obligations to elaborate networks and institutions of concrete support. These in turn face more proficient instruments mobilized to monitor migratory flows and to assess the veracity of claims made to access external spaces.

In much of the continent a long-term normalization of cross-border movement as a way of life interacts, sometimes with marked complicity and at other times with marked turbulence, with population displacement as a tool of regimes, rebellions, or private forces consolidating power, thereby populating or emptying out contested regions.[13] The status of particular regions or territories within competing popular imaginations, competing claims on the part of both local and multinational companies, and the exigencies of "domesticating" actual or emerging conflict render increasingly larger numbers of people expendable or objects of manipulation. These dynamics severely complicate the resettlement of displaced populations. This is particularly the case in situations where there is the persistence of strong arguments regarding not only where specific populations rightly belong but also their various positionalities in these places, as well as the popular perceptions of the rights and resources that they can legitimately claim.[14]

Although movement is performed by seemingly disconnected individuals uprooted from their homes and stable places of belonging, the agendas and motivations that reflect those of autonomous individuals do not necessarily drive it. Rather, the danger posed by individuals as disconnected agents constitutes a persistent and deep-seated concern of many African societies. If stabilizing particular configurations of social and institutional life within the confines of specific territorial placements is either materially not viable or generates unacceptable levels of internecine conflict, social stress, or unmanageable reciprocal obligations, then local institutions should be flexibly shaped to incorporate shifting social compositions. Thus, a sense of stability is forged from the very instability of the compositions and relations of those institutions that try to provide a platform for social connectedness and collaboration.[15]

To "place" individuals, then, does not mean to incorporate them as permanent members of a specific locality, but rather to orient the construction of "locality" to an ability to continuously, if only temporarily, root specific persons to a series of collaborations and obligations. Not only do social institutions accommodate themselves to such assumed and potential mobility, but they also become drivers of it — as the principles and terms of affiliation and cooperation are more heterogeneous and contingent.

Movement reflects a growing inability of individuals to remain in place. Yet the very sustenance of specific places themselves requires movement. This requirement exceeds the narrow sense that remittances derived from earnings away from "home" are required to maintain a functional sense of "home," or at least a continued sense of ancestral identification. The need goes beyond the injection of funds. Rather, the logic by which many of the critical local social institutions operate cannot be sustained without the continuous ebb and flow of specific populations or without the coming and going of diverse members plying diverse networks in various locales. Without understanding movement as part and parcel of the very lifeblood of particular local social institutions, analysts miss possibilities of policy and programmatic engagements with an important social infrastructure — albeit of limited visibility due to its dispersion and complexity — that cuts across rural, periurban, urban, national, and regional boundaries.

Populations appear more rootless and rooted than they may be in actuality. The efficacy of mobile and flexibly structured local institutions still depends on a sense of anchorage or emplacement. Yet, policies oriented toward making the many facets of populations in movement less problematic act to undermine this limited but necessary anchorage, and do so in ways that turn such population movements into the desperate meanderings they have too often inaccurately been taken to be.

Within many Sufi traditions, the *zawiyyah*, a lodge where accommodation for traveling "brothers" is provided, plays an important role as a service to members of a specific "brotherhood" and as an embodiment and facilitator of the translocal character of this affiliation. The zawiyyah is also a site where *zikhr*, worship, can be performed according to the practices of a particular brotherhood, and it also acts as a referral agency where information about various opportunities and resources might be accessed.

When a man joins a particular Sufi order, or *tariqa*, he is obligated to take a *wird*, an oath of loyalty. The loyalty is directed not only to the order as an abstract framework of religious practice but also to the leadership, the *shaykh*, and the hereditary right and passing on of this leadership. The order is thus anchored in an unyielding focal point of mediation between the earthly and the divine.

The hierarchies involved are more textured than simply the shaykh at the pinnacle and his followers in a position of devotion and access. Nevertheless, a strong sense of the equality of all before the shaykh does exist and enforces a practice where the *talibe*, the followers, must be responsible for the welfare of each other. The zawiyyah is the key institution through which this responsibility is expressed, for while in travel individuals are operating outside of the confines of their local anchorage and support systems. Temporarily freed from these domains, the zawiyyah becomes the most salient place through which the sense of connection among members of the tariqa can be expressed and also mobilized for various forms of collective action.

In many cities throughout West Africa, the zawiyyah is an important site through which migrants could be incorporated into the city. Through the zawiyyah they might be connected to preexisting economic activities as apprentices or laborers, or they might be availed some small sums of capital with which to launch enterprises, and in this way expand the network and diversity of economic activities engaged in by the order. At other times, they were provided with goods to sell back to their home regions, as a means of strengthening both trade and religious links. Given the specific political circumstances, the zawiyyah could also be used as a site for the dissemination of political analysis and organization.[16]

By establishing places of hospitality and support, travel was implicitly encouraged. Increasingly, zawiyyah became centers through which travel was tracked. The objective of monitoring was not so much geared toward keeping tabs on the activities of the "faithful" as it was to cultivate a means through which their movements could be used as a resource. After all, various talibe staying in a particular lodge would talk about what they were doing and what they had seen. To the extent that their successes and opportunities would bring glory to the shaykh, and thus to themselves in the "next life," there was a strong impetus to engage fellow members of the tariqa in various projects and opportunities where possible.

The zawiyyah acted as a circumscribed domain of publicity. It became a place where devotees could gather a sense of the wide range of locations and activities in which the tariqa was involved, be stimulated to take on new activities, and conceive and assess individual possibilities in the larger context of what the order was doing.[17]

When I visited a Tidiane zawiyyah in Treichville, a large quarter of Abidjan, during 1993, a large world map was positioned on a wall in one of the common rooms. On the map, hundreds of cities were circled with magic markers and "tagged" with numbers. Heavily worn and numbered cardboard files, corresponding to the numbers on the map, were placed on a table below. The files contained various lists of names of the followers living in these cities, along with brief profiles.

Some of these profiles had been written by talibe passing through this particular zawiyyah over the years. Others were stories and notes compiled by visitors regarding other followers whom they had met or knew about in their own travels. Still others were, in essence, photocopies of profiles that were compiled by zawiyyah in other locations. The term profile is a very rough designation for these documents — they were not prepared, compiled, or used in any systematic way. Indeed, given the fact that many talibe are functionally illiterate, certainly only a small portion of the tariqa are actually engaged in this type of record keeping.

What is significant about these notations is not as much their systematic character or use. Rather, they point to a practice of articulating discrete individual stories and activities into a larger network of interconnected pursuits and opportunities. What exists within the scope of these written records may only serve as a reminder to talibe of the possibilities of reciprocity and collaborative action. In some circumstances, these graphically apparent indications of networked activity may actually mask the nature of the "real" exchanges and collaborations taking place.

They may incite talibe to seek out interactions with fellow devotees in other places. These interactions may take place under the auspices of religious comradeship and a purported knowledge about what other talibe might be doing. Where such interactions might lead and whom they might involve remain something to be negotiated. At one level, the turuq (Sufi brotherhoods) seek to establish means through which collaborations and mutual support can be exercised among talibe who are strangers to each other. In other words, the turuq have to assert the viability of such cooperation. At the same time, they seek to fine-tune such collaborations. This is done so that certain economic activities, especially those that are illegal in specific contexts, can be pursued by talibe who find a means to trust each other and use their different skills and histories.

Reinventing Sufi Tradition

Until World War II, the zawiyyah remained an institution for all talibe, despite their economic capacities and social status. This was to change, however, after the war. In the acceleration of urban modernization in the postwar period, and then again in the period after independence, the zawiyyah became primarily an institution for small traders and the poorer members of the tariqa in most cities. The wealthier members of brotherhoods developed new associations and networks: they joined or formed political parties, welfare organizations, business clubs, and built special mosques and schools, as well as Islamic institutes and centers. These served as a base for consolidating the local and national power of specific tariqa, but also for accessing opportunities in and attracting funds from the larger Islamic world, particularly the Gulf States.

The traditional zawiyyah, then, has been increasingly incorporated into the orbit of these new organizations and objectives. How this incorporation takes place and the subsequent role of the zawiyyah in a new network of institutions and entrepreneurial activities varies, of course, in specific urban and national contexts. There are also differences in the extent to which different turuq cooperate or compete with each other, depending on their relative strength in particular regions. In northern Nigeria, Tidiane, Qaddriyyah, Bruhaniyyah, and Sanusiyya turuq have strong pockets of adherents in a context where there is an enormous diversity of Islamic expression, institutions, and entrepreneurship. As such, cooperation often remains minimal. In Abidjan, where Muslims have made a concerted effort in recent years to become a more predominant sociopolitical force, various turuq have joined hands in many activities.

New institutions have proliferated, including schools, mosques, various enterprises, and political and cultural associations based on class, ethnic,

and national distinctions. Yet the relationships among Sufi institutions retain a large measure of the spirit of the zawiyyah. In other words, the ethos
of how the zawiyyah has operated throughout hundreds of years is infused
into the operational practices of Sufi turuq as a whole. These are turuq still
dominated by the leadership of a shaykh and the incumbent responsibilities
of the talibe to take care of each other.

The rest of the Islamic world has maintained a largely ambivalent attitude toward the predominance of Sufism in West African religious practice.
The orthodox Sunni Wahabi traditions that prevail in the Gulf are largely
critical of this practice: they view it as an essential deviation from the
sunnah, the way of the Prophet Muhammad and the normative frameworks of *makhtab*, the guidelines that inform how the religion is to be
practiced.

In practice, a wide range of mutual engagements among Islamic orientations has taken place. With its large Muslim population and relatively fluid
political and economic environments, West Africa is an important place of
operation for the major Islamic powers. In the past two decades particularly, reform movements emphasizing a more political role for Islam in
national and international affairs have been active through various formations of the Jebha Islamiyyah, or Muslim Brotherhood. Various Shi'a
groupings based in Lebanon and Iran have used elements of the large Leba-
nese community in West African cities as nodal points in their political
and economic operations. Through its well-endowed welfare association,
Dawa Islamiyyah, the Libyans have also been extremely active in building
mosques and schools throughout the region. They have also funded a variety of political groups and have trained local leaders.

Urban West African communities have been the targets of sizable amounts
of external funding, in part through an ongoing struggle among the major
Islamic powers for predominance. While I was living in a Muslim household
in Nima, a mostly Muslim quarter of central Accra in Ghana, three of the
sons were taking money from different countries — Saudi Arabia, Iran, and
Libya — to work as organizers in the community. There, conflicts among
local groupings with different external affiliations could get quite tense and
competitive; although serious neighborhood disruptions could still be tem-
pered over long dinner conversations among the brothers at home.

Loyalties shifted according to need. The kinds of ideological and political
distinctions that external "allies" sought to enforce were never deeply
rooted in any community of which I was aware. Additionally, substantial
amounts of external assistance were capable of diversion. In another exam-

ple from Accra, the Muslim Judicial Council bought and sold large stores of rice in 1990 with funds intended to develop new Islamic secondary schools in the country. I know this because I was to assist the council in creating a strategic development plan for these schools.

Agencies such as the African Muslim Agency (AMA), which is largely funded by Kuwait, were established to disseminate religious materials and support religious education in each African country. While much of the effort of this agency is indeed focused on such pedagogical activities, it also has developed substantial business interests in many countries. Even some of the scholarships it offers for advanced religious and secular studies are "sold" on the open market, and many Christian students attempt to access such scholarships by pretending to be Muslims.

On the other hand, such "converts" are frequently sought out by the various Muslim agencies themselves. For example, the African Islamic institute in Khartoum, Sudan, is a large, well-endowed center of secondary and tertiary education. It is well known that if a student does well there he is likely to access opportunities for advanced professional training in the Gulf States. Many of the students from Nigeria and Ghana in particular are "converts" who are provided these opportunities in exchange for their participation in a wide variety of illicit business ventures by entrepreneurs in the Gulf States. These states provide the bulk of funding for the institute. The belief is that these "converts" are freed from particular family and community obligations and are more amenable to taking risks. As converted Muslims, they are also in many ways not viewed as "real" Muslims. This view prevails despite the Islamic injunction that says that Muslims, whether they are born to Muslim families or not, can only be Muslims through taking the *shahada*, the profession of belief.

The AMA is simply one element of a network of interrelated Islamic institutions and private corporations in the Gulf States. This network operates with significant scale and reach, and includes institutions such as the Islamic Development Bank, both the Saudi and Libyan "versions" of Dawa Islamiyyah, the Fahd Foundation, a venture capital operation, as well as a network of banks, construction firms, clearing houses, and import-export firms. The underregulated banking, customs, and market structures of most West African countries play an important role in the recirculation of money and commodities used by the Muslim Brothers, in particular, to repeatedly launch forays into financial markets with more capacity in Asia, Europe, North America, and Latin America.

My point here, however, is not to discuss how these Gulf-based economic operations work but to note some ways in which various turuq have sought to engage them in order to advance their own interests. Through a well-elaborated system of seminars, meetings, religious convocations, and, of course, the annual pilgrimage to Mecca for *haj*, West African Muslims have long been availed opportunities to travel to and throughout the Islamic world, particularly the Gulf States. As in the past, preparations for the haj can take many years. The pilgrimage involves a sizable investment of personal resources, and local savings mechanisms are usually relied on in order to generate the resources needed to fulfill this obligation. The Saudi government allots a specific number of "places" and requires specific plans for accommodation and travel on the part of national "delegations" to Mecca. This means that national organizing committees need to be formed. Payments are made to these committees for handling all the logistics involved in the pilgrimage, as well as negotiating who goes and under what circumstances.

Struggles over who controls these committees can be intense, because control means that large amounts of money are availed to committees, usually some time before the actual pilgrimage is made. There are frequently controversies over how these funds are used and invested prior to their deployment to cover the logistical costs for national delegations. In Benin, for example, there have been repeated controversies over the extent to which haj funds have been used to cover a variety of precarious pyramid schemes. In other circumstances, the Tidiane taruq, through organizing separate deals with the Saudi government, has used haj funds to support various takeover activities of European properties and companies by Saudi-based firms. These investments are made in return for a specific portion of the profits and for access to employment opportunities and markets for the commercial interests of major Tidiane businessmen.

In recent years, some turuq have become heavily involved in the transshipment of narcotics, counterfeit currencies, credit cards, and various types of software. They have also organized bartered exchange on a large scale—for example, where gold supplies are bartered for weapons, machinery, and vehicles. These economic concentrations require dispersed networks capable of plying distinct national regulatory environments, with differences in banking rules, customs procedures, and laws governing corporate formations and trade. The wide-ranging networks of zawiyyah, mosques, and Islamic centers scattered around the world can be appropriated as potential nodes for this specialization in "unconventional" trade and economic activity.

Every year during the haj, there is a meeting of what is popularly known as the "twelve tribes." These twelve tribes include (as well as roughly correspond to) the major West and East African turuq, syndicates based on personal loyalty to a major religious-cum-business leader, to leading commercial families associated as patron or funder of a specific network of Islamic welfare and education institutions, and to various other actors tied to particularly large youth councils, haj committees, and even political parties.

By saying that these tribes roughly correspond, I have several things in mind. First, the use of the notion of tribes points to the arbitrary composition of these interest groupings. For example, Tidiane interests are not consolidated within the boundaries of a single group. The Tidiane tariqa is in actuality made up of many diverse figures, tendencies, and institutions. While acknowledging nominal loyalty to an overarching history and shaykh, the tariqa is much too large and dispersed to fall under a single administrative rubric. There are also many different economic interests and activities within discrete Tidiane networks. In part, this heterogeneity has to do with the very different situations and histories of various Tidiane orders in West Africa. It also relates to deep divisions about the political, economic, and cultural orientations of Tidiane orders, not only across countries but within them as well.

The notion of roughly corresponding also reflects the ebbs and flows of who talks to whom and who is willing to deal with whom, as well as the changing fortunes of particular businessmen and syndicates, and the ways in which these syndicates change. For example, the Malian businessmen and marabout Bameni Cissoko, who had amassed a fortune through highly suspect means, lost most of it through a variety of legal troubles and overly visible efforts to become a major political actor within the West African region. The Patel family in Abidjan, once an important funder of politically oriented Islamic reform, has relocated much of its commercial activities out of the continent.

Shaykh Mohammed Al-Amoudi is head of the Swedish consortium of thirty engineering and construction companies, Midroc Scandanavia. He is also head of the ABV Rock Group; chief investor in the primary African ITC company, World Space; owner of Capitol Bank and the National Commerce Bank; and owner of most of Ethiopia's economic assets of any note. Al-Amoudi once was an active player in these African networks — reputedly through a massive trade in weapons. However, he no longer plays an active role since moving back to Ethiopia several years ago to become the country's, and perhaps the continent's, preeminent business figure.

In fact, it is never certain whether the designation twelve tribes actually represents twelve discrete groupings. On the one hand, as I indicated before, turuq are religious brotherhoods that vary in terms of their cohesiveness and spread. Some remain almost exclusively mystical orders devoted entirely to religious revelation. Others are widely dispersed. They may maintain an overarching sense of a coherent religious identity, yet how that identity is "implemented" and organized in specific national, political, and economic contexts can differ widely. On the other hand, the substantial investment made by normative Sunni Islam in Africa, through various national and international agencies, has had a significant effect in solidifying spaces of Islamic practice and organization outside of the turuq. This support has cultivated sizable networks of professionals, students, and entrepreneurs operating throughout the Islamic world. Different turuq now often seek affiliation and support from these networks as a means of accessing new opportunities, under the guise of proffering reform movements within the turuq.

Various businessmen and entrepreneurs who operate as local agents of various banks and corporations based in North Africa, the Gulf States and Malaysia also intersect. Additional prominent players include large import enterprises, particularly those in Dubai and Bahrain, which have become important places for the acquisition of commodities and for money laundering through commodity purchase. Often these businessmen and agents have little direct interest in the religious orientations of the turuq but participate within them because they provide an advantageous framework for their economic activities. The leadership of the turuq, in turn uses its expertise as a means of expanding its own economic capacity. These dealings are particularly important to the organization of sugar importation in Guinea, Benin, Chad, and Mauritania. These configurations are by no means stable, however, and there has been concern since the 1980s about ensuring a stable access to the Gulf States.

Africa in Jidda

The twelve tribes began as a way to deal with the increasing concerns on the part of Saudi authorities that Jidda was being "overwhelmed" by illicit African business activities. Saudi authorities were also worried that the

130 *For the City Yet to Come*

increasing African presence in several of the city's quarters, such as Mahallet al-Yemen and Mahallet al-Shan, was changing the character of the city. To a large extent, the Saudis were looking for scapegoats with whom to attribute the negative dimensions of urban growth in the country's primary urban center.

On the other hand, a variety of smuggling and illicit economic activities did take place. These activities included the importation of the so-called red mercury with which Saudi rials were supposedly counterfeited, increased narcotics trafficking, and the use of the port of Jidda to divert and repackage a wide range of commodities. These activities were the cause of increased concern among royal family members. While Saudi commercial interests had long taken advantage of many of these activities, they had grown to a scale that was becoming increasingly visible. Given the exceedingly tight way in which Saudi society is organized, an unusual opportunity was provided to African interests in Jidda to exert greater control in policing themselves.

What is particularly significant about this process is that the tradition of the zawiyyah was reappropriated as a primary reference point for how such control was to be actualized. Competition among groups using Jidda as some kind of commercial base, place of trade and exchange, or node in the transshipment of commodities could have been amplified. Instead, different interests, again roughly corresponding to the lines of demarcation described above, began to discuss mechanisms for keeping Saudi urban space open to their operations.

Through the course of these discussions, at first held through a variety of intermediaries, the interlocking relationships between turuq, nationally based commercial interests, transnational commercial operations of the different turuq, and common affiliations with discrete banking structures, religious propagation, and welfare institutions became increasingly clear. Like the function of the zawiyyah as a place for hospitality, mutual support, and accountability, the twelve tribes developed into a loose-knit council. This council was ready to accommodate travelers from different regions, Sufi orders, and institutional affiliations in order to keep track of the activities of diverse Africans in Jidda. It attempted to use an accounting of these activities as a means of maximizing the resourcefulness and opportunities available to different yet loosely configured interests and actors making up the twelve tribes.

During the few opportunities I was able to witness these discussions in 1994–1995, the primary focus was the situation in Jidda. The discussion of

Jidda also led to a lengthy and often convoluted global overview of the various political, economic, cultural, and religious dynamics at work in shaping the commercial interests and activities of these key religious and commercial leaders.

There was little discussion of the details of specific businesses and commercial ventures, except as they related to specific problems that had to be solved in the behaviors of particular operations in Jidda itself. No effort was made to prohibit specific activities. The only exception to this was if such activities posed an immediate risk to the ability of anyone of the major interest groups to continue their operations within a specific city or region. Rather, there was a complete accounting of what was possible to do within a specific ministry, company, city, or country.

Rather than focus on detailed discussions of what was actually taking place in the specific commercial activities of those represented, the focus was on assessing what was possible and not possible. Thus for example, if money laundering through Islamic commercial banks in Egypt was deemed not possible, it was assumed by all that from that point on no one at the gathering was actually doing so or would attempt to do so. It was through this discussion of possibilities that specific activities were both inferred and disciplined.

In addition, the different interests groups discussed areas of need. These discussions focused on the need for cheaper transportation, government connections, labor, financing for deals, real estate investment, and even the need for new infrastructure in the respective countries. It became clear to all that different interest groups could successfully retain a space of operation in Jidda only by adopting a practice of open-ended information exchange. It was a practice that also entailed identifying opportunities for collaboration among different African actors and interests within Jidda. When such an exchange worked, it was used as evidence that a much broader level of collaboration might be possible.

The primary objective — to ensure collaboration and to sustain the mixture of African strangers, travelers, and residents in Jidda — never exceeded Jidda. In other words, there was no obligation to try to transfer to some larger scale this zawiyyah-like practice of regulating African behavior in Jidda. When the different interest groups were convinced that collaboration was really working in Jidda, however, this confidence did allow them to "try out" collaboration of other kinds.

Rumor has it that the twelve tribes have been crystallized into a major council of African "mafia," dividing up territories and sectors for expanding illegal trades. While such may be the case, I presently have no way of verifying the truth of such rumors. Moreover, I am not so much interested in the way in which unconventional trade may be taking place as I am in showing from this sketch the way in which Islam provides a vehicle for mutual accommodation among actors from substantially different cultural and political contexts. Of course, this accommodation is sometimes reluctant, awkward, and contested. There are very different actors and institutions paying attention, adapting themselves, and often manipulating and using each other. Yet, this mutual accommodation provides a platform through which the specific commercial and political interests emanating from distinct African cities can be resourced and extended.

Because of its combined religious and commercial significance, Jidda constitutes an important site of African operations. A process unfolds in which there is an attempt to stabilize the interaction of the diverse characters and purveyors of those interests. The process entails Africans "reaching" deep into their traditions to take essential elements of a once-important Sufi institution, the zawiyyah, in order to inform how such regulation might take place. Throughout all of these deliberations, Islam remains a consistent reference point. What Islam may mean to various African actors and institutions is, of course, not consistent in itself. Nevertheless, Islam remains an important platform through which many Africans of various capacities and walks of life attempt to access and operate at the level of a larger world.

Reaching toward the Larger World

What I hope I have been able to show through these various case studies is the ongoing capacity of urban actors to make something of and with the city. What I attempt to point to is something beyond the confines of either Africa's enormous problems or the usual well-worn solutions.

In Pikine, we saw how a complex attempt to install new processes of community management and to articulate distinct quarters served to reinforce a broad range of local particularities. This reassertion of particularities happened in such a way that made some of them elements in new forms of collaboration among different types of residents in different quarters. As a systematic effort to define and mobilize individual and associational actors and to work out specific roles in the development of communities, the Projet de Ville provided new spaces of public action and economic opportunity. In some circumstances, it made ordinary citizens feel more included in the decisions that impacted community life. It also added many new complexities to communities whose residents tend to believe that the city is the proliferation of obstacles to be overcome rather than a place of resources to be mobilized. By bringing together both the obstacles and the opportunities generated by the project, we saw how distinct groups of women converge in the search for new economic opportunities while actively leaving the business of cohesion to others.

The story of *La Nouvelle Liberté* in Douala points out the importance of concrete images capable of valorizing specific local practices for making and managing the city. It also points out how image making can be a locus of intense contestation. Intricate maneuvers, appropriating what resources and actions are available, often enable quarters to work out complex relationships with their own diversity and a metropolitan space that "spills over" available physical structures and economic capacities. These maneuvers, however, are often implicit. Formal and self-conscious efforts at development on the part of quarters are, instead, usually caught in incessant deliberations about consensus, about actors knowing their "place," and about working out the relative "equivalence" of places.

While balances between opportunities, solidarity, accumulation, and loss are important, these deliberations often deny what it is that quarters and networks are doing already to work out those balances. That these ways of working out balances are usually outside of conscious intention makes them no less powerful in their influence on the city. Images amplifying the sense that urban coherence can be assembled from discrepant, "recycled," and fragmented resources, points of view, identities, and histories become critical dimensions of a commitment to the possibilities of what a city could become.

Winterveld is a community that could never truly cohere, for it was a community subject to an almost absurd history that did what it could to keep its various diversities apart. In my discussion on Winterveld I showed how the consolidation of specific notions of what is urban and what is not is used as a basis for specific interests to dominate the political and development agenda of the community. I also described how the Winterveld Crisis Committee became an almost all-purpose grouping of constantly shifting interests and actors. The WCC made itself into a kind of limit to all development projects and trajectories and every attempt to "govern" the community. The WCC also took on a somewhat ghostly presence — that is, something to which so many dimensions of community life, both bad and good, could be attributed; something that was omnipresent, but in ways that could never be precisely specified. With the WCC, Winterveld established a highly mobile and, albeit often destructive, vehicle for including and intersecting, at one time or another, all of the community's residents.

In the example of Jidda we see how a historical modality of assemblage deeply rooted in many West and East African societies is given a new lease on life through its application outside of the continent. Here, a tool that has long passed in urban Africa is treated as embodying important principles for extending urban Africa outside the continent.

A vast world of unofficial economies is one of the few real opportunities for substantial wealth creation in the continent. Nevertheless, it is a world that involves practices that increasingly rely on cutthroat competition and that have generated increased levels of insecurity and conflict. Here, many of the traditional tools and social institutions and reconciliation and cooperation simply don't work. Still, when efforts are made to secure an external base whereby actual or potential competitors at home can collaborate and reduce their vulnerabilities abroad, aspects of these same social institutions can potentially work to great effect. Such effectiveness instills greater measures of confidence that potentially can be reapplied to difficult dilemmas faced at "home."

5

Reconciling

Engagement and Belonging

Some Matters of History

In the remainder of this volume I analyze some of the critical social, economic, and historical conditions that have set the stage for the particular trajectories of urbanization explored in the case materials. In this analysis I attempt to address how Africans make cities they feel they can belong to, while at the same time open up multiple possibilities of becoming — particularly those possibilities that are capable of being "conversant" with a larger world. In other words, I take up issues related to the challenge of configuring modalities of belonging able to facilitate the capacity of urban Africans to operate at larger urban, regional, and global scales.

In the following discussion, I attempt to situate emerging forms of social life and collaboration in a complex history of belonging and becoming, visibility and invisibility, and possibility and impossibility. This is a history of attempts to enfold these apparent binaries into each other and keep them from being forced into static polarities. I will look at how the modalities of collaboration exemplified in the case studies are wrapped up with a proliferating informalization of urban space and activities. Further, I will examine how they are linked to specific economic dynamics and policy environments, focusing particularly on the ways that formal governance regarding land use, shelter, and service provisions is frequently set against the inclinations and resourcefulness of urban residents. In light of increasing urban hardships, I will then turn to an examination of how the basic inclinations to connectivity within urban life operate as sites to mobilize forms of collective action into new practices of transformation.

The Dilemmas of Engagement: The Emergence of Cities

Many times I have participated in conferences about African cities where over and over again it has been said that Africans have a limited sense of belonging to their cities. The claim is that because they don't really feel that they belong they don't make a real commitment to the development of these cities. I don't want to argue the validity of this claim, but it is important to stress that belonging has something to do with the economies of making connections and of being connected.

Connections are productive. They exert a force that acts on things and bodies. Cities are places of thickening connections. Urban connections have often been understood as a function of proximity. In other words, if people exist side by side, then somehow they have something to do with each other. The colonial urban experience in Africa both confirmed and disputed this understanding about proximity. Europeans and Africans, at one and the same time, had both everything and nothing to do with each other. The terms of interaction were continuously altered, forcing Africans to always reorient themselves to the city. As such, African urban history emphasizes both disarticulation and a kind of metissage, but above all it emphasizes ambivalence. It is an ambivalence about where the urban and rural, the customary and civil, and the traditional and modern begin and end. It is an ambivalence of using the city as a context for conventional modernization and of using it as a way of actualizing memories of what specific African societies once were or could be.

The case studies in the preceding chapters have emphasized tentative, sometimes highly experimental, orientations to composing workable urban socialities. In part, these emergent forms of social collaboration ensue from urban histories where African urban residents were increasingly turned toward a future of progressive individuation. Although much of colonialism acted to deny any basis for African subjectivity, it nevertheless imposed a series of policies, legalities, economic practices, and administrative systems that disconnected African urban residents from each other wherever possible.

The enormous growth of the African urban population is also a growth of ambivalence, notably about where one is and where one belongs. As such, economies of connection are increasingly contestable. What is connected, to whom is one connected, to what degree, with what flexibility, and to what extent connections are visible and knowable all become important points of contestation.

In the following section I discuss aspects of African urban history relevant to the production of ambivalence. What does it mean to belong to a city over which there was from the beginning incessant struggle of whose city it actually was? What does it mean to engage the larger world, when the larger world was to some extent always very directly present at home? What does it mean to be urban, when often the only place for Africans to demonstrate an "urban competence" was in areas away from the city? Is it possible to remake African cities in ways that are unprecedented and that go against the grain in terms of our conventional understandings of urbanization, particularly in the characterization of social life? In order to address these questions, it is necessary to review some history.

By no means here do I attempt to offer a summary or systematic account of the complex developments that have been at work over time in the diversity of the continent's cities and towns. Because the focus of this book has been on examining more ephemeral, emergent, and cross-cutting forms of sociality, the review following will largely emphasize the historical constraints incumbent in the cultivation of sociality within African cities under various moments of colonial engagement.

The major urban areas that are the focus of this discussion operate from different legacies and engagements. Abidjan (Côte d'Ivoire), Kinshasa (Democratic Republic of Congo) and Nairobi (Kenya) were completely colonial inventions, whereas Lagos (Nigeria), Douala (Cameroon), and Kampala (Uganda) had precolonial existence. Urban consolidation was always in many senses both ordering and rupturing. Whether African cities could be said to share a history of highly problematic engagements between often vastly different local and external orientations and powers doesn't change the fact that urban forms cannot be accounted for only on the basis of pinpointing structural relationships.

Nor can urban life be accounted for only in terms of relative industrialization. Perhaps the key reason for citing the existence of a precolonial African urbanity is to mark a distinction between urbanism as a way of life and the conventional understandings of urbanization as a process.[1] In William Bascom's discussion on Nigerian Yoruba cities, he emphasizes the way in which urbanism was made possible through the intersection of farming, trade, and, most important, occupational specialization.[2] Weaving, dyeing, iron working, brass casting, wood carving, calabash carving, leather and bead work, pottery, creating medicines, and performing ritual services all required specialization. This sense of specialization was extended to the practice of trade, and it required each occupation to be dependent on others. The key element of cohesive urban growth, according to Bascom, was that formal political control mechanisms operated at supra-kinship levels. This level of operation enabled intense market competition and occupational differentiation. Nevertheless, kinship bonds continued to situate individuals in clearly demarcated positions and responsibilities within support and authority networks.

For the most part, the long period where different versions of colonialism operated was, of course, critical to the shaping and present-day capacities of most African cities. The importance of colonialism was not that it gave rise to cities in what was for the most part considered to be a rural continent. Rather, the crucial move was to shape urbanization so that cities would act instrumentally on African bodies and social formations in ways that made various endogenous forms of and proclivities toward urbanization possible only within the context of an enforced engagement with the European world.

The ways in which this "urbanization for engagement" was accomplished and manifested varied in different settings and time periods and with the degree and kind of urbanization that proceeded colonialism. Further, it varied with the different ways in which distinct African societies used the creation of new cities and/or the transformation of precolonial ones for their "own" objectives, however diffuse, coherent, varied, or contradictory they might have been. This is not to say that urbanization or engagement with the larger world did not exist prior to the colonial period. The medieval urban mixed economies of central and western Sudan, centered largely on trans-Saharan trade, certainly pursued a politics of relations with external powers — often manipulating the ideological conflicts between Christians and Muslims concerning the use of trade routes. Indeed, the unwillingness to sustain such mixed economies and multiple external engagements, through the allure of the lucrative slave trade, was largely responsible for the rapid decline of these precolonial urban centers.[3]

The period of formal British occupation in South Africa, 1806 to 1910, witnessed the founding of a large number of towns. However, only Johannesburg and Cape Town attained populations that exceeded one hundred thousand. Cape Town remained the largest city in Sub-Saharan Africa into the 1950s. In the most urbanized African country at that time, South Africa, 25 percent of the population was considered urbanized, but only fourteen towns had more than fourteen thousand inhabitants, and South African cities contained only one-eighth of the African population. As of 1950, almost all Sub-Saharan African cities contained fewer than two hundred thousand inhabitants. Between 1950 and their respective dates of independence, the capital cities grew 110 percent on average, with some cities, such as Lusaka (Zambia), growing as much as 400 percent.[4] Between 1950 and 1990, there was a 1,017 percent increase in the growth of capital cities.[5] Presently, cities like Dakar (Senegal), Abidjan, Luanda (Angola), Maputo (Mozambique), Douala, Cape Town, and Nairobi are each verging on three million people. Ibadan (Nigeria), Conakry (Guinea), Dar es Salaam (Tanzania), Kano (Nigeria), Yaounde (Cameroon), Lumumbashi (Democratic Republic of Congo), Lusaka, and Harare (Zimbabwe) are verging on two million. Kinshasa has anywhere from five to six million depending on who is counting and how they are doing it. Greater Khartoum (Sudan), Johannesburg, and Addis Ababa (Ethiopia) have roughly four million, with Lagos approaching twelve million.[6] Many of these figures are undoubtedly underestimates of real population sizes.

Linking the Urban and Rural   There have been many explanations for this urban growth, and for the massive rural to urban migration that took place from the end of World War II to the onset of the global recession in the early 1970s. In some instances rural migrants were forced to the city by land shortages or by the collapse of rural economies. Here, it is important to keep in mind the heterogeneity of rural circumstances. Increasing differentials in wealth and capacity had varied impacts on different rural regions and categories of urban residents, and so did the increasing differentiation of land use and production for domestic consumption as opposed (or alternating with) domestic production.

In other instances, and for specific categories of migrants, economic advancement, freedom from the social constraints of rural life, education, prospects and enhanced social status, the connections between the attainment of education and urban work, and varying government policies related to cultivating an established urban population became factors.[7] The complexion of migration also varied among regions. The migration of entire families took place more often in West and Central Africa, where women's role in farming was no larger than that of men, and where there was a strong tradition of trade.[8]

The degree to which the elaboration of rural-urban linkages facilitated migration and the extent to which the linkages, in and of themselves, intensified a sense of difference between places were also significant. This sense of difference could potentially be converted into a resource for both rural and urban life. Kinship ties provided a link that enabled people to find a place in the city, as well as an opportunity to return if things didn't work out. This linkage was reinforced by communal land tenure systems and a gendered division of labor, where women were generally responsible for food production.

The sense of linkage went beyond these kinship ties, however. The concentration of administrative power in cities was so sudden that it had a jarring effect on the rural areas, which were also the objects of this administration. Rural areas were forced to change, particularly as substantial amounts of low-cost imported foodstuffs began saturating urban markets.[9] Rural areas also resisted the various ways in which they were to be incorporated into more nationally focused production and political systems. Administration was limited in its scope and ability to incorporate rural areas within its ambit.[10]

Thus, urban and rural areas existed, in part, as disarticulated spheres. Structuring and plying linkages among them have not only been necessary to reduce "mutual estrangement" and facilitate some sense of overarching coherence, but linkages have also become economic instruments in their own right. Linkages are such that they can be used and manipulated to facilitate a better life in both domains, compensate for difficulties, and circumvent various social and governmental controls. Increasingly as people faced conflicts around changes underway in rural areas the city became a place of refuge, a source for tipping the scales in favor of one party or another, and a place for the short-term accumulation of resources. For urban residents, rural areas became a place to send family members in times of difficulty, to hide assets, to feed urban households, or to garner support or inputs for various urban projects.

In Dakar, for example, escalating rural and urban crises intensify the need to maintain various kinds of networks and linkages. Sociocultural and regional networks have long been depended on to receive migrants coming from the rural areas. However, because migration is largely a collective strategy to diversify the sources of household income, migrants can't simply operate within these reception networks but rather must also seek footholds in a broad range of other, more urban-based, affiliations. These include occupation and institution-based networks, local neighborhood-based associations, informal sector networks of various apprentices and entrepreneurs, and confraternity networks of various kinds.

In fact, relationships among these networks operate as channels of interchange. They channel information and resource flows, with confraternity networks operating as vehicles to support informal sector economic networks, and vice versa. Movement from one network to another enables the migrant to broaden and make more complex their social interaction with the city. This enriching of the fabric of their urban lives puts them in a better position to reinvest in rural areas. This investment, in turn, helps reproduce a rural population, a portion of which continues to migrate and thus need various sociocultural solidarity networks.[11]

Accommodation, Incorporation, and Ambiguity Even under the general assumption that the cities were for Europeans and the rural areas for Africans, economic necessity meant that supplies of African labor had to be located in the city. Thus, an ongoing tension ensued between the cultivation of stable African quarters, behaviors, and identities and the maintenance of a certain instability that would deter Africans from making the city their own. As David Goldberg points out, recourse to perpetual removal and turnover of populations prevents the consolidation of solidarity or the development of cultures of resistance.[12] Providing sustainable urban environments for African habitation would thus make it more likely that Africans could generate and reproduce a specifically urbanized existence. Such existence could be delinked from the rural domains that fundamentally were to be African domains.

The provision of housing, then, operated as a subsidy to wages and an instrument of social control. It was designed to accommodate the specific needs and character of labor for the ports, mines, and administration. Planning policy was geared toward the elaboration of a dual city. This dual city attempted, albeit uneasily, to mediate divergent tensions in how African urban residents were to be conceptualized and accommodated in the city. The so-called modern or Western parts of the built environment were those linked to carrying out organizational and managerial functions. These functions serviced the link between African cities and the capitalist world economy. Although Africans were to be mobilized as labor for capitalist production, their lives and the reproduction of this labor were still to be situated in an indigenous, precolonial economy. Thus, the traditional or cultural had to be accommodated or incorporated into the urban built environment.[13]

This accommodation would accord a space of relative autonomy for Africans right next to the work and residential domains of the colonial apparatus. Given this, and given that the costs of colonial administration and the competition among colonial enterprises were increasing as time went on, a more disciplined and comprehensively assimilated workforce was needed. Thus, the built environment was used as an instrument of spatial articulation and for configuring specific identities and stability. Housing—its design, layout, acquisition, and financing—was used as an instrument to break down specific symbolic meanings of space operative in the village or in "rurally oriented" African urban quarters so as to establish new forms of sociality, which was attempted through the provision of specific types of dwellings. These dwellings were situated in particular physical layouts and were accessed and secured through a specific financial system.[14]

Cities as Experimentation, but for Whom?   Throughout the colonial project, control was always tentative, contained, and contested. It was exerted over a patchwork of territories. The sporadic and fragmented character made the colonial project no less insidious or persuasive. These limitations on control, however, were always revealed in the city's own spatial structuring. As Fred Cooper points out, cities entailed "expanding an ill-controlled urban economy that offered opportunities to casual laborers, itinerant hawkers, criminal entrepreneurs and providers of service to a migrant, largely male working class, thus creating alternatives (for women, as well as men) to the roles into which colonial regimes wished to cast people."[15]

The present emphases on decentralization, local management, the exigencies of poverty alleviation, and regionally articulated local economic development are all a reformulation of familiar instruments. They have already been used in an ongoing effort to ensure the engagement of African cities with nonlocal worlds, particularly non-African worlds. These were instruments that were geared toward securing specific conduits of engagement through the remaking of African identities and practices. Equally important, this process involved the (hyper)visibility and crystallization of "traditional" selves and social formations so that they could be the objective and concretized targets of remaking.

Individuals and groups did refuse to cooperate or assimilate with one or more aspects of the multifaceted and frequently loosely knit intermeshing of discourses, institutions, and actors that constituted the colonial enterprise. Yet the resistance against this remaking became an important aspect of producing this visibility of the traditional. Cities simultaneously could operate as arenas for the consolidation of a wide range of local practices, initiatives, and identities. But as soon as neighborhoods or associations showed their cards, for the most part they became an occasion for the applied scrutiny of mission societies, private companies eager to take advantage of local skill, or the state administration itself.

There were possibilities to function in the interstices between overt assimilation and resistance to these remaking operations. Indeed, through ruse and dissimulation, many "alternative" subject positions could be temporarily enacted. Nevertheless, a powerful form of "captivation" was still put in place. To refuse the consolidation of endogenous capacities meant that they could not be drawn upon or referred to as self-conscious incentives to pursue specific collective aims in the face of European power. To unreservedly submit to the remaking process meant that there was no basis on which to get European power to at least make gestures toward showing its cards.

Cities came to be the means through which bodies were turned into individuals. They were to have an individuating function. Even though at earlier stages colonial cities depended on distorting communal practices and endogenous social formations, at the beginning there was little interest in the differentiated capacities, histories, and desires of African "individuals."

The realization that the continuing productivity of colonial economies would require a thoroughly urbanized African labor force, uprooted from the social enclosures of extended family, clan, and village, emerged only after World War II. Even to this day, cities reflect an uneasy tension in the persistence of communal orientations and the pursuit of individuated destinies. From the beginning, these communal orientations played an important part in enabling Africans to live in cities. Indeed, cities were appropriated as domains to reinvent such collective ways of being through the very instruments of modernization.

Making Individuals: On Responsible
Individuals and Tensions in the Mobilization of Labor

The various efforts to work through appropriate ways of mobilizing labor and how labor was to be deployed for production had significant relevance to the shape of urban development. Making colonies productive, maintaining political control, satisfying different constituent parties regarding various aspects of the colonial endeavor, and limiting the costs of administering colonial territories never fit into a seamless apparatus. Indeed, there were marked tensions in efforts to address these often countervailing agendas.

The aspirations of economic progress on the part of the metropole relied primarily on conservative conceptions of the social organization of production. The capacity to mobilize inexpensive labor largely rested in continuing to valorize what were understood to be local chieftancy-based rural orders. The objective was to access labor without encouraging wage labor.

In Central Africa, the mobilization of labor was a major problem because of the region's mobile population whose numbers were made more vulnerable by the epidemiological impacts of colonial incursion. More pronounced than in other regions, the Central African states tried to turn over much of the administrative costs to concessionaire companies, whose repressive styles frequently backfired and thus in turn escalated the costs of securing control. Instead of facilitating the incorporation of their domains into capitalist circuits, these companies tended to treat export goods as a form of tribute. This was especially reflected in the way concessions were taken up often for stock-market speculation in Europe and also for quick profit taking.[16]

The extent of labor needs meant that much of it had to be coerced, which in turn had the effect of disrupting the social relations of local social orders. These were the very social orders that were to be valorized in order to enhance the long-term productivity of the colonial economies. Support was accorded to chiefs capable of delivering consistent and "precise" accountings of those under their jurisdictions. As a result, many of the complex power-sharing relationships embodied by local orders were disrupted in favor of intensifying authoritarian control. Such control succeeded in providing labor to colonial enterprises. A loosening of the population from its former social and political ties was also set in motion, giving rise to populations accountable to no one.

This loosening was particularly the case in Central Africa. There polities were largely based on "big man" systems operating more as commercial firms than as states. Power had been derived from dominating trade routes — a function now displaced by European-controlled transport systems. In order to stay in power chiefs had to invest in Western education and in the economic systems that Europeans were creating, because otherwise the resources availed to chiefs remained limited. They had to depend on particular political alliances with colonial authority, but these alliances were unreliable because of the duplicity of the colonial administrators and because the administrators didn't remain in their jobs for long periods of time.[17] Thus, the strategic orientations through which local chieftancies sought to remain in power implicitly laid the groundwork for escalating demands on urban resources and access to urban space. Accordingly, more opportunities were created for increasing numbers of Africans to be made into "responsible" individuals.

Depending on the character of metropolitan politics at the time, the methods through which Africans were assimilated into individuality var-

ied. The ebbs and flows of these efforts, as well as various forms of resistance to them, elaborated an arena through which urban residents were,
nonetheless, progressively individualized — that is, in the very process of
working out some form of being distinct within the colonial project.

For example, the French were interested early on in cultivating a sense of
metropolitan civility. The granting of citizenship to the Senegalese communes of Gorèe and St. Louis in 1848 was a means of tying the struggle for
rights to the inextricable application of the French civil code. Urban-based
Islamic religious and social structures provided a form of resistance to
being absorbed within this civil code; Muslim autonomy in matters of
family law was officially acknowledged in 1857. This concession was primarily a ploy to win urban Muslim support in light of the threat to the
French posed by rural-based Muslim marabouts. When France consolidated its grip on Senegalese territory, its tolerance and accommodation of
Muslim institutions waned.

Yet Muslim rights were reaffirmed again in 1912. This reaffirmation was
part of an ongoing negotiation over the applicability of the French civil
code to communities that were officially accorded French citizenship. These
negotiations gave rise to a particular form of urban citizenship. As Mamadou Diouf emphasizes, this form of citizenship embodies acquiescence,
assimilation, and resistance.[18] Incorporation into French citizenship became a domain where fundamental issues were reargued. These arguments
took varying shapes. Some claimed that citizenship could become a vehicle
where the power of cultural differences wielded over the Senegalese as
a basis for domination could be defused. Others argued that citizenship
meant the demise of values and religious practices that had been important
to the Senegalese. Alternately, citizenship could become the locus through
which these very values and religious practices would be revalorized. Not
only would they take on an equivalent status to those values of European
derivation but they also would become influential in helping them define
the very characteristics of that citizenship itself. Thus the mark of religious
difference, and its accommodation by both the French and Senegalese, kept
open the question about who could say to whom whether they did or did
not belong to some common political entity.

African Approaches to Capitalist Relations   While forced labor was a critical aspect of colonial economics in the post–World War II era, during this
time it became politically and economically unsustainable. For many years,
the colonial authorities had attempted to circumvent the connotations of

"forced" labor. For example, the 1926 provisions were made to recruit labor as if it were a military obligation — a practice known as the *deuxième portion*. In this case young men were drafted for labor on public works for three years and paid the equivalent of a military salary. This provision, however, was abolished by decree in 1950, and its end had the effect of revealing just how much compulsion had permitted the perpetuation of ill-conceived projects that could not have been sustained in any other way.[19]

Colonial administrations sought to limit the expansion of wage labor up until the decade prior to the onset of World War II. In addition, the prevalent ideological position was that Africans were reluctant wage laborers. Nevertheless, Africa was being systematically incorporated into capitalist relations. An economic structure based on "peasant" export production and the initial elaboration of a mass market had already begun to emerge in West Africa at the beginning of the nineteenth century. African producers had begun to make fundamental changes in agricultural production, and they did so by relying on and innovating endogenous social and economic institutions.

The progressive elaboration of such export economies introduced its own differentiation of labor. As such, conditions were established for further engagement in expanding and diversifying economies, which were linked to international markets through colonial structures.[20] Indeed, the chief function of expatriate firms was to provide and display the consumer goods that were to be a primary incentive for export production. Large expatriate and multinational firms squeezed out medium-scale entrepreneurship by the 1920s. Yet, market expansion during the first decades of the twentieth century was made possible by the substantial increase in the number of African intermediaries. Small African export producers played a significant role in expediting the predominance of monetary exchange within the overall economy.[21]

Monetization Labor was not only involved in producing for colonial economic machines, but the progressive incorporation of labor into some form of quantitative assessment was necessary in order to support a viable system of regulation over the relations of production. Even in forced labor regimens, the amount of labor, its exertion, and productivity was to be codified. Such quantification then had to be linked to the various forms of remuneration accorded to customary authorities and the amount of taxation applied. As production systems moved to incorporate various forms of paid labor, workers had to demonstrate a basic sense of the equivalence between how they labored, how much time they devoted to labor, and how much they were then capable of consuming with what was then paid to them.

Colonial production systems were always vulnerable to labor shortages. Workers had a tendency to impose their own work rhythms: they would either walk away during or after specified "contractual" periods, or simply earn what they felt they needed and then disengage from their status as laborers. Given such orientation, colonial authorities increasingly attempted to dictate the contents of those needs. This was done through systematizing taxation. Africans were obliged to convert valuable economic resources into monetary form through selling their labor. This alienation of endogenous value resulted in many Africans acting against their own economic interests. For example, large tracts of rural land were frequently left untended and became economically depleted.

The social universe of most Africans became increasingly parceled. Power fragmented among the domains of cash crops and money, diplomas and certificates, status and offices, and trades in medicine. In contrast, the initiation rites of many local cultures had once concentrated all-important knowledge into a single locus of physical transformation. The incorporation of local cultures into capitalist circuits intensified notions of substitutability — that is, where various domains could be substituted for each other. This sense of substitutability is itself an individuating process. Persons are "extracted" from a state of being encompassed by the community or lineage as a whole.[22]

Colonial authority attempted to consolidate territorial holdings through extending and institutionalizing monetary-based transactions. Money was also used to incorporate African economies into an export, cash nexus and inculcate the notions of abstract individuated valuation associated with currency. Currency was not based simply on how many concrete tokens or instruments of currency one accumulated, but rather on the value that any particular instrument represented. Taxation was to be the primary means through which the colonial administration was funded. Therefore, it was imperative to codify how much the individual African (invariably male) earned, how he earned it, how he paid his taxes, what he bought with his money, and above all, how much he understood about money, prices, and circulation.

Prior to World War I, so-called interface currencies could generally be used for tax payments, the market, and other financial transactions. These currencies were specific to transactions among various endogenous groups and between those groups and the various agents of colonial administration and economy. The operations of currency, as such, were tied to and operated through specific local assets held in iron, gold, cowries, copper, and cloth. In face of the demand that tax and commercial transactions be negotiated solely in cash, most African societies suffered a major loss of assets. This loss came at a time when Western economic practices generated significant asset formation. These stores of wealth would, in turn, underpin an exponential increase in the potential for economic growth through various instruments of credit.[23]

Africans were almost never extended such credit. Colonial economies were linked directly into the currency circuits of the metropole. As such, Europe was vulnerable to possibilities that financial crises in the colonies would have a direct bearing on currency valuations back home. This would especially be the case if money was hoarded or suddenly released, and thus currency was to be tightly controlled. The production of money was to be rigidly linked to demonstrable reserves in sterling or to export levels. This stringent monetary policy severely limited currency supplies, kept credit institutions weak, and subsequently resulted in low levels of investment.[24]

Thus, colonial regimes attempted to steer African workers into a situation where they would accord their needs, aspirations, sense of time, and obligations with particular notions of monetary value. African needs were to have the same metaphorical relationship as particular material instantiations have with the exchange relational values of money. In this way, African workers were compelled to participate in an ongoing and fluctuating assessment of their situations and positions vis-à-vis others. In other words, they were to participate in a differentiated and individuated framework of well-being that is never inherently stable.[25] It could be argued that well-being is never a stable state, and that many African societies have always sought to recompose themselves with the resources brought through incorporating new groups. So even if well-being is something incessantly mutable, here it was to be based on taking into consideration a progressively enlarged space of factors where there could only be individualized mediation.

Export Faced with international pressure as well as domestic pressure from the new metropolitan political orders of the post–World War II period, legal frameworks were instituted to prohibit forced labor recruitment. While areas of British control had been more urbanized and proletarian than those under French control, both concentrated on providing incentives and improvements to wage labor. Initially, this policy emphasis further bifurcated urban and rural domains and economies. More agricultural work was shifted to so-called customary labor. Customary labor was deemed to be outside the purview of the state and outside its domain of regulatory power.[26] These policies had the effect of watering down judicial prohibitions of forced labor, yet they also provided an expanded space for fuel, labor, and exports to be provided outside the colonial state apparatus. Such provision occurred through innovations made on various customary social formations.

For example, Côte d'Ivoire introduced a harvest-sharing approach, known as the *métayage* system, where laborers retained fixed percentages of the proceeds, varying according to specific commodities. New, African-based production networks, such as the Société Agricole Africaines, largely made expatriate agricultural producers and suppliers irrelevant. In the Ghanaian Gold Coast, farmers migrated specifically to grow cash crops for export. Established forms of "traditional" cooperative enterprise were harnessed and adapted to finance the migration itself, to acquire land in new areas, and to mobilize labor. The irrelevance of expatriate actors was also reinforced by what had been a long-term reluctance on the part of expatriate trading firms to acquire land concessions for private commercial agriculture. For they feared that if certain firms were able to establish plantations, these firms would gain a monopoly over the supply of export crops.[27]

The colonial apparatus intensified its control over an agricultural sector largely being elaborated and improved on by Africans themselves. At the same time, the volatility of cities posed a problem to any semblance of seamless colonial control. This volatility emerged from the extensive restructuring of rural areas, an enhanced interlinkage of urban and rural communities, and a simultaneous widening of an urban-rural divide. Ongoing investments in railways and roads substantiated the possibilities, if not the actuality, of territorial integration. In West Africa, the expansion of the railways signaled the decline of the former, north-facing, trans-Saharan trade routes and reoriented the markets of the interior toward the coastal cities. Two centers of exchange were linked that formerly had only been in sporadic contact. Still, lateral linkages, territorial integration, and the articulation of areas remained largely underdeveloped. The chief reason for this lack of development was that transportation investments were largely made in areas that already demonstrated substantial export potential. In addition, infrastructure development focused almost exclusively on resource evacuation.

Cities were "officially" linked to highly segmented regions of the interior. Other domains were drawn into urban orbits through modalities and actors that remained largely underregulated and through dispersed institutional forms and economic practices. Prevailing investment patterns also fostered this disarticulation. Prior to World War II, investment tended to follow rather than cause growth. Differences between rich and poor colonies were amplified as borrowing capacities fluctuated with trade cycles, and roughly half of colonial budgets were spent on administrative costs. A further substantial portion was locked up in repayments on the capital and interest on loans — especially as almost the entirety of the West African rail system, for example, was build by public enterprise.[28]

Expanded export production in the rural areas raised per capita incomes and increased labor specialization and population growth. In some regions, this expansion had significant restructuring effects. For example, groundnut production, with its requirement for increasing amounts of land, tended to crowd out domestic food production, resulting in expanding volumes of rice imports into the Senegambia region. Cities, in general, began to import food from farther afield. Particular areas maintained their agricultural specialization in part because of new, extended, and regionally based marketing opportunities.

Thus the depression in world trade affected not only export regions but also the complex network of domestic production and trade. Although the effects of the Depression of the 1920s and 1930s were spread throughout the regional economies, it was specialized labor that was particularly hard hit. Diminishing terms of trade for export commodities led to increased production costs. In compensation, Africans had to step up the volume of cash crop production to maintain existing levels of import consumption. In the process, however, Africans experienced substantial declines in real incomes. Urban wage earners suffered major declines in earning power between 1930 and 1945.[29] Faced with increasing shortages of basic consumer goods, urban workers demanded raises. The lack of commodities, however, meant that wage increases were largely eaten by inflation. This situation was further reinforced by the monopolistic structure of the import-export nexus and wholesale trade.[30] These conditions posed severe constraints on enlarging the labor force and improving its conditions — both prerequisites to diversifying and expanding urban production. Even though farmers regained high producer prices following the war, there were few available imports to spend money on and thus less incentive to provide food to urban workers.[31]

Urban Unrest and Autonomy   Urban and worker unrest had grown during the Depression years but remained diffuse and sporadic. After World War II, however, the situation changed. The recent memory of Depression hardships, combined with the political openings and economic restructuring necessitated by the postwar period, ushered in a more substantial, sustained, and politicized period of labor militancy. This militancy had a significant effect on the direction of urban economies.

The general strike of Dakar in 1946, which cut across nearly all of the city's fifteen thousand wage earners, demanded equal pay for equal work across racial lines. While this principle was not concretized in the strike settlement, provisions were made for the payment of family allowances to most levels of government workers. In the process, the needs of the African family were acknowledged as similar to those of the European family. That the state should accept the responsibility for reproducing its African civil service was also acknowledged. Previously, wage differentials between different types of urban jobs amounted to little. As such, the African urban labor force tended to be homogenized as some kind of undifferentiated social mass. The strike settlement introduced wider wage hierarchies for each occupational category. Perhaps more important, however, was that the state implicitly recognized the urban working force as a complex and differentiated social entity whose conditions of work and everyday life were critical in terms of urban control, order, and productivity.[32]

The recognition of social differentiation was also implicit in Zambia's urban land policy of the late 1920s. Plots for self-construction were provided in order to re-create aspects of rural life. Efforts were made to facilitate urban adaptation through "mixing" long-term urban residents and new migrants. In the Zambian copperbelt, towns were basically divided between mining and administrative economies. Both had their own territories, housing estates, infrastructure, and regulations. Given the lack of houses for families in the official mining compounds, the mine companies also established their own plots for self-built housing. These plots were much more restrictive in terms of regulation and surveillance than were other comparable areas across the city. Still, they were popular destinations of residence because many saw them as a step to employment in the mines. Only those who could clearly demonstrate they were family members of miners were allowed to settle there. Although sporadic efforts were made to clear out the many residents who had no family connections to the mines, these regulations could never be thoroughly enforced.[33]

Bruce Kapferer points out that on the municipal plots there was no single authority capable of totally affecting the lives of those residing there.[34] The lives and economies of those who worked in formal wage labor (as clerks, porters, maintenance workers, cleaners, etc.) and those who worked as small-scale traders, cultivators, and artisans were heavily intertwined and interdependent. There was no single basis on which individuals could be unilaterally aligned or divided. The use of the informal economy to sustain a growing population provided a ready pool of reserve labor that buttressed exploitative industrial policies. On the other hand, the same informal world of work enabled urban residents to move out of specific jobs in the formal sector that they found unsuitable and subsist until they found other jobs, better pay, or an opportunity to develop their own trades or enterprises. This process, according to Kapferer, deterred the formation of a stable work force locked into fixed economic structures and with fixed interests that would then bring it into continuous opposition with identities and interests outside itself. This situation is in contrast to the discipline of the mine, where distinctions between staff and nonstaff were repeatedly marked, territorialized, and enforced.

As a result, political parties were only able to instantiate themselves into the city by taking on the wide diversity of interests that affected its membership; for example, domestic affairs, housing, employment, and urban services. This political participation, although split among opposing parties, nevertheless reinforced the sense of interconnection among different categories of formal and informal workers. When mining compounds increased their formal housing stock after World War II, the movement of miners out of the plots greatly reduced their ties to the nonmining population. This population was under threat of constant eviction by the companies and had increasingly fewer opportunities to find employment in the mines as the labor force became more stable and mining more mechanical. As a result, large concentrations of unemployed youth were to turn these "former" mining plots into major areas of insurgent political activity.[35]

The labor strikes in Mombassa and Dar es Salaam in 1947, the Nigerian national strike of 1945, and the Gold Coast riots of 1948 demonstrated just how cities could bring together different migrant labor systems. These strikes also demonstrated how different crises of social reproduction could articulate themselves in what Fred Cooper calls "a single, demographically dense, socially connected locus."[36] Here, intensified production combines with increased pressure on urban resources, and then combines with inflation to raise different sets of difficulties for different sets of urban residents who are, in turn, usually treated as a homogeneous mass. The problems of

reproduction are subsequently seen as the problems of circulation and production in ports, commercial centers, and mines. Accordingly, the emphasis
in the postwar period is on using urban resources and services to promote
some kind of integration of African workers into an urban modernity. This
integration centered on breaking up local social orders and modalities, for
it was through these local orders that African urban residents were able to
compensate for the hardships occasioned by the limitations of capitalist
production and create spaces of livelihood formation outside it.[37]

In some cities, these efforts certainly did not remain uncontested. Douala
grew more during World War II than it had in the previous twenty years, in
part because of the intensification of forced labor for warfare production.
Following the war, the city faced massive unemployment and reductions in
purchasing power for salaried workers. The advent of trade unionism extended by the Free French Government of Algeria in 1944 also heightened
the organizing efforts on the part of white settlers in the face of growing tax
burdens and wage demands by unionized African workers. The white *colons*
(those of colonial descent) argued against the role of high finance in colonial
matters, against industrialization beyond the manufacture of semifinished
products, and against the emergence of a black working class. The colons
argued that the black workforce had to be protected against urbanization.[38]

An insurgency broke out in 1945 in the slums of New Bell, where large
numbers of recently out-of-work immigrants were concentrated. This insurgency was followed by a second group of white rioters. Some of these
rioters were already armed and some attained arms under the auspices of
being members of a defense group publicly sanctioned during the heat of
things. The second group started shooting Africans on sight. Then, they
moved, albeit with a clumsy effort, to seize control of the colonial administration and establish a trust territory. While the colons came nowhere
close to their intended objectives, they did manage to get rid of most European communists and labor organizers. In the long run, however, this eviction had the ironic effect of giving rise to endogenous trade unions capable of manifesting both a nationalist and Marxist worldview — something
unique in French Africa at the time.[39]

Economies of Urban Growth The ways in which the European powers
compensated for economic contraction usually lacked imagination and efficacy. Expatriate firms largely took the defensive posture of disinvestment,
which occasioned more African hostility. Public works were retrenched,
and increased custom duties were applied to imports in order to maintain

revenue levels for administration. These measures ended up simply increasing the costs of imported goods for African consumers. Attempts were made to strengthen bilateral trade links, but again this proved to be a high-cost, high-price trading regime that limited where Africans could buy goods. Additionally, the balance-of-payment difficulties faced by Britain and France after the war reinforced policies of imperial preference. In some settings, the demand of equal pay for equal work became a rallying cry for white workers. These workers attempted to maintain their share of skilled jobs in the face of companies that were replacing them with Africans at lower pay.

The British introduced marketing boards that fixed commodity prices and became the official buyer of products. In francophone areas, stabilization funds were introduced that were aimed at fixing producer prices and guaranteeing minimum incomes in light of fluctuating world market prices.

Marketing boards were supposed to set producer prices below the world price in times of prosperity. This was suppose to create surpluses that could be applied to supporting producer prices when the world market was depressed. Even in difficult times, marketing boards still set prices below international levels so as to keep on acquiring surplus funds, albeit on a reduced scale. Producers lost a high proportion of their potential income because surpluses were supposedly being used to fund development.[40] Even in the development boom between 1946 and 1951, West African marketing boards maintained sterling balances six times higher than the disbursements made under the Colonial Development and Welfare Act.[41] Although intended to stabilize income, marketing boards and other stabilization measures made incomes unstable. The boards couldn't control the volume of production, which is a key factor in terms of price stability and fluctuation across seasons.

Despite these impediments, there was substantial economic recovery, particularly in West Africa. Between 1945 and 1955 the volume of exports quadrupled, with a sixfold increase in importing capacity. There was a concomitant expansion in the role of economic governance: investment between 1947 and 1956 was more than twice as great as in the forty-three years prior, and with a larger proportion of grant funding than had been seen previously. The French initiated the Fonds d'investissement et de développement économique et social des Territoires d'Outre-Mer (FIDES) as a large-scale development fund, and FIDES money was primarily spent on the development of road networks.

In Central Africa, these funds usually continued a paradigm of economic growth based on increases in the prices of existent commodities rather than on any fundamental change in the framework of production. The distortions inherent in this paradigm were amplified as multinationals began to play a larger role, particularly in the minerals sector. Multinationals were to have few links with African enterprises, and local profits were absorbed by the state.[42] Urban development projects were centered on construction, and inmigration to cities increased. There was little deliberation and planning about how to bring about the long-term economic development necessary to support an increased population once the artificially induced construction boom was completed.

Expatriate firms, faced with expanding competition as economic expansion and diversification made West African trade attractive to newcomers, began to turn themselves into specialists. They focused on a limited number of goods, curtailed handling costs, cut back on retailing operations, and concentrated on wholesaling. Retailing, importing, and distribution in certain sectors became increasingly the purview of Africans, largely in order to secure the firms' long-term interests. Some firms also became manufacturers as increased competition reduced profit margins on the trade in many staple imports and as domestic markets expanded. These manufacturing activities were largely concentrated in processed food, drinks, clothing, and construction materials. They tried to cut production costs by processing at source heavy raw materials, such as minerals and timber, in order to save freight charges.

The colonial enterprise was faced, however, with wide-ranging dilemmas. Urban growth was expanding rapidly and in ways that could not be adequately anticipated or controlled. Rural producers compensated for unpredictable prices and markets in ways that were neither adequately understood nor engaged. Labor militancy and urban unrest were becoming increasingly politicized. The policy of increasing African participation in local governance placed the administration of larger domains of everyday life in African hands. At the same time, the inequities and the more base and banal aspects of colonial administration were amplified. Additionally, nationalist strivings were largely carried forward by an often tentative and problematic alliance of farmers, traders, and wage earners. These constituents all shared various degrees of commitment to the exchange economy. These interest groups, however, constituted only a small proportion of the overall population.[43]

These identifiable and modernist constituent interests largely took European notions of prosperity and well-being as their references. The references of the bulk of rural and urban populations were more uncertain and fluid, and they demonstrated an increased capacity to straddle occupations, territories, forms of livelihood, and cultural orientations. The inability of the coalitions of proprietary classes to sufficiently act in concert, along with their "distance" from the realities of the bulk of the population, established the grounds for various postindependence difficulties in many countries. They led to intense public sector leakage and the conversion of the public sector into a privatized arena of rent seeking used to placate competing factions.[44]

Social Embedding and Differentiation   Up until World War II, efforts continued to be made to sustain and reproduce the links of urban workers to the rural areas, especially in terms of providing a place to go after a career of work was finished. These efforts led to several initiatives to ruralize cities and reconstruct certain aspects of the social and juridical dimensions of village life within an urban setting. In the end, these efforts were largely viewed as complicating matters, especially because "modern" and "traditional" institutions could be played off each other. Following the war, the prevailing policy was to separate African workers vertically and horizontally in hierarchies and occupations. This structuring was to be part of the larger agenda of cultivating urban-based, responsible workers and citizens. The aim was that these workers and citizens would consider their interests on an individualized basis in the pursuit of greater well-being to be derived from greater individual productivity. As such, African workers needed to be delinked from their involvement with the village — as a specific site, cosmology, and set of cultural references.[45]

Much of the policy deliberation on the part of formal administrative institutions at the time focused on how African workers were to be detached from a collectivist social field and turned into individuals — as if there were some overarching social fact of social embedding that prevailed across diverse African populations. The institutionalized acceptance of the possibility that such urban, modernist identities could be cultivated in African populations also meant a progressive demonizing of other endogenous social orders and practices. This demonizing took on a particular geographical location: the rural village. Any residual elements of that "village," with its associated universe of social practices, ties, and discourses, had to be removed from the city where they did not properly belong.

The dilemma faced by colonial administrations, whatever their national origin, was just how much they were prepared to pay for such policies of modernization. The continued productivity and profitability of colonial enterprises were increasingly predicated on the cultivation of responsible, modern urban identities. Yet the concrete programs of urban stabilization that were implemented — focusing on sustaining disciplined, nucleated households — were never sufficient to remake urban society. The prevailing ideology, largely a recirculation of well-worn disciplinary regimes, considered that the rise of a new generation of fully urbanized workers depended on rooting male labor into nuclear families, where women would assume the role of wives and mothers attending to educational and health needs of children. These women would also implicitly discipline the behaviors of male workers, who now had a family to support, outside of any available extended family or "customary" arrangement.

Even though urban wages increased substantially in the postwar period — at an average of 116 percent increase between 1949 and 1955 — top wage levels for Africans in 1962 fell well below the bottom wage for Europeans.[46] There was just not enough money to support a massive project of resocialization. Given the large number of unemployed workers already on the copperbelt, for example, officials could not afford to substantially underpay miners in relationship to Europeans nor overpay them in relation to agricultural workers.

In Nairobi, the situation was made more acute by the substantial land grabs undertaken by white settlers, who used mechanized export agriculture to consolidate their position. As landless and jobless migrants poured into the city, unskilled laborers who had been established in the city for a long time had little more chance of being able to sustain family life than did the casual worker.[47] Trade unions had conventionally been seen as organizations that would deepen and complete the fundamental resocializing project of turning workers away from the village. Yet, they were often repressed as being too political before they could even establish an adequate foothold to concentrate on "industrial" matters.

Therefore, urban workers of all kinds, even though linked to structures of social and occupational differentiation, typically had to fall back on various "neotraditional" or provisional modalities of association in order to secure basic livelihoods. Substantial repression on the part of colonial authorities in the years immediately preceding independence reinforced these tendencies. Examples of this repression include the expulsions of Kikuyu from Nairobi, which once again imposed an imaginary of an undifferentiated African multitude.

The Power of Urbanization   What we find in the diverse trajectories of African urban development are the different ways in which urbanization was grafted onto inhospitable domains. Once grafted, however, urbanization had a significant effect in reordering territorial relations beyond the scope of the immediate territory of which these cities were a part. However, the extent of this reordering was limited. In all regions, particularly across Central Africa, large swathes of territory remained outside of functional colonial control. In the region of West Africa, Senegal, Côte d'Ivoire, the Gold Coast, and Nigeria contributed almost all of the region's recorded total economic output.[48] While cities primarily served to organize the evacuation of primary products, the ongoing development of this function opened up spaces for Africans to elaborate livelihoods outside of European supervised wage labor.

These opportunities largely derived from the configuration of other geographies, concretized through the movement of populations back and forth between urban and rural domains. Opportunities were derived from the expanding transactions that these population movements were able to establish and into which increasing numbers of people were drawn. Eventually, evolving networks of various African local associations in both cities and rural areas were able to coordinate more complex networks of relationships among these transactions. There were, however, insufficient amounts of consistently reliable material resources to draw on in order to provide solid infrastructure for these alternative spaces of livelihood formation. Relations and practices had to be continuously renegotiated.

Practices of making the city something other than what was expected by a more complete incorporation of capitalist production had to locate different organizational forms and auspices under which to operate. Such practices increasingly depended on the identification of loopholes and underregulated spaces in changing colonial economies. Once identified, these practices acted as compensations and alternatives potentially capable of being appropriated by diverse actors with different agendas.

Fluidity thus remained both a fundamental strength and weakness. These "alternative" economic and cultural practices were unable to remake the city in ways that could serve the objective of expanding agricultural activities for the bulk of rural residents. Nor could they expand the integration of the bulk of the city and its residents into capitalist circuits. Instead, these practices acted as a limiting constraint to both endogenous and capitalist economic expansion. They found ways to urbanize relationships derived from ruralized solidarity and to identify possibilities for urban sustainability in particular ways of engaging undersupervised rural domains. Thus, urban Africa's pursuit of "independent" agendas and aspirations largely took place in this "closed" circuit. These agendas both intersected with and ran parallel to the narrow ways in which the overall urban economy was linked to global capital.

Urban Plans

In a discussion of urban history in Madagascar, Gwendolyn Wright talks about the complex position of trying to mobilize and regulate labor while at the same time enticing local cooperation, by offering modern products and urban services.[49] In some ways, such provisioning was occasioned by the sheer threat of disorder that ensued from changing labor policies. At the point at which slaves were freed in Madagascar nearly half of the population of the capital city, Antananarivo, was made up of slaves. The French made significant investments in establishing networks of articulated market centers that could help regulate population flows, yet the colonial authorities were periodically compelled to reinstate forms of forced labor to avoid chaos in the large cities. This labor was deployed in large public works programs and infrastructure development, much to the dismay of the entrepreneurial class who feared that their access to cheap labor was being compromised.

Unlike British colonialism that emphasized segregation as a means of dealing with the continuous concerns about health issues, the French — in principle if not usually in practice — initially focused on the need for proper urban environmental management. Systems regulating garbage collection, drainage, slum clearance, public health, and venereal disease registration were established during the early part of the twentieth century in order to mitigate significant health hazards. The tropics were a health nightmare for Europeans — a situation that was only compounded by urbanization. These moves toward the proficient structuring of space and the registration of populations, supplemented through the procedures of military conscription, ushered in a period of near obsession with building and its associated designs, codes, and regulations. Cities in Madagascar were further marked with an emerging sense of segregation that could be accomplished with recourse to racist ideology.[50]

Across the continent, both the French and British eventually used the language of health concerns to engineer racial and ethnic divides in the city.

Further, they instituted classifications of building materials appropriate for particular kinds of settlements. In the emerging segregation discourses prior to World War I, the configuration of exclusive residential spaces focused largely on elaborating a specific ideal that would be suitable only to European occupation. In Freetown, Sierra Leone, for example, the development of hill station communities outside the city followed the identification of the origin of malaria. Not many in the non-African population, however, were convinced that hill station living was really worth the trouble and expense. These communities therefore did not attract the anticipated private investment or residents from the entrepreneurial class. While the French were not as inclined as the British to invoke racial language, segregation was effected through the demarcation of specific zones whose occupation was contingent on specific per foot expenditures.[51] As the history of Conakry, Guinea, demonstrates, however, such regulations were not strictly applied until the introduction of reserved lots for "natives" in 1912. Rather, these regulations became a legal basis to acquire specific tracts of land when needed.

Aesthetic concerns began to replace those of health as a mechanism of segregation. Attempting to replicate various trappings of European life in Africa was, of course, a way to accommodate an expanding European population. More important, it signaled that Europeans were there to stay permanently. To shape the city in a European image was to affirm the long-term commitment of the colonial enterprise to shaping the larger regional spaces. Such shaping also reflected the general trend where the growth of market economies everywhere spurred the multiplication of nucleated households. These households were to be increasingly accommodated in separate, single-family detached dwellings.[52]

This preoccupation with aesthetics — of building parks and scenic roadways, of appropriating larger tracts of land for more housing and recreation — often had a detrimental effect on African urban residents. In Brazzaville, Republic of the Congo, long faced with periodic and severe food shortages, urban cultivation was entrenched as an important strategy in feeding the city. With the introduction of aesthetic criteria into urban planning and with subsequent restrictions placed on where and how cultivation could take place, a growing urban population faced even more severe food shortages, particularly in the Depression era.[53]

Segregation was not a coherent frame of spatial organization applied intact on the city. Rather, specific forms of segregation evolved in response to particularly local combinations of several factors. These factors included the specific growth patterns of cities, available urban budgets, the implications of substantial residential mixing, and a growing recognition that cities would require substantial resource investments. Segregation also was expensive: its pervasive growth and self-evidence was thus used to defer having to spend money on the African sections of the city. As Joseph Uyanga argues, the Township Ordinance of 1917, which legalized an ipso facto segregation of European and African residential areas in Nigeria, also ushered in a process of continuously "passing the buck" in terms of who would take responsibility for the maintenance and governance of African urban quarters. Planning processes were subject to cumbersome town planning committees that accomplished little and left much room for the application of a variety of informal processes.[54]

In the Malagasy context, the appearance and spatial organization of at least certain parts of cities had to reflect local sensibilities so that the French could demonstrate their flexibility and accommodation of cultural difference. On the other hand, the proliferation of images of modernity was to lay the groundwork for an economy based on standardized goods and mass production. Malagasy cities thus were to be arenas for incorporating local populations into a "modernizing" world. The parameters of this world, however, were not fixed but remained a work in progress. The fluidity of this modernity was demonstrated by the extent to which colonial cities were used to discover technologies that might be able to transform the metropolitan societies of Europe. This experimentation took place through the very process of identifying those aspects of the local population that were most amenable to change, those that resisted change, and those that potentially could precipitate revolution.[55]

Thus, local populations were compelled to integrate themselves into a modernity being worked out to a large extent on the basis of their own actions. For the most part, however, these actions were denied a more direct and autonomous role in shaping that modernity. Cities were staging areas to produce benefits that would be exported and then redeployed back to ensure a deepening of power differentials between the local and the external, African and European. To break this circuit, then, in large part meant using the language of modernity to argue that these cities, and of course the larger territories of which they were a part, would have only limited use to Europeans in the future.

Akin Mabogunje, in a comprehensive review of urban planning in post-colonial Africa, points out how African cities have been shaped by particular assumptions and paradigms of development.[56] While I will not review them in detail, a few points are worth stating here. That the African city could, in one sense, be created without the validation of historical processes as part of a colonial system of exploitation was also by many Africans seen to imply that a countervailing urban system could be constructed.[57] This countervailing system could be capable of advancing and embodying a nationally centered agenda after independence. Such efforts had to confront the syncretism of the evolving urban economy. Precapitalist social formations and endogenous economies persisted. This persistence acted against the full commodification of land and labor. An additional assumption was that the reaffirmation and extension of ethnic ties that enabled migrants to get used to city life would eventually be transformed into a growing class consciousness.

Strict housing and land development standards were established across most major African cities, and urban planning and labor stabilization was linked. These articulated policies were attempts to connect an emerging working class into a direct and long-term relationship with capital and the state. Access to urban space was to be contingent on regular participation in wage labor.[58] Such attempted linkages had the effect of producing sprawling and "illegal" settlements. The postcolonial state did progressively assume more responsibility for the social reproduction of urban populations. Still, the bulk of such social reproduction remained the purview of social orders denied official recognition and was usually misinterpreted as "traditional," "irregular," or "spontaneous."

The continuous deferral of the transformation of endogenous social orders into modern urban identities limited the scope of effective intervention for a capitalized local state. Cities across the continent, for the most part, still don't have appropriate forms of local governance. In anglophone countries, municipalities were given broad legal powers a long time ago, yet they seldom demonstrated any real political or economic accountability. In francophone countries, local municipal authorities had few powers as well as intricate controls over finance and elaborate bureaucratic supervision.[59] Thus, a piecemeal approach to development has prevailed, which usually entails selective interventions that, above all, constitute a rationale for turning land into a commodity. This is exemplified in slum clearance, the building of new estates for civil servants, sites and services schemes, and the general tendency to downgrade, over time, the role and the responsibility of the state in the provision of shelter. When systematic planning was attempted, it often occurred only at the level of master plans informed by Western assumptions that had little correspondence with reality.

The focus on import-substitution policies following independence failed to cohere domestic industrial development. Instead, these policies reiterated colonial distortions as industries tended to center on the same port cities of the colonial period in order to access imported raw materials. Industrialization was often undertaken without long-term assessments concerning the supply of inputs, the prospective growth of domestic markets, the institutional structures to ensure productivity, and the policy environments necessary to ensure concrete articulations between manufacturing and agricultural development. Trade unions were also unable to contribute effectively to the elaboration of urban-based industrialization. Nor did they deal effectively with collective consumption issues as they became increasingly co-opted into national political structures or repressed or subsumed by nationalist considerations.

Mabogunje points out that this piecemeal approach is also demonstrated in the prevailing process of urban problem solving. Specific issues regarding how economic surplus is to be shared are dealt with in largely symbolic ways, including gestured increases in the level of local reinvestment of surplus, the indigenization of enterprises, or the nationalization of key industries. Rarely have issues been addressed that deal with collective consumption or neighborhood struggles. According to Mabogunje, because class conflicts and formations are so diffuse, "state power is under no compulsion to intervene to minimize through urban planning and policy any disruptive conditions arising from class struggle nor to seek to secure a degree of spatial orderliness because of the disorderly forces emanating from the market place."[60] This process engenders opportunities for clientelism, sector straddling, and the beginnings of neighborhood activism.

Cities and the Faces of the State Following independence, primary cities were thrust into a series of overlapping yet incongruent roles. Recognizing the profound differences in the various nation-building strategies employed by different states, as well as differences in capacity, external alignments, and the character of territorial encompassment, I want here to remark on a few general trends. My intention was not to review postcolonial urbanization; in the text following I will discuss in more depth the social and economic dynamics associated with contemporary urbanization.

Cities were increasingly to be experienced as the purveyors of modernity, with schools, health care, cultural institutions, and the crystallization of the state. They were, moreover, to be the domain of men. Rural areas were to represent the continuity of tradition — the hearth and spiritual home of the nation and, as such, the domain of women. States in a rush to produce at least the trappings of modernity often manipulated and depleted the good will of rural areas. They were quickly intolerant of their persistent parochial attitudes and practices. Mahmood Mamdani has talked about the ways in which the city represented the elaboration of the law, the code, and the structures of differentiation between public and private, civil and state — that is, the ideological, bureaucratic, and normative underpinnings of modern social organization.[61] Rural societies, although no less resistant to colonial impositions, were less inclined to frame that resistance in the language of nationalism. As a result, these societies were suspicious of urban-centered administrative and political logic.

Most postindependence cities presented states with a complex social terrain as well as with relatively new social divides and emerging social formations. The rapid growth of cities at this time generated social dynamics that were difficult to track and assess let alone control. The historical differentiation of education, religion, language, and region of origin were all to a certain extent intertwined. This intertwining led to the reproduction of clear ethnic distinctions within urban settings, particularly in southern Africa.[62]

Urbanization, however, was articulated to ethnic practices in different ways. In some instances, the city tended to solidify certain values and practices for some ethnic groups. This strengthening permitted not only the establishment of strong rural-urban links but also a confident occupation of the city as an increasingly important site for the reproduction of specific local cultures. In contrast, other groups experienced the city as more of a disjunction. Accordingly, these groups sought either other modalities of support and identification or adapted customary practice to urban mores in ways that still enabled them to adhere to customary practices. The variety of such responses marked a larger gap between rural and urban worlds. More important, the variety of responses also amplified the incipient divisions within a particular ethnic group regardless of whether its members lived in rural or urban contexts.

Urbanization sometimes tightened the relationship between economic interest and traditional obligations for some groups. In others, urbanization stabilized or widened a preexistent segmentation. For example, a bride price would increase for certain groups on urbanization given the sex ratios prevailing in the urban area. This increase in bride price would, in turn, serve to increase the frequency of intravillage marriage because it was perceived that cultivating trust among fellow villagers concerning payment schedules would be easier if financial outlays were increased. Here, the urban would "stretch" rather than necessarily "modernize" extended family relations.

The urban context could also reinforce ties between women and their families of origin, making them more autonomous from their husbands. Conversely, given the dependency of many urban women on their husbands' economic position, there could also be a greater convergence of male and female points of view. This convergence was a major change for ethnic groups where wives were characteristically distant from their husbands. Thus, a broad range of traditional sources of tension were accentuated or altered for specific groups living in increased urban proximity.[63]

In addition, symbolic participation in the system of modern social stratification provided ways of mediating rural-urban and traditional-modern divides that otherwise were unavailable. For example, Terrence Ranger cites the use of the *mbeni* dances. These dances were essentially a performance of European social mores and norms; not only did they offer the potential for subversive mimicry and mockery but also occasioned new and extensive social networks. While these networks were originally established to provide instruction and orchestrate dance performances, they were later used to pave the way for adaptations in other aspects of life as well.[64]

Urban living arrangements were also highly varied, bringing together different identities in sometimes nebulous "corporate" formations. Jean La Fontaine describes a not atypical situation in a compound in Kinshasa during the early 1960s.[65] The owner of the compound, who also owned a small neighborhood shop, was from a family who came from northern Angola. He had acquired the compound from his mother, who relinquished her widow's rights to it. She had living quarters on the parcel and was supported by the owner-son as well as by another son and a daughter who lived elsewhere in the city. There were five other tenants, four of whom paid rent. The tenant who did not pay was a refugee from Angola belonging to the same ethnic group as the owner, and for whom some kinship connection was claimed. Another tenant from the same ethnic group did pay rent — he worked as a domestic servant and lived on the parcel with his family and wife's sister whom he supported as she minded the children while the wife pursued trade. One tenant worked as a clerk and lived with his lover. The other two tenants were single women; one basically living with her lover and the other involved in a string of mostly commercial relationships with men. The collective living arrangement combined both mutual support and a large measure of agreed-on noninterference in each other's lives. Thus, the compound not only demonstrated an ability for a mix of related and unrelated individuals to operate in concert but also to go their own separate ways without mutual responsibility when needed.

Urban elites were relatively young, while customary authority tended, for the most part, to valorize age. The attainment of urban elite status was largely derived from personal achievement in modernist occupations rather than social ascription. As such, another potential fault line was established in terms of competing vectors of authority. In most contexts, everyday life was not pulled between these apparent polarities of authority. While potentials for interelite conflict loomed over most cities, mutual accommodation and co-optation had a substantial history.[66]

Modernist elite and their groupings often needed a coethnic political base and, therefore, religious, ethnic, or regional ascription was maintained as an important category. The need to tap into the evolving state and accumulation regimes led traditional elite to adapt to discourses of modernization.[67] The modern and traditional were by no means stable categories of elite formation. The trajectories of ascendancy and decline varied; different kinds of elite dominated urban scenarios at different times. There were also various hybrid forms of authority situated in the changing dynamics of local contexts. Urbanization was not necessarily perceived as a loss of the customary or traditional for all ethnic, cultural, or regional groups. Therefore, different actors could embrace new political dispensations and urbanization. New constellations made up of diverse sources of authority were subsequently produced.

Lawrence Frank, in his discussion of various forms of ideological competition in urban Nigeria, demonstrates how recruitment criteria changed in the late 1950s. The importance of wealth and education as political markers shifted to ethnicity and origin once long-term lower-class urban residents began to seize control of local councils in Lagos, Ibadan, and Port Harcourt. Ethnic identity, of course, can be highly situational, evidenced by the way in which lower-status Igbo migrants from less advantaged areas abandoned broader Igbo solidarity to develop a more restricted communalism in order to win seats on the Port Harcourt local council during the years just prior to and following independence. Ethnicity could prove a highly mobile vehicle for challenging specific configurations of authority, whether modernist or traditional. As such, ethnicity became a vehicle for expressing populist resentment of the dominant elite. In a situation usually without the requisite money and education to translate a growing numerical following into power, the use of ethnic ideology could act as the principle of differentiation least disadvantageous to the bulk of lower-status urban residents.[68]

Self-survival and Informal Economies Perhaps the biggest change in the complexion of urban life during the postindependence period has been the reorientation of the city from being the center for a modernist elaboration of formal public and private employment to an arena for highly improvised small-scale entrepreneurial initiative. This initiative is often highly survivalist in nature. Yet, the sheer fact that nearly everyone across all social classes has been forced to configure an economic project of some kind gives rise to a remaking of the social and spatial formations of the city. This remaking occurs in ways that no public policy or formal institutionally driven development agenda has yet to match.

Aili Mari Tripp has documented just how extensive this transition is in her work on Dar es Salaam.[69] This is a city where the government has assumed most of the wage bill through the nationalization of industry and the proliferation of parastatal companies. Where heads of households were wage earners, these publicly derived wage earnings had constituted 77 percent of total income whereas private incomes accounted for only 8 percent. By 1988, informal incomes constituted roughly 90 percent of household cash income. Low-income household expenditure on food exceeded the monthly minimum salary eightfold, whereas ten years earlier food expenditure roughly equaled income.

By the late 1980s, the average worker's salary could pay roughly three days of the monthly household food budget. From 1978 to 1991 there was a 28 percent reduction in the employed labor force, which primarily was composed of people leaving wage employment because it was no longer viable. Where wage employment is maintained, it is almost never because people perceive it as providing an adequate income. Rather, such jobs provide a supplement of security for often highly vulnerable informal sector activities. Depending on the character of those informal activities, the maintenance of wage labor jobs can provide opportunities for private work, inputs for one's business, subsidized housing, and access to telephones, transport, and clients.

In urban Zambia, survival often means engagement in high-risk collaborations based more on chance taking than on trust. Employers are used as loan banks to supplement meager wages in return for tacit agreements that employees will not steal or inform others about the employer's resources. Such employee-employer relations thus depend on the conflation of trust and threat, which makes the relation insecure for both parties. Yet the borrowing is not just a way of getting by, it is also used for *kaloba*. In kaloba the employee uses what they have borrowed to lend money out at high interest rates so as to pocket a small profit. There is also the widespread use of *chilimba* arrangements, where two people alternate handing over to each other an agreed-on portion of their salary every second month in order to be able to afford basic provisions. This, too, is a high-stakes arrangement: people often lose their jobs and can't continue with their part of the bargain or, alternately, run off with the money.[70]

Urban areas are arenas for a protracted struggle over the legitimacy of self-employment and of the right to survive in the city. When it became clear to many states that cities could not support their populations, many efforts were made to send "unproductive" people back to the rural areas thus forgetting the reasons why people came to the cities in the first place. Urban residents from various walks of life found an implicit commonality in not complying with various ordinances, and repression that sought to limit how people could earn money and where, as well as where they could live. As Joseph Lugalla puts it: "In every item and issue one has to struggle. It is a struggle to get good housing. It is a struggle to secure employment, to get medicine in a public owned hospital, to deposit money in a bank or withdraw, to get a telephone, an electrical or water connection. It is also a battle to board a bus to and from city center, pay the normal official fare, and to come back home safely."[71]

In many cities, male residents had to prove that they were employed, and women residents that they were married. Ranging from the Nigeria War against Indiscipline in 1984, the Human Resources Development Act of 1983 (Tanzania), to the destruction of the Accra market in 1979 states have attempted to limit the use of the cities for the expansion of small-scale entrepreneurship. These actions are usually carried out under the guise of getting rid of loiterers, saboteurs, and racketeers. Discourses of health and sanitation, reflected in licensing procedures, were once again involved to segregate populations and territorialize activities. The state regulation of space became a vehicle of accumulation as, at every turn, bribes were demanded.

In the end it was a losing battle for the state: for the clearest demonstration of popular will, and of a coherent urban culture and urban citizenship, was the persistence of people to survive in the city. And to survive meant to revise and improvise informal activities and to put together the provision of a vast domain of foodstuffs, services, shelter, consumables, transportation, health care, and education outside of the institutions, frameworks, practices, and policies sanctioned by the state.

Public space was appropriated as a source of employment and livelihood. Children, especially, would position themselves at bus stations, markets, and roadways, to beg, shine shoes, sell cigarettes and food items, wash cars, or steer customers to transport. Those who were at the bottom tier of official employment (e.g., janitors, clerks, and messengers), and who also operated at the surface and interfaces of institutions, used these positions as "gatekeepers" — that is, intervening into what came in and out of these institutions. In response to this "seizure" of public spaces, the upper social strata privatized their lives and immersed themselves in various enclosures — walled private housing estates, private schools, and exclusive clubs.[72]

As Tripp indicates, the Tanzanian government by 1994 had little choice but to come up with a national policy to assist informal sector activities. This assistance took the form of financial services, appropriate technology, and market and skill development. The growth of small-scale private economic activity may have its correlates in urban colonial economies, yet the substantial shift in the way the majority of urban residents made a living — from the prevalence of wage employment during the first twelve to fifteen years following independence to the prevalence of so-called informal sector activities today — has brought with it an equally substantial change in the complexity of urban social formations.

Self-responsibility for urban survival opened up spaces for different ways of organizing activities. Communities became increasingly involved in one or more aspects of the provision of essential services, while advocating for more effective urban planning and management. Many local associations have been formed to improve sanitation, provide shelter, improve marketing, provide microfinancing, and advocate for a broad range of rights. Moreover, more diffuse forms of social mobilization and coordination have come to the fore. Many of these more provisional associational formations have their antecedents in the practices of shaping cross-cutting networks, urban secret societies, and the closed associations that were prevalent in many cities during the initial spurt of urban growth following World War I.

The provisional character of associational forms is also reinforced by the dearth of realistic policy initiatives to deal with the dynamics of contemporary cities. Rather than dealing directly with what is taking place in cities, the general policy thrust seems to be that the economic processes capable of contributing to real and sustained urban development can only be set in motion by making African urban areas less important and less privileged. Emphasis should be placed on the development of food and agricultural production and on the elaboration of secondary cities as processing and regional marketing centers. Despite declining inequalities between rural and urban incomes, urban areas account for nearly a half of the gross domestic product (GDP) in some countries. There remain net resource flows from rural to urban areas — as evidenced by the urban share of overall national and public investment and trade balances — as urban centers account for almost the total of negative balances,[73] although there are some preliminary indications that this may be changing as urban-generated rural investments may be expanding.

An "Africanization" of the Urban?

In some ways, a piecemeal approach to nation building and urbanization may be necessary as a way of balancing the profound tensions that exist in most African cities. The limits to capitalist penetration in African urban centers and the undermining of industrial development through the persistence of neocolonial economic relations, which keep African economies as primary producers in highly unfavorable trade conditions, combine to curtail the development of modernizing economies. In the limited institutionalization of these modernizing economies, the familial domain remains the crux of social security. Networks of connection that are based on extended family systems or "invented" out of a patchwork of conventions, memories, and contacts must be maintained as the real locus of economic survival. The most common form of this dimension remains the actual extended family, with its kinship ties, rights, and obligations.

Extended families have enabled urban residents to survive precarious economic conditions, which in the absence of family would have been inconceivable. These same conditions, however, make nearly impossible the ability to satisfactorily tend to kinship obligations. Meanwhile, the number and complexity of obligations and ties are increasing. While this increase may differentiate and extend available safety nets, taking care of one's participation in them now requires more work. The size of primary household and residential units also seems to be growing in many urban areas.[74] This increase is not because nuclear families are themselves getting larger but rather because increasing numbers of extended family members, affiliates, and boarders are consolidated within a single compound or unit and, more important, enact their ties with one another on a "kinship" basis. As such, the political intricacies of extended family relations become more difficult to navigate and more easily conflicted.

At the same time familial ties are also loosening. Some 11 percent of the residents of Lagos are now living on their own.[75] The long period of colonization had the effect of enforcing more individualized approaches to accumulation, status, and negotiating livelihood. Urbanizing trends everywhere now mark out an excessive recourse to individualized ways of handling everyday life. Increases in the mobility of African urban populations among locations marked by ever-increasing disparities in economic capacity mean that a city's population witnesses oscillating rhythms of the substantial accumulation and loss of material wealth. In sum, the pressures for maintaining functional cohesion within the framework of extended family systems and the practices of resource distribution that go with it are enormous.

It is for these reasons that Peter Geschiere, in his discussion of contemporary practices and discourses of sorcery in Cameroon, amplifies the popular conviction that the most dangerous forces come from inside the house, from the very heart of the possibility for survival.[76] This conviction, according to Geschiere, expresses the desperate need to maintain good familial relations, and the lengths to which people will go in order to do so, even though no matter what is done the individual remains vulnerable. Sorcery is deployed both as a way to level apparent inequities in the distribution of resources and as a strategy for gaining wealth. Illness and misfortune, then, are largely attributed to the failure of individuals to share resources with kin. By implication, the failure to do so invites misfortune and even death.

Demons are understood as an index of incessant connectivity; that is, that which ties people or events to others despite what they do and without their intention.[77] Accordingly, there is a preoccupation on the part of many residents in African cities with the extent to which they are tied to the fates of others whom they witness "sinking" all around them. At the same time, they hope that the ties around them are sufficiently strong to rescue them if need be. Sorcery comes to the fore, then, as a discourse that attempts to both disconnect and defend connections. It attempts to mediate two equally powerful "versions" of the contemporary social terrain — that is, as spaces where connections proliferate exponentially and as spaces where all ties are disjoined and fragmented.

Given the prevailing economic conditions, individuals are often compelled to seek out the assistance of sorcery in order to gain the income necessary in order to meet kinship demands so as not to be a victim of that very same sorcery. Such circuitry also motivates an incessant search for new sanctions against sorcery and new forms of protection against it. This is a process that has come to dominate life in many African cities. After all, the historical process of urban construction in much of Africa has been about people trying to fit increasingly complex social and economic networks into the frames of kinship.[78]

Urban Uncertainties and the Importance of Women   Uncertainties have been embedded within African cities for a long time. They have always existed as domains of unscripted and underregulated potentialities despite the rigidities and objectives of colonial power. As Catherine Coquery-Vidrovitch and others have indicated, the colonial town was always predominantly an African town, despite the intentions of Europeans.[79] As such, it has continuously been a place for the reformulation of both old and new influences. Even if created by decree, it is a hybrid in its inception. Even as colonialists sought to limit the urban black presence, there were multiple struggles to etch out spaces in the city. Ironically, the locus of such urban struggles was the market and the right to trade. Under anglophone colonialism in particular, the protracted efforts made to secure an economic niche in the city through the market constituted an important aspect of the overall struggles for independence.

These efforts were also gendered. Women escaping from a variety of rural coercion were often the primary targets of removals, detainment, and expulsions. Their few goods were seized, and a link between female urban presence and prostitution was cemented.[80] As Emmanuel Akyeampong points out for Ghana, "prostitution" was a concept that described more than the sale of sexual and domestic services — it included female assertiveness and accumulation in general.[81] Urban women were in a precarious situation not only because they often had no "formal" status within urban economies but also because they had removed themselves from the traditional and spatial constraints usually placed on women in general.

Women's urban roles have been crucial to ensuring spaces of operation in the city outside of colonial impositions and designs. This has been the case even though it was largely the colonial disruption of social systems in the rural areas, particularly the loss of land for subsistence production and other forms of social support, that forced many women to the cities.[82] Women largely paved the way for alternative forms of accumulation. They provided for urban residents who lived outside the formal circuits of colonial economies, and thus enabled informal workers to establish a foothold in the city. With their accumulated savings women often became significant property owners, and thus in turn provided sources of shelter outside of both municipal developments and industrial compounds.

The nature of African urban investment was largely a consequence of political economies where specific forms of land holdings and economic activities were constrained by the colonizer. Investment in production was severely curtailed and earnings had to be put elsewhere, and so were often invested in urban real estate and construction. The elaboration of footholds in the city helped to maintain investments in networks that were relied on to mobilize labor for large-scale agricultural work, demonstrate status and prestige, and forge matrimonial alliances.[83]

Institutionalizing a significant presence of women in the city was a hard-fought struggle in many contexts. Caught between the traditional authorities that sought to maintain control over their bodies and livelihoods and the often highly ambivalent colonial authorities, women's economic position in cities was precarious from the start. At times, colonial administrations facilitated significant changes in family and communal relationships by providing opportunities for greater autonomy for women. Relevant measures included guarantees of personal safety, the encouragement of native courts to permit divorce, and the enabling of prospective husbands to pay their own bride price through wage labor.[84] This support, however, often constituted an underhanded way of accelerating the fragmentation of social systems in rural areas. This fragmentation was often compensated for by the control of women as the most salient means of preserving cultural integrity. At other times, colonial authorities aligned with the efforts of native authorities to exert direct control over where and how women could work and live.[85]

In her exhaustive history of trade in Nairobi, Claire Robertson paints an intricate picture of how women attempted to progressively win more control over the sources and dispositions of their income.[86] She also shows how women were situated in a complex field of complicity and antagonisms between native and colonial authorities. Nairobi was significantly shaped by a series of almost constant skirmishes between frequently shifting political and economic interests. These skirmishes produced small incremental victories for traders who did everything possible to pursue trade.

Following World War II, the colonial administration forced most women to carry passes in order to be present in Nairobi. This policy reflected the obsession with prostitution, both as a sign of the native authority's loss of control over women's bodies and as a health and economic issue for colonial authorities. As the city witnessed the growth of more formal retail outlets, European consumption became less dependent on hawking. Accordingly, a variety of stringent regulations governing commercial activity in Nairobi were put in place. These regulations had to be continuously revised, ignored, or withdrawn as both traders and hawkers adamantly pursued these activities. Because women were generally the only ones engaged in cooking food, this service was vital for the large numbers of single men who resided in the city.

Perhaps the last and most desperate efforts on the part of the colonial regime to regulate economic activity occurred under the auspices of the state of emergency instituted in face of the Mau Mau rebellions of the 1950s. Thousands of traders were expelled from Nairobi. As traders and hawkers eventually returned in mass during the late 1950s and early 1960s, struggles centered on conflicting interests among various scales and types of commercial activity. Struggles occurred between trade that was centered on the highly mobile and unregulated sale of produce and that centered in regulated distribution and marketing systems. These struggles took place between small-scale trade and the consolidation of a commercial class that was substantially capitalized and politically conservative.

Up to the present, the practice of trade involves increasingly larger numbers of people as well as strong gender segmentation in terms of goods sold and their relative profitability. As Kenyan land transactions have become more profitable, contested, and corrupt, the prospect of being without land has driven more men and women to the city. Women eke out profit margins that usually average less than seventy-five cents a day in the dry staple trade.[87] More recently, younger men are now entering this trade. Urban reform agendas, the search for investment, the rechanneling of profit by large-scale entrepreneurs into real estate, and greater domination over retailing combine to encourage greater levels of harassment against traders. Protection from this harassment and efforts to secure various aspects of the right to trade also lead to organizational efforts based on and reinforcing gender segmentation.

Much of the former modalities of solidarity, support, redistribution, and security are less and less available to individuals. Both men and women increasingly have to assume responsibility for their lives and the lives of their children as individuals. Hence, trade becomes even more important as the predominant means through which individuals and households sustain themselves. The frequency with which postindependence governments have attacked these very means through which most urban residents sustain themselves is an assault against the coherence of the city and the nation — especially as this attack makes the very process of feeding the city even more precarious.

Investments in Sociality   This pushing of residents off the map continues a process where colonial administrations moved Africans to the periphery. Popular neighborhoods were not even considered to be urban, yet from the beginning they became a structural part of colonial realities, infused with transformations of precolonial forms of livelihood and renovations of links to the hinterland and to international trade circuits. Popular neighborhoods became places for the expression of discontent and resistance, and they became places of refuge for the poor. As Coquery-Vidrovitch points out, popular neighborhoods are now places for the "integration of households into new networks of capitalist production; the invention of new webs of concepts and practices of land and land laws; new patterns of foodstuff consumption; new regulations governing social and political life . . . all these processes involving new relationships to the broader economy which is neither Western nor traditional behavior."[88]

Older quarters became centers of African leisure, with cafés, dance and beer halls, cinemas, and community centers together forging an urban cultural life. Associations of all kinds proliferated, both reflecting and elaborating differences of class, religion, age, gender, occupation, and regions of origins. Football clubs became key instruments in bringing together various quarters of the city and channeling the competitive impetus that could characterize many of the relationships among different social strata.[89]

The *matanga* is an example of a waning rural ritual that was resuscitated in the city and then became identified as an almost exclusively urban practice. The matanga is basically a huge party thrown any time during the six-month period following a person's death; because death itself involves a series of transitions, it is felt that it should be commemorated on more than one single occasion. The widest circle of people who had had relations with the deceased in any category is expected to be involved. Music is obligatory, and thus the matanga has helped sustain the growing number of bands and orchestras that were vital for solidifying emerging urban cultures. By casting the social net as wide as possible in these ceremonies, it would be possible to demonstrate the shifts in social relations taking place across the city and provide new opportunities for networking.[90]

As the older quarters were often close to European residential zones, they frequently were "invaded" in order to increase the space available for European settlement and economic and recreational activities. Following World War II, however, many of these quarters were sufficiently entrenched and consolidated to resist efforts to remove local residents. This resistance greatly attenuated further moves toward segregation on the part of colonial authorities in most cities.[91]

The character of associationalism was neither entrenched nor static. Ways of associating had to be sufficiently flexible in order to adapt to the changing realities and fortunes of different groups of residents as cities grew and experienced political change. It was possible for quarters that were once socially and culturally homogenous to become more diversified and cosmopolitan, as it was for heterogeneous neighborhoods to become objects for the consolidating efforts of single ethno-cultural groups. The fortunes of specific groups and quarters would wax and wane. Consequently, the character of associations would themselves change, and participation in various forms of associationalism itself was increasingly turned to as a vital social and economic resource.

David Clark provides a good example of this situation in his study of associations in the Kibera section of Nairobi.[92] Sudanese Nubian soldiers who served in the British colonial army originally settled the quarter. They operated as important landlords in expanding urban settlement opportunities for the poor. By the 1970s, however, this Nubian community faced many strains. Slum clearance programs and housing developments undertaken by the city council and National Housing Corporation diminished Nubians' role as landlords. Subsistence agriculture was largely foreclosed as new housing developments and mushrooming squatter settlements consumed available land. Other ethnic groups increasingly filled the jobs that were once available, such as night watchmen, messengers, and office boys. As a means of social reconstruction, therefore, the community participated in a wide range of associations, football clubs, and local chapters of the ruling political party. This participation served as a vehicle of collaboration and alliance with other groups, particularly those living in Kibera, in order to influence events and the disposition of resources.

The objective of associationalism was not only to affect the disposition of resources but also, in significant ways, to "domesticate" those resources. Alternately, the issue of how resources are produced and consumed was used to make substantial claims about values and norms. As cities were the locus of contests among various ways of interpreting issues of propriety and belief, economic changes in cities became occasions of often highly conflicted reflections on what was to constitute the proper life.

6

The Production

and Management of Urban

Resources

Much of the current emphasis in African urban development centers on reintensifying efforts to configure appropriate modalities of urban governance. Such emphasis includes not only the evolution of effective municipal institutions but also the rationalization of land markets, investment in infrastructure, and more coherent laws, taxation, and planning. Throughout this discussion on African cities, I have placed clear priority on provisional and ephemeral modes of sociality. I do this in part because these modes embody the kinds of social forces and ways of being social that have emerged historically as a means of trying to keep African urban residents simultaneously in different worlds and in different agendas. I do this also because despite the past decade of concentrated reform, African urban politics remains a rough-and-tumble world. Cities are neither generating nor have other access to the kinds of finance needed to pull off the sweeping restructuring necessary to substantially increase the number of jobs, opportunities, and services. As national and local states have long regulated urban spaces with such unreality and arbitrariness, this inability to provide at least a basic framework for sustainable urban livelihoods means that public authority is rarely taken seriously.

My task in this chapter is to situate African cities in a larger overview of economic constraints and possibilities. In other words, I attempt to review just what African cities are up against in terms of their long-term economic viability. In the text following I delineate a general picture of rural life and macroeconomics, as well as recent trends in urban policy formulation and the impact of policies on land use and tenure, shelter, and infrastructure. I also briefly situate these concerns within the prevailing logic of urban governance and the management of urban services. In these reviews I provide some sense about how prevailing paradigms of urban development in Africa may work against social arrangements that have been effective in terms of providing opportunities for livelihood under precarious conditions. This working against what has often been effective not only impacts on what residents consider possible or impossible but also shapes how residents set out to try to accomplish a wide range of tasks. It shapes their sense of what can be shown or must be hidden; what can be institutionalized or must remain provisional.

The analysis in this chapter builds on some of the groundbreaking work led by Richard Stren and the Global Urban Research Initiative (GURI). One facet of the GURI work was to document the existing knowledge base on African cities and to substantiate it with a series of regionwide research projects that might suggest new formulations of urban governance from the ground up.[1] This work in turn stemmed from research coordinated by Stren and Rodney White in the 1970s and 1980s that incisively points out the limitations of prevailing management paradigms in relationship to African urban realities.[2]

Shaping African Urban Space:
Issues of Macroeconomy and Municipal Administration

Much of rural Africa is in crisis. The degradation of environments due to climatic change, the attenuation of local knowledge systems, and a more desperate approach to resource use all undermine livelihoods. But perhaps more important, the institutional structures of rural life, which served as a locus for resource regulation, social reproduction, and the production of new adaptive knowledge, are being depleted.[3] These structures managed complex interchanges of actors and could ensure a balanced approach to the need for productivity and equanimity. As specific territories are less able to provide for the basic needs of tenant populations, and as violent political conflict becomes entrenched as a mode of economic accumulation, these populations become more transient and the subsequent destinations more prone to contestation over rights of use and settlement.[4]

At the same time, as James Ferguson powerfully argues, there are no clear linear connections between the rural and the urban, because neither indicates a specific unfolding of temporality or capacity. There is an oscillating relationship where both rural and urban offer always transitional sites for the remaking of the other, depending on their respective economic fortunes. Ferguson adds, further, that what he describes as "a unilinear evolutionary progression immanent in the urbanizing process" seemed clear until the last two decades.[5] However, the interpenetration of urban and rural actors and spaces, at the same time that their distance increases from each other, makes the categorization of clear lines of interaction among them difficult. Nevertheless, whereas perhaps more is asked of the rural, the rural is less able to make some kind of functional response.

As the socializing capacity of local institutions declines, so does their capacity to structure productive activities. Nonfarm related employment in the rural areas increases as agricultural activity among urban residents increases. Extended family systems are less able to draw on their members for labor, thus instilling a greater dependence on wage labor for agricultural activities and providing individuals with a greater range of exit options when faced with intrahousehold tensions regarding the use of available assets. The trade in secondary rights to land thus becomes more prevalent but remains an insecure form of tenure, especially as land market transactions are increasingly lucrative in the escalating demands by the political elite for land, urban housing, and corporate agriculture.[6] At the same time, the deployment of remittances from migrants into land investments wane as the costs of education, health care, and consumer goods increase.[7]

A shrinking public sector, and the concomitant phasing out of agricultural subsidies, extension programs, and marketing programs attenuates the links between local rural institutional life and larger markets and institutional spheres. Incentives for export-led primary production have tended to intensify the marketization of land and production at scale, constraining small farmers from expansion, boxing them into overuse of limited land holdings, and often disrupting the various ways in which rural actors could negotiate access to opportunities and resources.[8] The emphasis on enhanced procedural clarity and rationalization of land production, as well as adjudication of claims and resource rights, has eroded intricate complementarities among diverse actors, making it difficult for them to rely on those complementarities as a means of securing some access to livelihood, no matter how limited.[9] Competition is intensified, but without new inputs and capital such competition seldom produces more efficient and sustainable resource use. Instead, it exerts a debilitating effect on the coherence of rural communities. Even when new national policies provide for varying forms of communal ownership, security of tenure, and long-term usufruct agreements, they tend to further incorporate rural domains into the purview of the state and its administrative structures.[10]

With only limited access to credit that can be used to upscale production activities, coupled with the continuous high costs of transportation and storage, small farmers are always vulnerable to a range of external shocks. This situation can tighten the hold on land exerted by customary tenure systems that usually impose narrow terms of inheritance and entitlement. There are few opportunities for local investment in infrastructure and thus limited opportunities for capturing investment-level remittances from migrants. As the levels of remittances decline, in part due to increases in the cost of urban living, the absolute dependency on them for daily rural sustenance increases.[11] It is clear that in many rural areas the moral economy that links rural and urban and local and migrant residents remains strong, and remains concretized through financial means. There is even the elaboration of more reciprocal relationships in the flows of resources — monetary, consumable, symbolic — between rural and urban areas.[12] Still, greater rural social differentiation begins to emerge as larger numbers of migrants operate at greater physical and emotional distance from their places of origin.[13]

In their study of the Limpopo Province in South Africa along with five regions in Botswana, Arjan de Haan, Johann Kirsten, and Juliana Rwelamira found a persistence of largely circular patterns of migration, with migrants maintaining rights to land use and other assets, although the lengths of stay were growing longer.[14] In this study household wealth is positively correlated to both the incidence and capacity of migration, as remittances continue to play a critical part in improved rural livelihoods. Concomitantly, greater availability of land or other assets to less endowed persons or households does not appreciably slow down out-migration.

As the cost of urban living has risen enormously in the poststructural adjustment period, a twofold character to urban provisioning has emerged. On the one hand, trade liberalization regimes have flooded local markets with cheap imports, undermining what limited manufacturing sectors did exist in urban areas. On the other hand, the diminution of national economies has been in some cases so extensive that even these cheap imported provisions have become too expensive for local consumption. Dependency grows on the urban hinterland for most basic consumables. Depending on the geographical positioning of cities, as well as the characteristics of the built environment, transport and communications systems, natural resources, and institutional proficiencies, the implications of this burgeoning reliance on urban hinterlands may have severely negative ecological consequences or may posit new opportunities for urban sustainability.[15] A critical issue remains the enlarging footprint of the city, because it must draw water and the sources of biomass fuel, for example, far beyond the city boundaries and thus compete more directly with rural uses of land.

The recent surge in the diversification of rural incomes, with the vast majority of rural households now having one or more nonagricultural income sources, leads to a greater individuation of economic activity. The structures of economic rights and responsibilities are changing within peasant households, and they take an increasingly ambiguous character.[16] As economic individuation spreads, the labor-intensive mechanisms of negotiation that have come to characterize local institutions in many rural settings become less viable. Whereas these negotiations tended to attribute clear roles to rural actors, a certain ambiguity in roles is now necessary in order for these actors to access a diversity of resources and opportunities.[17] Diminishing viability is also a result of the continued cultural and political valorization of rural existence as an agricultural one, even if farming makes up increasingly less of the total volume of livelihood. There is thus a subsequent disjunction between social and economic realities as agricultural work continues to constitute the basis of social status in most rural settings.[18]

The factors driving diversification are also complex. To some extent weak financial markets and social insurance must be compensated with the pursuit of diverse sources of income in order to mitigate consumption variability, as rural dwellers must compel as much as they can from a limited range of assets, which may in turn be generating diminishing returns.[19] Diversification also stems from the fact that as economies of scale are rarely operative in African agricultural production, agriculture itself must be practiced across heterogeneous landscapes and climatic conditions.

What is critical is that diversification in its own terms does not stem from or guarantee a larger asset base. While nonfarm income is clearly associated with higher welfare, access to high-return nonfarm activities can be significantly constrained by a preexisting lack of land, tools, resources, and status.[20] For example, better-off farmers frequently seek labor-saving technologies in order that household members can be freed to participate in better-paid nonfarm labor.[21] Because women often assume primary responsibility for subsistence food production, policies that have emphasized liberalization as a mechanism to capacitate export-oriented agriculture cause them to suffer from increases in the price of inputs yet benefit little from rises in producer prices.[22] Left with a limited diversification of assets and income portfolios, the poor are trapped in low-return activities, while those of greater capacity use the increasingly diverse cross-sectional portfolios to acquire a larger share of available assets in land, labor, and capital equipment. As as result, social differentiation within rural domains becomes more marked.

It is estimated that 70 to 75 percent of the rural population in Sub-Saharan Africa lives on fragile lands, whose phosphorous deficiencies, low rates of water infiltration and retention, and low organic content severely limit agricultural production.[23] The actual proportion of national territories constituting arable land is contracting. This is particularly the case in the countries of South Africa, where, for example, the proportion of arable land in Zambia and Zimbabwe is presently no more than 7 percent of the total.[24] The volatility of land politics in Zambia, Zimbabwe, and Malawi, coupled with adverse climatic conditions, is presently compromising food security and spurring significant population movement.[25]

Whereas rural institutions were largely oriented toward amplifying a concrete reciprocity among actors, with an attendant effort to minimize the visibility of disparities in access and income, the sense of a disparity has grown. This may not be attributable as much to changing local dynamics as it is to a greater awareness on the part of local actors as to the larger political and economic context in which they are situated. A procedural democratization of most African societies has generated new economies in information flow. As a result, citizens are much more aware of fundamental inequities. When the distribution of inequity is spatialized, actors will attempt to relocate themselves in contexts where incomes are expected to increase.[26]

At the same time rural orientations and even rural agricultural production in some countries are reinforced by specific trajectories and constraints of urban operation, which make clear divides between the rural and the urban ambiguous. For example, in Jens Andersson's work examining Buhera migrants in Harare, Zimbabwe, rural investment as a sociocultural disposition — that is, as a means of elaborating particular frameworks and practices of belonging — becomes a basis for different ways of working in the city. Access to work, shelter, and sociality in urban areas is contingent on how Buhera urban residents relate to particular rural resources, such as land, rural livelihoods, and local politics. In other words, what urban residents are able to do in the city — for example, how they can acquire urban shelter or how they can work collaboratively with others to elaborate urban livelihoods — remains in large part a function of how they position themselves in relationship to their rural historical ties.[27]

In Ligongwe, Malawi, Harri Englund found rural and urban areas linked in complex moral economies that simultaneously required clear differentiation between the two domains and thick interlinkages that made clear distinctions between domains difficult. Residents frequently tolerated poor urban living conditions as a means of maintaining relatively prosperous rural positions, while many rural residents were clearly dependent on a range of inputs derived from urban social networks. As the price of food and shelter has increased substantially in the city, and in light of structural adjustment policies that eliminate price subsidies and permit a liberalization of trade, attachment to rural areas is reiterated as a means of access to food production. Given an overarching context of economic hardship, such complementarities require both the reiteration of reciprocal obligations between rural and economic households as well as a means of modulating the degrees of mutual demand. Such a task requires moral economies that both efface the "distance" between the urban and the rural as well as amplify it.[28] A translocal topography predominates that incorporates urban and rural, not as clearly defined and opposed domains but rather fractured ones with different connotations, expectations, practices, and strategic orientations.[29]

Stalled Globalization Despite some notable successes registered by many developing countries in adapting to and actively engaging with global changes, Africa has largely been left out of most facets of economic globalization. The so-called new international division of labor has largely bypassed major parts of the African continent. Real incomes have fallen at an annual rate of 1 percent since the 1980s. Minimum wages have fallen between 50 percent and 70 percent during this time. The anticipated 22 million jobs that will have been created between 1985 and 2020 will fall far short of the 380 million necessary to get unemployment below 10 percent.[30]

Put simply, economic globalization has largely stalled in Africa. The consequences for urban economies have been severe. Stalled globalization weakens the capacity of the formal economy to generate jobs. In most countries of Sub-Saharan Africa regular urban wage employment constitutes only a small fraction of total employment. Starting from the early 1980s, regular employment has fallen and by increasingly wider margins has failed to match the growth of the nonagricultural irregular labor force.

Even though 60 percent of African countries were able to experience economic growth rates in excess of population growth — and half of these registered growth rates of more than 5 percent — in the least-developed African countries GDP declined from 4.9 percent to 2.4 percent in 1997.[31]

Despite growth in the majority of the countries, there remains concern as to whether the process of correcting bad macroeconomic policies itself enables the productive output of a country to bounce back without factor accumulation. This is a process that yields rapid growth that cannot be sustained over the long term.[32] Further, slightly more than 350 million Africans (more than half of the population of Sub-Saharan Africa) continue to live in poverty.[33] Aggregate per capita income, US$665 per annum, is now three-quarters of what it was in 1980. Assuming stabilized population growth rates, the overall African economy would have to grow at a rate of 10 percent per annum over the next twenty years just to double the present level of per capita income.[34]

While the continent's aggregate economic performance continues to improve — as GDP growth moved to 3.3 percent in 1998, compared to 2.9 percent in 1997 — the distribution of growth is uneven. The Economic Commission for Africa has posited several indicators to

— Examine directions in current account balance, inflation, and per capita income, and the extent to which the population benefits from performance improvements or is negatively affected by decline;
— Determine a country's capacity to maintain long-term economic growth;
— Assess the appropriateness of government monetary and fiscal policy in terms of sustaining growth.

According to these measures there has been little improvement for the majority of Africans, even in countries experiencing accelerated growth rates.[35] Only those countries that have substantial levels of resource endowment, coupled with small and/or highly skilled populations, such as Botswana, Mauritius, South Africa, Tunisia, and Equatorial Guinea, demonstrate any significant capacity to maintain long-term economic growth.[36] The conclusion that over two-thirds of African countries are rated as having low sustainability is particularly worrying. This includes countries that are both large and small, natural-resource poor and natural-resource rich, and with both good policies and bad policies.[37]

At the beginning of 1998, twenty-two African countries were engaged in structural adjustment agreements brokered by the International Monetary Fund. These agreements emphasized reduced inflation rates, reduced budget deficits, elimination of current account and balance-of-payment deficits, and efficient debt management. These actions are purportedly undertaken to create a platform for human resource development and poverty alleviation. Despite an allocation rate for potentially productive public expenditures, which exceeds that of the rest of the developing world, the record of the African public sector is not impressive. In part, this situation is due to the fact that the public sector has been used mainly to create employment rather than to deliver services; and in part it is the pressure to create jobs that stemmed from rapid growth rates in the stock of education. Thus even when social service allocations do end up in the hands of the relevant providing institutions, the bulk of this money is used to cover wage bills.[38]

Limits to Industrialization and Investment The widespread implementation of structural adjustment programs continues to have a deleterious impact on urban-based manufacturing. Crippling shortages in imported materials are created, investment is reduced, and effective market demand is depressed. In the past, firms that were forced to hold large inventories to guard against unreliable supply networks usually acted only within trusted business relationships. They invested in costly infrastructure to guard against disruptions in power and water supplies. Firms also focused on state contracts as a means of protecting themselves against the risks associated with these costs. Now, structural adjustment has removed much of this protection, even while liberalization has reduced some of the costs.[39]

Although large-scale manufacturing enterprises have created an impressive volume of jobs in the newly industrialized countries of Asia and Latin America, they have generated only a small number of employment opportunities in urban Africa. Confronted by increased market uncertainties, high interest rates, rising import costs, and shortages of raw materials, African industrialists have adopted new accumulation strategies. These strategies involve a process of informalizing production activities and work relations.

Moreover, reductions in the size of the civil service, subsidy cuts, privatization, and deregulation under structural adjustment programs have eroded the state's capacity to intervene effectively in the economy and in social policy.[40] Structural adjustment programs have swelled the ranks of the unemployed. In many instances, the weakened state has been unable to implement the policies of the international financial institutions. Uncertainty in the investment climate is thus exacerbated, and investor confidence plummets.

The situation is compounded by low rates of domestic savings and investment. Compared to the 1975 to 1984 period, gross domestic savings on the continent declined by 34 percent during the first half of the 1990s. Yet, savings are difficult to register given the large amount of external obligations. As Africa moves toward a more positive trade balance, current account deficits continue to increase (US$8.6 billion in 1996 to $9.5 billion in 1997). This is largely due to interest payments on external debt and trade-related services. The overall external debt has risen from $340 billion in 1996 to $349 billion in 1997, with debt servicing absorbing 21.3 percent of export earnings.[41] It is estimated that an investment rate of 33 percent of GDP is required in order for Africa as a whole to register the growth rates of 7 percent needed to reduce the ratio of people living in poverty by 4 percent per annum.[42] Because the current domestic savings rate is 15 percent, this means that 18 percent would be needed from external sources. Current levels of official development assistance for Africa average 9 percent. When these figures are disaggregated by region, however, the residual financing gap in, for example, Central Africa is about 27 percent.[43]

Urbanization is conventionally associated with progressive levels of in-dustrialization. As industrialization is increasingly oriented toward export, an assessment of African urban futures seems inextricably linked to under-standing the constraints on the continent's capacity to export. Real trade as a share of GDP declined by an average of 0.35 percent annually between 1980 and 1993.[44] Africa's openness to the world has been much more constrained than that of other continents; during the 1970s and 1980s governments tried to avoid adjusting exchange rates as long as inflation remained manageable. By avoiding exchange rate adjustment, these coun-tries effectively limited their participation in international trade. A wide range of protective barriers simply took away from the market the alloca-tion of foreign exchange and other productive resources and placed it in the hands of the state.[45]

Unlike the situation in Asia, the protections that were instituted were neither time bound nor performance linked. Thus, they could not be used to guide newly developed domestic industries to larger scales and help these industries become more competitive. With an extremely narrow tax base and limited tax-collecting capacity, African governments became overly dependent on taxing international trade transactions in order to generate revenue. State management of the overall economy thus came to center on trade policy instruments as a means of both compressing imports and in-creasing revenue.[46]

It must be remembered that in many urban contexts, manufacturing activities were compartmentalized and curtailed to support only a limited number of ventures consonant with specific colonial interests. British rule after World War I in Dar es Salaam, for instance, segregated access to improvements across sectors. Industries were limited to sisal decortication;

cotton ginning; rice, sugar, and timber processing; and groundnut, co-
conut, and sesame seed oil pressing. Other attempts to generate industries
were suppressed. Significant small, geographically scattered, and family-
owned industrial establishments did exist, although they experienced high
mortality rates due to licensing requirements that favored foreign-owned
companies. In addition, marketing ordinances tended to impose higher
tariffs on goods produced by African-managed establishments.[47]

Donors, Trade, and the Private Sector Historically, governments have
used tax and taxlike policies to support the special interests of favored
groups to the detriment of the development needs of the larger population.
Even when conditions for accessing finance from donors and banks have
been imposed, many governments continue to trade growth for transfers to
favored groups. These trade offs occur especially when favored groups are
able to secure substantial links with private interests in donor countries.
Donors often believe that when governments are alienated, impoverishment and political turmoil may be accelerated beyond acceptable levels. If
turmoil increases so does the levels of immigration to donor countries.

Even when new policies, stressing trade liberalization, budgetary reform, and strict monetary controls, reduce the room for executive discre-
tion, a country's political situation often becomes more contestable and potentially volatile. This volatility adds uncertainty to the sustainability of
reforms. In such an environment, the poor gravitate toward safer self-
insurance mechanisms. These mechanisms curtail more profitable, yet
risky, behaviors, which in turn contribute to lower growth. The private
sector thus concentrates on maintaining a liquid portfolio of assets, rather
than on investing in infrastructure or future capacity. Therefore, even when
a new generation of political leaders and institutions is cultivated, much
uncertainty remains as to whether they will be able to carry policy changes
into the future.

The proportion of primary production to manufactured output has been
conventionally identified as a key impediment to economic growth. The
small volume and slow pace of the continent's total aggregate output is
perhaps a more significant factor — that is, where low exports reduce overall output and low output reduces exports.[48] Rapid expansion in total
output would require more concentration on both unprocessed and processed primary exports. At present, such concentration takes the form of
expanding mineral extraction, which requires significant investment in in-

frastructure. These investments are almost always only attainable through politically sensitive transactions with transnational mining companies.

Toward Municipal Proficiency   Given the truncated way in which African cities are linked to global economies, what should the purveyors of urban policy do? Conventional wisdom says that a more proficient mobilization, organization, and deployment of local resources and resourcefulness is best accomplished through a comprehensive decentralization of governmental authority and financial responsibility to the municipal level. The conventional thinking is that only when urban citizens take responsibility for the management of their political affairs will they feel secure enough to become proficient entrepreneurs and forward looking in their individual and collective initiatives.

In this process of "subsidiary" — that is, of bringing the management of public affairs and goods down to the most immediate and practical levels of where they actually take effect, municipal authorities are also supposed to act with increased measures of fiscal autonomy. Municipal authorities are to take on more responsibility for covering larger shares of their operating costs. In this respect, nascent municipal governments in many African cities are caught in a persistent bind. Improvements in physical and administrative infrastructure are necessary in order to make peoples' activities more productive. By being more productive, these activities can generate increased amounts of revenue, which municipal governments can then use to improve the overall urban environment. Because the tax base of most cities remains very limited, however, municipalities are not able to raise sufficient funds in the interim so as to have some kind of working capital to make these improvements. Addressing this dilemma has been one of the main features of externally induced policy and project initiatives.

Local urban economic development once concentrated on effecting the locational decisions of foreign investment. Tax breaks were offered, as well as other inducements, in order to attract firms that would then create jobs. This strategy is, however, presently in decline. The reasons for this include, first, the fact that an inordinate amount of time and money were spent on "boosting" the attractions of a given city. The payoff, in terms of the amount of investments secured, just wasn't there. Second, new GATT regulations prohibit any domestic subsidy that could displace inputs in domestic markets or in the exports of other countries in international markets. These regulations deter local governments from offering subsidies to specific industries within their jurisdictions or from using tax breaks to attract particular firms.[49]

The current trend is toward sectorwide strategies. These strategies focus on creating economies of agglomeration: that is, basically taking what exists and finding new ways to organize, link, and substantiate it. Fostering greater links between training and job creation is an important component of these economies of agglomeration. Theoretically, these links will, in turn, bring about virtuous cycles. Targeted investments in human capital creation, employment, and entrepreneurship, largely managed outside of the public realm, will result in better health and living conditions. Improvement in these conditions will then result in a more solid base of human capital and so forth.

Local governments now rely heavily on various forms of municipal development funds. Here, the central government uses its credit rating to access funds on capital markets for municipal development. Alternately, a more privatized formula is used, where the government provides liquidity but does not assume the subsequent risk.[50] Now, most states and international organizations promote mixed funding—for example, grants, loans, internally generated revenue, governmental transfers, foreign direct investment—for urban development needs. In fact, most urban development projects now necessitate mixed funding. Grants are conditional on accessing loan financing, which is itself conditional on governmental guarantees. Such development financing assumes the existence of suitable credit markets for municipalities and attractive repayment conditions, both of which, however, are rare.

So far, decentralization has encumbered municipalities with increased burdens of tax collection that are not compensated for by an increased share of national revenue. This is particularly the case in francophone countries. Composite figures for West Africa show that local government budgets represent less than 1 percent of GDP, and 3 percent to 5 percent of state budgets in economies where public revenues are only 15 percent of the GDP.[51] While US$20 per annum is spent for residents in the somewhat better-off cities of Abidjan and Dakar, only $4 to $6 is spent on average for other African capital cities.[52] West African local authorities spend one-hundredth the amount per capita as do their European equivalents.[53] If medium-size West African cities were to set aside 3 percent of their budgets for routine maintenance and 2 percent for larger operations and renewal projects, they would spend twice the amount of their overall budget and more than twenty times what they actually do spend in these areas.[54]

In most African urban contexts, a variety of revenue burdens predominate. Rate-of-return targets are too high; loan repayments tend to exceed local government capacity; and municipal governments are often bogged down with time-consuming cadastral projects that will only increase revenue generation in the long term. Additionally, indirect taxes are the only real source of cost recovery for nonrevenue-generating services such as road maintenance, waste management, and drainage.

While municipalities in "normal" conditions would be expected to rely heavily on revenue generation through taxing property, such practice proves difficult in most African cities. Reliance on property as the locus of taxation is often constrained by inadequate land registration systems, lack of formal property titles, excessive exemptions available to those who develop land, and a lack of compliance due to poor delivery of services.

There has been a significant devolution of responsibility to the local level, yet there has not been an equivalent devolution of political and fiscal power. While states may now have more options to access development and operational financing for municipalities, they are not generally providing a fair share of the national fiscus for cities. In most francophone countries, the state has first claim on whatever resources are available. The state is supposed to raise money for municipalities and inform them well in advance of the budgeted allocation. But this is seldom the case. The system becomes distorted with too many tax exemptions and too much incorrect information. As a result, cities find it difficult to generate realistic plans, leading almost always to excessive amounts of deficit spending.[55]

In Guinea, 40 percent of business taxes and 60 percent of property taxes go the state, with the rest shared between Conakry and its constituent districts. Central government transfers account for only 10 percent of the capital city's budget.[56] As large urban centers are also decentralized into multiple municipalities, a skewing of capacities within the urban centers is also taking place. In the Côte d'Ivoire the ten municipalities that make up Greater Abidjan can borrow from a local public fund to complete district-servicing projects. The aim of these projects is to bring in rapid returns through the construction, for example, of markets and bus stations. This fund was established with 71 percent World Bank and 29 percent national government funding. Yet, there are increasing disparities among districts. For example, while the per capita capital budget of the former European district of Plateau was sixty times higher in 1987 that that of the peripheral district of Attécoubé, it was ninety-nine times higher in 1990.[57]

In order to deal with the lingering problems of balancing responsibility and financial capacity and to deter further fragmentation within urban systems, a general agreement among multilateral and other donor groupings has coalesced around several objectives:

— To coordinate municipal and national regulatory frameworks so as to promote greater municipal autonomy, as reflected in the trends to establish municipal accounts;

— To diversify the character of state-local transfers — for example, investment funds, shared tax revenues, global operating grants, devolution of property gains;

— To focus on realistic taxation — for example, to center on the use of property and facilities rather than on ownership;

— To identify new modalities of taxation — for example, asset ownership, asset appreciation (capital gains, property appreciation), transfer of property, use of property (such as "residential" or "housing" taxes);

— To assess the extent to which the administration costs of specific interventions outweigh the potential gains — for example, the problem with investments in cadastral systems is that instead of generating a working understanding of the social composition and profiles of urban districts, attention has been paid to the spatial positioning of specific population centers and other urban assets, which are much less useful for taxation purposes.[58]

While these objectives inform most policy discourses throughout the region, many substantial difficulties remain in terms of implementing them in the day-to-day practices of municipal administration.

Urban Land

Perhaps the major challenge related to the financial sustainability of cities entails the conceptualization and disposition of urban land. Who has access to it, for what purpose, and under what circumstances? Concomitantly, what kind of valuation is attached to its status and use, and under what circumstances can rents be appropriated from it? All of these questions have proven to be particularly intricate political, cultural, and administrative challenges in most African urban contexts. After all, land remains the most important resource and source of status and well-being for most residents. As such, it is a key site and locus of urban contestation. In response, the state has frequently tried to minimize land disputes by putting all land in its own hands.[59]

In most of Africa, land persists in being viewed largely as a public good. It is to be collectively owned by those who use it and can elaborate a social history on the basis of it. As colonization became the dominant force engineering urbanization on the continent, specific discourses of land management were introduced and enforced as law. In other words, the access to urban land, the ways in which it could be used, claimed, divided, and be a part of other exchanges became the purview of codification and law. While "law" was certainly not a foreign notion to most African societies, subsuming relationships to land within legal frameworks was largely viewed as a distortion of the status and meaning of land within these societies.

Efforts to regularize land tenure and shelter systems in African cities took place within a complex tension between forging cities that were conversant with the larger urban world, but also conversant with local inclinations about land and sociality. In addition to mediating this tension, there were also difficulties involved in accommodating the large influx of rural dwellers in the city. Urban population sizes are now such that even as inward migration abates, internal population growth overtaxes the availability of land, to say nothing of services. As such, access to land and plotted domains in most cities has been subject to substantial speculation and irregularity. The popular response to this irregularity tends to invoke a past where land belonged neither to the state nor private parties.

Such responses point to the situation where even when lands came under direct state control during periods of nationalization, they could be sold several times over through a variety of land agents. Land settlements served to constitute emerging patronage systems. While governments usually made some efforts to regularize tenure, the articulation of local, largely nonstatutory authority to competing national political groupings impeded regularization.

What seems clear is that the way in which most popular neighborhoods were once settled and organized is no longer accessible to most low-income urban households today. This is due, in part, to the very rationalization in land markets and policies that have been progressively introduced in recent years. Many popular neighborhoods were situated on private or communally owned land. The land was developed and serviced outside of legal channels. While the sale of property itself may be legal, either the substandard nature of construction and provision or the absence of permits allowing letting or authorizations for habitation may make the marketing of a particular built environment illegal.

While land submarkets in Africa are often varied and opaque, a few generalizations are possible. As I have indicated, individual ownership of land does not run deep in African societies, and is a precept that by now is a well-worn stereotype. The ability to dispose of land was not the same thing as owning it. Customary political authorities might bestow land or distribute rights of tenure to groups and individuals, but only in the name of some larger group. In Islamic societies land was largely accorded *wakf* status — that is, to be held in trust for the general welfare of the community.

Land was often subject to an intricate web of complementary and competing claims. These gave rise to multiple genealogies that, in turn, anchored the intersection of overlaying collective identities. Thus land was not readily available for purchase and sale on the market. Within urban contexts, land submarkets were complicated by various patterns of coownership and customary and colonial frameworks. Municipal and national authorities were often bogged down trying to unravel different logical and historical forms of documentation to piece together workable land transactions.[60]

The difficulties in such land brokering eventually led half of Africa's states (with 75 percent of the region's population) to assume some form of control over land ownership and/or disposition.[61] What ensued varied greatly: from comprehensive and exclusive nationalization to reparceling of land to private ownership according to standardized regulatory frameworks. Yet in almost all policy environments, the provision of land in urban submarkets remained exceedingly problematic. Further, it was complicated by the pursuit of rent-seeking strategies by most African regimes.

In addition as the poor require immediate occupation of space and access to construction at variable standards, national land policies were seldom able to circumvent widespread informalized practices of land disposition. Even with widespread decentralization and the proliferation of municipal governments, land disposition remains almost exclusively a matter of national regulation and action. One of the common areas of contestation between municipal and national governments is over the control of the cadastral — that is, over who gets to control documentation regarding land registration and about who lives where.

The Insecurity of Tenure Many Africans exist in an incessant state of tenure insecurity. In Ethiopia, for example, this insecurity was initially constructed through an imperial system. Land was held in eminent domain by the state and the vast majority of peasants were highly exploited tenant farmers. When this long-term system was overthrown by the Derg revolution in 1974, land was nationalized and the bulk of rural farmers were resettled in agricultural collectives. Even in the present regime, which overturned the Derg in 1991, the state retains control over the redistribution of most land, and maintains usufruct rights with limited, short-term transfers now permitted.[62]

In many situations, powerful individuals are able to flaunt various land and building regulations at will, putting up poorly designed structures in areas not appropriate or zoned for residential use. Regulations and zoning laws would then have to be reformulated in order to accommodate this situation. Poor areas have been frequently subject to slum clearance. Policymakers tended to mistakenly believe that these areas were composed solely of marginalized and homogenous sociocultural groups. As a result, it was assumed that these communities could replicate themselves intact under better circumstances somewhere else. It was also assumed that they had to be dispersed and integrated into the larger urban society. In almost all instances of slum clearance, resettlement schemes were badly planned and woefully underfinanced. Settlements grew whose conditions were worse than the original ones or that brought greater density to already dense areas.[63] The legal accommodation of irregular building activity on the part of the elite and the frequently illegal breakup of poor settlements usually served to deepen a dual form of urban land development.

One of the most notorious examples of "slum" clearance was the sudden eviction during 1990 of residents from Maroko, one of the largest settlements in Lagos.[64] Between 1973 and 1995 there were to be thirty-six major forced migrations in Nigeria, two-thirds of them in Lagos. Claiming the existence of horrible living conditions in a makeshift, illegally occupied quarter, the state used its power of eminent domain as contained in the 1978 Land Use Decree to acquire this occupied land in the "public interest." As a result, residents were forced to disperse across the city.

In actuality, Maroko had been a settlement for eighteen years. Most tenants paid annual rent to the customary owners of the land or purchased plots on ninety-nine-year leasehold and were in possession of state-issued certificates. Perhaps the key factor is that Maroko is located close to the highly priced neighborhoods of Victoria Island and Ikoyi. Partitioned and repartitioned to their limits, there was no room for expansion in these upper-class quarters.

A resettlement committee was only set up after the demolition had already taken place. The few residents declared eligible for official relocation were placed in unfinished housing estates without services. Even here, there was a great deal of speculation in how sites were allotted. In a follow-up survey of a cross-section of former Maroko residents, almost all of them reported facing more severe overcrowding, poorer environmental and sanitation conditions, and higher prices for shelter. While Maroko was not connected to the national electricity grid and most residents did not have publicly piped water, sizable numbers formerly had access to both piped water and electricity through private commercial providers and community ventures. Now, few of the resettled have access to electricity, and most rely on well water to supplement that provided by commercial tankers.[65]

As mentioned above, it is now a well-known story about how African land disposition is often a confusing mixture of public ownership, customary rights, and private holding. Most land parcels fall under multiple and often-competing jurisdictional frameworks, setting up a situation where multiple claims can be made on land. This mixture may ensure that urban residents may be able to access land in many different ways. On the other hand, there are also many different ways in which land distribution can be manipulated — resulting in hoarding and speculation.

In Kinshasa, for example, illegally developed plots outnumber the legal ones by tenfold. It is often not clear in these situations who is taking advantage of whom. Proofs of ownership produced by various customary authorities are often unreliable and varied because they are based simultaneously on traditionally invested powers and on those conferred by the former colonial authorities. In addition, the identity of the seller is often not clear, especially when the supposed head of a household is aged and/or illiterate.[66] Also in Kinshasa, public officials working with cadastral maps have acquired substantial power by working a parallel land market for land expropriation. Here, land problems, particularly related to the entangling of competing ownership claims, are reinforced by civil servants so that they can offer their services on a private basis so as to resolve the issue.[67] In Lagos, it is also possible to identify innumerable instances where the "need" for proper land management and the "impediments" to such management has opened up a highly lucrative economy of compensation and intermediation.[68]

Land as an Instrument of Urban Institution Building   At the same time, local land disposition systems are often quite adept in terms of addressing various dimensions of urban growth. D. R. Aronson provides an interesting example of land negotiation in Ibadan prior to quasi-land nationalization. In this rapidly growing city, investments in land and building construction were one of the few available investments. As such, land was the object of intense speculation and potential manipulation. Most available land was located on the outskirts of the city. This available land remained largely under the jurisdiction of customary arrangements exercised by extended family systems. These extended families usually resided in the overcrowded inner city, where the density and proximity of family habitation allowed family members to keep an eye on each other's business dealings. Such inner city residency also reflected a long-term Yoruba practice of "urban" farmers living away from their land holdings.

Because this land was shifted from agriculture to the development of new urban neighborhoods, there were few structured ways to determine the reputations and trustworthiness of potential landlords, neighbors, or tenants. As formal institutions governing these matters remained new and often corruptible, there were few guarantees about any facet of land transactions. These facets would include the assurance that one was purchasing land from the real owner, that counterclaims wouldn't arise, that the demarcations of property would be respected, that building materials wouldn't be stolen, and that tenants would be reliable and landlords reasonable.[69]

Given this situation, the various parties entered into usually intricate negotiations. These parties included the different factions of owner families, speculators operating as middlemen, prospective buyers, and contractors. Often, families had to officially demonstrate that they were the rightful owners of land within the prevailing "modern," as opposed to customary, regulations. Once such ownership was established, different factions of the family would often deal with different speculators. These speculators tried to steer land deals in ways that would maximize their own status, if not immediate financial advantage. Families tended to prefer dealing with outside middlemen rather than parceling out land among family members. These middlemen tended to be closer to networks of surveyors, lawyers, and prospective buyers, which would enhance both security and value in the disposal of the land. In addition, "internal" sales might lead to the accumulation of unfair advantages for specific family members, thus introducing intolerable inequities into the family system.

Speculators would work hard to cultivate and maintain the "allegiance" of owning families to ward off other possible claims and speculators. Owning families frequently negotiated with various middlemen, including conflicts as a means of soliciting various payoffs that increased the value of the land. This practice was also a way of facilitating the spread of income across the family network. All parties wanted to be seen as powerful and cunning, yet reliable. Although there was plenty of bluff, threats, pretense, and payoffs in order to arrive at definitive claims and purchases, negotiations also aimed to establish reliable future partners.

Such partnerships were themselves viewed as valuable resources because they could be used to influence the disposition of resources and attain influence in urban emerging institutions. Urban development also meant putting together new institutional and political arrangements. Effectively negotiated participation in land deals could be parlayed into the attainment of status and income-generating possibilities elsewhere. Thus, land negotiations were used as a way to elaborate a structure of personal influence and social constraints capable of shaping the intensifying and expanding competition over urban resources of all kinds.[70]

The persistent contestation and ambiguities related to the ownership and use of land are important factors in shaping most African cities. In the years following independence, locally deliberated land management systems of an ad hoc nature could provide effective mechanisms of socializing land transactions, and those of other important urban resources. As cities have grown larger and resources more precarious, new, more systematized, frameworks of resource management may be necessary. Squatting and land invasions, the manipulation and/or commercialization of customary rights, and de facto landowners who build outside the law all can combine to distort urban growth processes. Such practices deter the establishment of mortgage markets and taxation of property, both of which are potentially crucial sources of urban revenue. It is important to keep in mind, however, that African cities have mixed histories of public and private ownership and development. These histories make it difficult to come up with fixed generalizations about the efficacy of particular land management frameworks.

In the case of Mozambique, the decommodification of land and housing stock following independence gave rise to a distinct urbanized fraction of the population. This urban population was able to live in cities for little rent. Following the revised 1990 constitution, private markets involving properties were progressively sanctioned. This has led to various forms of property revalorization, especially in Maputo's central "concrete city," thereby forcing growing numbers of households to the peripheral areas.

Mozambique's ruling party, Frelimo, initially established grassroots organizations to assist the party in exerting its authority and to provide information on the suitability of land occupation. These same organizations are now playing a major role in the allocation of land and in contributing to the development of an illegal land market. But this illegal market often does a better job of ensuring a wider access to land and a more diversified use of it than do formal and legal markets. Informal mechanisms tend to converge a broader range of actors and resources and force potential users into more negotiated dispositions of land. Subsuming that disposition to the courts, although having the potential of ensuring greater equity, also overtaxes fragile legal systems, sometimes creating greater loopholes through which more insidious forms of corruption can prevail.[71]

The State and the Transfer of Land In most francophone countries, the state continues to exercise the rights of eminent domain over land. Property rights are thus negotiated with the state. As a result the state always has some role in land disposition issues, regardless of the various degrees of entitlement established. Title is often only granted if the land is developed. In this way, the state attempts to deter the withholding of land for speculative purposes, a practice that has frequently occurred in cities where land has already been marketed.[72] But the history of land management has repeatedly demonstrated that regulatory frameworks tend to compound and entrench the inaccessibility of land.[73]

The Nigerian Land Decree of 1978 placed the administration of all urban land in the hands of the state through the Land Use and Allocation Committee (LUAC). A complicated bureaucratic application process was put in place. Applications for certificates of occupancy had to be accompanied by proof that taxes had been paid up for the last three years. Because many landlords had not paid, they were afraid that attaining certificates of occupancy would lead to prosecution.[74]

Applications were then forwarded to the surveying division of the Ministry of Works and Housing. Afterward, the deeds section processed them before they were resent to the survey division. The application was then sent back to the LUAC, who then published the application in local newspapers to allow members of the public to file objections within a twenty-one-day period. If there were no objections, the application was then sent to the town planning section of the ministry, which undertook site inspection and confirmation of the information contained in the application. Once passed, the application then went to the state governor for approval and signature. Once land was acquired, plans for construction also were subject to a prolonged approval process. Given these complexities, many land transactions rely on a transfer of rights by sale, which is backdated to a time prior to 1978. In the end, access to land, housing, and financing relies heavily on political connections and assumes substantial individual wealth.[75] It also relies heavily on the persistence of community-level institutions that still provide the most salient framework for conceptualizing, mediating, and legitimating land transactions.[76]

The State and Its Missed Opportunities as Land Regulator   The formal ownership or trusteeship of land gave states enormous powers to plan, dispose of, and develop land in ways that would contribute to more balanced and equitable urban growth. Most states did little, however, with such authority. Despite the enormous economic growth, for example, of Kano, Nigeria, during the 1970s and 1980s, the overcentralization of land use planning and regulation, inappropriate building standards, the lack of policies to guide urbanization processes, and the lack of institutional capacity combined to severely restrict the supply of urban land. Responsibility for specifying how land was to be developed and the enforcement of these specifications were split between two authorities, neither of whom saw it as their responsibility to ensure the efficient functioning of the other. As a result, landowners were able to hold on to property for speculation purposes without developing the land within two years after acquisition, as was mandated by law. Resources for rationalizing public land management and the planning system were also limited by high levels of subsidy. It was estimated that US$3,300/ha was required to develop land for residential purposes in 1988, but that land would then only attract an annual rent of US$83/ha plus administrative costs.[77]

In Sudan, all planning power and responsibilities for land management were placed in regional town planning boards. Accordingly, officials spent most of their time deliberating whether someone could change the use of or make extensions to their property. Officials had to cover various parts of what are often quite large regions. In part, this centralization of micromanagement was undertaken because of limited expertise at the local level and a desire to guard against excess in the promotion of local private interests. In reality, given the profusion of minor details taking place across a broad physical territory, these boards were largely unable to administer their own decisions.[78]

The trend in land affairs is definitively away from public micromanagement and toward a more gradualist approach to working out ownership issues. This emphasis on gradualism delinks the rehabilitation of spontaneous and irregular settlements from the resolution of issues of land ownership. In part, this trend reflects an appreciation for the ways in which multiple vehicles of land disposition contribute to providing the shelter requirements of urban residents. It is clear that the operation of multiple rationalities as applied to land access was an important aspect of the vast cumulative investment in housing for West Africa from 1960 to 1990 — an investment that exceeded ten times the total net transfer of external resources for that period.[79]

Shelter

As the state steps out of managing land disposition in Africa, it is also less able to directly intervene in the provision of shelter. Conventional wisdom, reaffirmed through the United Nations Habitat II process of 1996, makes clear that the private sector should, and is most able to, assume the responsibility of shelter provisioning. The state's former role in this sector is an ambivalent one. While it contributed significantly toward facilitating the consolidation of an urban middle class, it was often at the expense of other social groups. For example, 20 percent of existing housing was bulldozed in Abidjan between 1969 and 1973 under the auspices of urban development. By 1988, so-called modern housing occupied 47 percent of residential land, even though the public sector urban market would house only 20 percent of the city's population.[80]

Most of public sector developments were available to a nonhomogenous middle class (e.g., white-collar workers, technicians, upper-level merchants and craft workers), which made up about 11 percent of the population.[81] Subsidized access to modern sector housing went a long way toward the consolidation of a professional class, because disposable income could then be invested in education, commerce, and the trappings of middle-class consumption. Self-employed workers, craftsmen, and small traders were largely excluded from this modern sector. Instead, the only forms of housing they could access were those typical of the colonial period in the so-called African town — that is, multiple household dwellings organized around a common courtyard and shared facilities.

Neighborhoods in Abidjan such as Treichville, Adjame, Marcory, and Point Bouêt became increasingly dense, circuitous, and socially entangled.[82] In many cities, "traditional" quarters became increasingly complex — both in terms of social arrangements and the convoluted use of grids and infrastructures. The complexity was a result, in part, of the very modernizing efforts the state made on the basis of its ownership of land and what it attempted to do with it.[83]

Today, public sector housing investments have basically disappeared in

Abidjan, and most public housing units have been sold off. This situation puts increasing numbers of the presently unemployed middle class in a precarious situation, while consolidating the positions of real estate speculators. Despite a variety of cushioning mechanisms (e.g., links with the external world and the use of public employment to cultivate a wide range of rent-seeking activities) the middle class has been hard hit economically. Since 1963, real household standards of living have dropped, despite the period of economic growth during the 1980s.[84] This downward trend puts additional pressure on the need to maintain significant levels of ambiguity and flexibility in terms of land disposition and use. After all, these diminished middle classes were important supporters of the political regime, which, until the military coup of December 1999, had ruled Côte d'Ivoire since independence.

Self-Built Housing It is estimated that 15 percent to 20 percent of Abidjan resides in informal housing. This informal housing is popularly referred to as "places," whether they be small plots, structures, or rooms within structures on these plots. These places are quite small: plots seldom measure more than one hundred square meters. Structures usually consist of single rooms of nine to twelve meters and typically avoid the use of permanent materials because all such places are situated in legally tenuous circumstances. However, although they are officially illegal they are tolerated by the state as a way of excusing itself from further responsibilities to provide shelter. Most places are usually acquired through offering "gifts"—that is, cash payments labeled as such to mask commercial practices. Informal housing and quarters in Abidjan are largely occupied by long-standing city dwellers drawn from the different waves of migration that have characterized the city.

Even in a highly cosmopolitan city, some informal quarters continue to reflect a connection between ethnocultural origin and occupation. Domestic servants and watchmen of Burkinabe origin usually live in settlements near the elite residential neighborhoods of Cocody. Those working in the fishing business, usually of Ghanaian origin, commonly locate themselves in the southern neighborhoods of Point Bouêt and other areas along the lagoon.[85] The growth of informal housing also reflects a wide range of motivations. In the often up and down nature of Abidjan's economy, personal economic capacities frequently fluctuate, as do family circumstances. The proliferation of informal housing is also part of a trajectory of settlement whereby many residents move from the status of being rent-free lodgers in the homes of friends or extended family to that of tenants, and then, sometimes, owner-occupiers. Residents often choose informal housing as an available means of going beyond the status of being tenants, even if it means relocating to precarious circumstances.

Self-built housing for multiple families remains the chief means of shelter provision in most African cities. It is a particularly significant provider of rental housing for those with limited means.[86] Even when the state provides public housing, the extensions and partitioning of that housing undertaken by residents make a major impact on the characteristics of these quarters. For example, Gergi, a relatively new quarter of one-room cement block-houses near the airport in Addis Ababa, has been totally transformed since initial construction. The state had originally intended to use the grid design of the quarter and its houses to limit population size, but by using indigenous wattle and daub construction techniques these small shelters have been thoroughly changed, and the quarter has doubled in size in less than ten years.[87]

Still, official housing policies remain focused primarily on the construction of large numbers of single-family dwellings. In Ghana, informal sector shelter provision of multihabited compounds with open-air courtyards for cooking and washing provide housing at half the cost of even subsidized formal housing programs. These courtyards are considered part of a built-up area in terms of permitted plot ratios. As such, these constructions are often deemed illegal. In general, formal construction is four and a half times the cost per room as that provided by informal artisans. There is little difference in quality — although formal construction now tends to emphasize large, multistoried single household villas instead of multihabited compounds. While the state helped promote a Housing Finance Corporation to assist lower-income buyers, applicants had to purchase new houses from real estate developers with loans that had concessionary real interest rates only 3.5 percent to 4.5 percent above the inflationary index. Thus this program ended up dealing exclusively with middle-income buyers who usually had access to other subsidies and assistance as well.[88]

As self-built housing owners have almost no relationship with formal financial institutions, houses are built on the basis of limited savings, windfalls (such as pension payouts), remittances from family members working outside the country, and, in some cases, family loans. On average, it takes about five years to build a house. Given that in Ghana urban households have an annual median expenditure of US$2,700, and that the average cost of a traditional compound house is US$8,800, households are somehow accessing additional income. In doing so they might be incorporated into long-term loan arrangements through formal financial institutions. Loans could be released in stages for the purchase of land lease, and then for financing the various stages of building. The key issue here is how to provide collateral to these financial institutions while maintaining community control over land.[89]

The Escalating Costs of Shelter In Lagos, where the state has largely relinquished de facto authority over land management, property speculation and housing costs have increased enormously. Constrictions in loan availability, waiting time, and land and construction costs all have combined to make the provision of shelter exceedingly expensive. From 1988 to 1989 alone, the price of iron rods increased tenfold, the costs of roofing sheets quadrupled, and the prices of cement blocks and tiles tripled.[90] The result is that only 1.5 percent of households have a residential building to themselves and a large number of tenants are always on the move.

Margaret Piel describes a study in Ajegunle, one of Lagos's largest popular quarters, that found that some 985 of houses with more than one household were ethnically heterogeneous. The heterogeneity of household composition reflected the desire to keep landlord-tenant relationships commercial and contractual, so as to circumvent claims of solidarity that might ensue from renting to tenants sharing the same ethnic identification.[91] It is presently difficult to find any rental accommodation in Lagos that does not require at least two to three years of rent payments in advance.[92] Consequently, there is little resale of existing housing stock. This lack of resale is also reinforced by the way in which housing is conceptualized as belonging to families and not individual owners.

In Benin City, Nigeria, the persistence of inappropriate building codes contributes to illegalities in housing construction and deters the use of more appropriate local building materials.[93] Accordingly, a one-bedroom flat that met all building codes and specifications would cost eleven times the annual salary of a newly fresh graduated civil servant. In 1998, 47 percent of Benin City heads of households earned less than US$909 per year, and it would take thirteen years of annual income to build a one-bedroom flat.[94]

When states and municipalities insist on unrealistic standards for housing construction and improvement, it is important to ask whose interests are being served. Postcolonial states have largely maintained and generalized the standards and procedures employed by colonial authorities to differentiate urban space into discrete zones of use and occupation, usually defined by class and, sometimes, race. In doing so, the state makes large swathes of the city vulnerable. Imposing this vulnerability gives the state leeway to arbitrarily support various means of compensating for that vulnerability and repressing others. In addition, groups of powerful clients in various professional associations, such as architects and contractors, are cultivated. As states have rushed to display their commitment to modernity, contracting has become a popular occupation, even for those who know very little about it. Large-scale housing development programs usually have more to do with elaborating opportunities for kickbacks and graft than they do with providing shelter.

Between 1975 and 1995, three Nigerian national housing programs were launched that were intended to produce a half-million units, but only 76,000 were built. The National Housing Program of Nigeria, 1994/95, is a good example of the way in which the process of building can constitute a fortuitous opportunity for accumulation. Instead of having building contractors procure materials through private arrangements, the housing program implemented a system where a chain of suppliers would provide specific inputs for building materials and then deliver them to contractors at specific sites.

For example, suppliers of cement and sand would provide materials to contractors making the molding blocks, who would then supply them to building contractors. This supply system was very expensive, and it also was vulnerable to substantial corruption because contractors could manipulate the volume and timing of supplies. Concessionaire prices on imported materials were given to contractors, and foreign exchange was provided at discounts to cover import duties that had already been waived by another agency. As each supplier of fittings (e.g., roofing materials, plumbing, electrical outlets, etc.) was mandated to install them, many different contractors could be working on a single house at the same time. This led to the frequent diversion of building materials. Compensation payments were often made for the acquisition of already public land requiring no compensation. In addition, by setting the prices of houses before construction actually began, the state ended up providing implicit subsidies to 84 percent of the cost of delivery for low- and middle-income housing.[95]

The insistence on unrealistic standards also ensures that only a few members of society will participate in urban housing production. These privileged few are usually the political, business, and military elite. This narrowing of participation maximizes the profits on new construction. It ensures reliance on imported building materials necessary to comply with prevailing standards, thus providing the state with additional sources of revenue.[96]

Shelter and Illegality Over half of Nairobi's population in 1993 lived in illegal settlements. Most owner-occupiers usually secure makeshift occupation licenses, letters from chiefs, or some form of documentation from private landowners that may at least operate as negotiating instruments. The majority of tenants, on the other hand, usually have no idea about the precise status of the plot or building they occupy. Tenants make up the overwhelming majority of residents in these areas. In addition, 94 percent of residents in illegal areas do not have access to adequate sanitation. Poorly constructed pit latrines are usually shared by twenty-five households. Households also use these pit latrines as places to dispose of other wastewater, which means they fill up quickly and frequently overrun.

Residents have little choice but to live in such a precarious state. During the 1970s and 1980s, in pursuit of an objective of decent housing for all, the government insisted on ensuring basic standards of health, privacy, and security in all housing programs in which it participated. In the end, the various components of these housing developments — contractors, financial institutions, residents, the state — could not meet such exacting standards. Residents had little choice but to seek shelter outside estates and projects that were officially sanctioned.[97]

According to Winnie Mitullah and Kivutha Kibwana, most urban-related law and policy is oriented toward the protection of the central business district or urban core.[98] The support they provide for residency progressively diminishes as one moves toward the periphery. The content of most Kenyan urban legislation is explicitly hostile to the situations faced by residents of illegal quarters. This hostility continues to pose a very precarious situation for a large number of Nairobi residents, leaving them vulnerable to being displaced and shifted around the city. To adapt to this precariousness, residents forego investing in long-term social ties in their immediate quarters, and instead seek out opportunities to spread their affiliations across the city.

Issues of land ownership may eventually have to be resolved and systematized. Perhaps the most important reason for this is that the lack of land title sometimes creates a variety of spatial mismatches. Here, low-income residents become trapped in areas far away from where jobs are located because they cannot sell property at a fair price. Other proposed developments can't then use this property for better-suited purposes.[99] Once questions of title are sorted through, it becomes possible for more proficient land use planning to take place and for municipalities to equip themselves with appropriate instruments in this regard. For example, municipalities are only just now venturing into land pooling and readjustment schemes. In these programs, owners receive smaller but equally valued and better-serviced lots in an exchange with municipal authorities. Municipal authorities, then, acquire larger tracts of land to create buffer zones, rights of way, and passive open spaces, a portion of which can be sold for cost recovery or service provision.[100]

On Negotiating Access and Making Urban Society   Attaining security of tenure, however, is more than simply the rationalization of land markets and the application of clear-cut juridical procedures to the disposition of land. In Ghana, land is owned by kin groups. These groups include deceased but "present" ancestors, so as to ensure the proper place of the material world within the larger scheme of things. Most homeowners not only must provide accommodation for an average of twenty people, but they must ensure that future generations have some base from which to operate. Because monthly urban rents average only US$8 per room, with the rent-to-income ratio of the median household only 2 percent of expenditure, self-built housing provision is not usually undertaken as a money-making operation.[101]

As lineage and custodianship is intimately linked to the maintenance of specific physical territories, disposing of land, housing, or any other real property is inevitably viewed as a serious disruption of lineage that is likely to be punished by ancestors. Land is gained through usufruct, and chiefs can allocate land to members of the lineage as their right or to outsiders in exchange for tribute. A small "modern sector" does exist in urban areas, where land is allocated through leasehold and administered by the state's land commission. Such arrangements, however, apply to only a small fraction of urban land.[102]

As Sara Berry has pointed out in several studies on land use in rural Ghana, it is the heterogeneity of possible claims to land that seems to ensure a sense of security. Beginning with the colonial period, land claims in Ghana have been adjudicated both by customary courts and by those of colonial administrators. Both types of jurisprudence form a record that has been added to information about genealogies, contracts, wars, migrations, and changing notions of local citizenship, all of which impact on the disposition of land. The entire process of disclosure — who can say what about certain "relevant" historical antecedents — is an important instrument for shaping what is to count as the important knowledge related to determining how a particular piece of land is to be used.[103]

How claims are structured and enter into negotiations therefore constitute a kind of power, for the particular way a claim is made affects the disposition of land and other assets. How a claim is made, and how particular memories, information, records, and knowledge are brought to bear on a negotiation, are also instruments through which alliances are built and social relationships are reaffirmed. The process of negotiation is an opportunity to redefine and reaffirm particular claims on people, property, and power. What occurs is a process potentially open to the participation of all, albeit in often highly unequal ways. Nevertheless, such participation seems to guarantee reasonably secure access to land and opportunity for people in ways that a system of unambiguous property rights may not.[104]

There is very limited knowledge of how land transactions actually take place in the bulk of urban land submarkets. It is often not clear, particularly to municipal authorities, where the money goes or precisely who gains or loses (and in what ways) from various routes to land and property valorization. In light of these ambiguities, it is not clear whether even today's preferred strategy of land development sequencing, beginning with the regularization of existing tenure, will provide more opportunities for shelter and security in the long run.[105]

How the negotiability of land use and shelter is made operational within large urban contexts is, of course, highly problematic. In many cities, a patchwork of disparate arrangements exists, depending on the inclinations of customary landholding groups, an expanding class of land agents representing those groups (or increasingly, their own interests), and the kinds of controls exercised by the state. Each patchwork not only indicates a disjunction in the overall effort to regulate the city but also indicates often highly innovative, if problematic, attempts to intertwine the public and private, the traditional and modern, and the formal and informal that may point to new ways of maximizing the resourcefulness of land and infrastructure. It may not be clear just what gets done and how, but in some ways, it is the very hedging of visibility that is a critical factor in determining the future viability of African cities.

It is evident that a large portion of Africa's real urban economy is being developed in the interstices between the formal and the informal, the traditional and the provisional, and between highly normative codes and improvised social arrangements. There are situations that convey unequivocal rules, identities, and procedures. There are other situations where fluidity in transactions and compensations make the consolidation of clear identities and procedures highly problematic. Given such phenomena, the management of what is visible and accessible to whom becomes an important process. In societies undergoing marked change, where arbitrary rules and continuously improvised social practices coincide with strong convictions and traditions, it is often difficult for individuals and groups to assess the implications of their actions or to clearly ascertain what is possible or feasible.[106]

It is one thing to talk about informality when it concerns the day-to-day livelihood of ordinary urban residents. It is another thing to talk about informal processes that concern accumulation of some scale and fall outside not only the regulatory apparatuses of the state but also its logic of regulation. Macroeconomic constraints on functional and sustainable urban growth prompt renewed interest in the possible ways that economies of scale are generated through informal mechanisms. Here, the interest is also in how the sheer heterogeneity of cities — their multiple social and ecological regulations, influences, alliances, networks, and identities — allows for the continuous reregistration of various aspects of everyday life within both smaller and larger parameters. What is seemingly marginal and isolated can become a domain through which translocal activities are conducted, just as global command functions are often highly localized.[107]

Religious brotherhoods and fraternities, ethnically based trading regimes, syndicates, and even community-based and multiassociation operations are functioning with increasing scope. Urban quarters not only serve as platforms for popular initiatives (e.g., waste management, microenterprise development, and shelter provision) but readapt local modalities of cohesion and sociality to more regional and global frameworks.[108] In many cities religious associations, fraternal brotherhoods, associations of people sharing a common village of origin, women's groups, and so forth become important in configuring new divisions of labor. They help coordinate the cross-border, small- and medium-scale trade of individual entrepreneurs and the work ways of pooling and reinvesting the proceeds of this trade to access larger quantities of tradable goods, diversify collective holdings, and reach new markets. Some localities, such as Nima (Accra), Obalende (Lagos), Texas-Adjame (Abidjan), and Grand Yoff (Dakar) reflect a strong relationship between the elaboration of local associations and the generation of new economic activities and resources.

The mechanisms through which local economies expand in scale are often murky and problematic. They can entail highly tenuous and frequently clandestine articulations among, for example, religious and fraternal networks, public officials operating in private capacities, clientelist networks mobilizing very cheap labor, foreign political parties, and large transnational corporations operating outside of conventional procedures.[109] Increasingly, these new modalities of association and economic accumulation operate in-between the conventional survival strategies that urban quarters have pursued for some time and the growth of more renegade economic practices. In many ways, these latter practices, integrating various scales, are a direct outgrowth of the strains placed on African societies by globalization. These strains manifest themselves in the intensification of civil conflict, the breakdown of public economic governance despite substantial public sector reform, and the shift of critical economic activities to border and frontier territories.[110]

As Béatrice Hibou indicates, the organizers and manipulators of violence are the important mediators of economic activity in many African countries.[111] The consolidation of rule and the mobilization of popular support can no longer rely on allocating public sector jobs or awarding special exemptions or advantages, such as access to foreign exchange or import licenses. The combined trajectories of crisis and reform have largely eliminated these instruments. They are replaced by the increasing use of tax and fiscal manipulation, trickery, and protection from and access to informal trade through games of chance, coercion and violence.

Furthermore, the problem of civil conflict takes on an increasingly economic character. Most African countries still rely on primary production. They are thus increasingly vulnerable to the predatory. Because civil conflict does not necessarily stop primary production, predatory forces can insert themselves in a long chain of trade and transport required in getting products to markets.[112] In economies of primary production, taxation can happen in-kind. Products such as diamonds, cocoa, gold, cotton, and so forth don't carry company brands. As such, they are easier to transport, their origins are easier to cover up, and thus the discount is taken off because their extralegal marketing is much smaller than it would be for other manufactured goods.[113]

The growth of transnational networks that specialize in mediating illicit transactions also facilitates the rise and sustenance of civil conflict or the ability of states to maintain conditions of internecine conflict. For example, when Sudan faced difficulties in disposing of its agricultural and industrial output on international markets, several trading networks intervened. In return for using certain Sudanese banks to launder money derived from drug and arms trafficking, these networks, masking the Sudanese origin of goods such as cotton and gum arabic, were able to sell them on the international market.[114]

In her study of the garrison-entrepôt of the Chad basin, Janet Roitman documents the growing "frontier" economies at the confluence of Cameroon, Chad, and Nigeria.[115] The appropriation of borders, military bases, cross-border flows, and fluidly configured social conflicts become critical elements in the elaboration of new economies that operate outside yet in tandem with national regulatory frameworks. These parallel economies intersect with national regulatory frameworks by reinventing economic and cultural practices that once predominated in this region — that is, raiding and smuggling. A sense of continuity or relinking is constructed, but one that entails a rupture with prevailing formal power relations. Here, as Roitman indicates, the real fiscal subject exceeds the fiscal subject of the state because it has moved into more diverse and unpredictable relations with emergent figures of regulatory authority. These newly reinvented (and largely familiar) modalities of accumulation — through smuggling, raiding, and parallel taxation — undermine the regulatory logic of development, national progress, social welfare, and their concomitant institutions. Accordingly, local populations invest in new forms of security and welfare.

As Roitman also points out, it is important to keep in mind that states of exception often emerge as a product of existing social regimes, for the precepts underlying that which appears new or as a rupture are often consistent with relations and activities prevailing in the existing order. The "new" provides unforeseen opportunities for existing political and economic regimes to reconsolidate authority, legitimacy, or efficacy at different scales or arenas. Arrangements that both link and disengage distinct domains for wealth generation and social regulation have endured in many places of the continent, particularly at such frontiers as the Chad basin.

These arrangements endure, in part, because they are not encumbered with having to sustain or operate exclusively within distinctions between near and far, inside and outside, or licit and illicit. Such binaries often act as internal markers of rather solid arrangements that take place over a broad set of diverse actors, territories, and identities. Something thus is always emerging, always in struggle to actualize specific connotations and outcomes.

Building Shared Urban Political Cultures If economic viability requires a more concentrated convergence of the activities undertaken by discrete groups of actors, how can an urban political culture emerge that is capable of leading the heterogeneous groups making up the city toward a sense of shared interest and greater collaboration? Many community associations argue that local actors are now engaged in systematic conversations with municipal authorities, as I showed in my discussion of Pikine. In some cities, these conversations have never before taken place. These associations go on to claim that the process of negotiating these conversations and the partnership necessary to administer a shared urban space will eventually give rise to a sense of common citizenship.

In recent years, NGO activists in Dakar, Abidjan, Ouagadougou (Burkina Faso), Bobo Dialoso (Burkina Faso), and Bamako (Mali) are participating with local authorities to establish negotiating forums from which it is hoped that new local government institutions will emerge. These activists argue that the constitution of new municipalities must be a framework for experimentation — that is, to experiment with various ways of linking identities, roles, tasks, viewpoints, and orientations. It is a process of extending the capacities and actions of specific sectors and identities.

This is a task where the primary responsibility of governance is to set up ways in which different associations, organizations, and institutions can respond to each other and work together. This collaboration is not based on putting differences aside or subsuming the collaboration to some common objective or task. Rather, the challenge is for different organizations and actors to work with substantial autonomy, but at the same time respond to, address, build on, and use what each organization does.

The first task of municipal governance is to ensure that spaces are maintained for diverse formations and initiatives to take place and to constantly search for arenas in which they pay attention to each other. The point here is not for actors to defend, mask, or hide from each other, but rather to see each other as sharing potentially uncharted and unclaimed spheres of activity and ways to maneuver.[116]

7

Cities and Change

Cities are places from which people potentially can change many things. Even when individuals and communities are defending themselves against the deprivation and harshness of urban life, change is often on their minds. But change is something that demands platforms and resources. If communities are always defending themselves against the city, how does the city become an instrument for change? When little is left besides the fact of one's physical existence, what can be mobilized to make conditions change? Moreover, how can urban residents avoid a sense of the world closing in on them and instead mobilize the will and skill to cross boundaries and scales in order to access the resources and experiences necessary to affect change?

As I tried to demonstrate in the case studies in earlier chapters, there is a need to maintain a sense of social cohesion and to dispense with it in order to secure opportunities for livelihood across multiple scales. In other words, there is a need to maintain a sense of place while at the same time reach a larger world—even if neither place nor world correspond to easily distinguishable scales, such as local or global.[1] If we are to talk about what is to be done in terms of the emphases of urban governance and investment, we have to understand the nature of the dilemmas posed by these apparently conflicting needs. If we are to think about concrete strategic directions for urban development in the future, what are the key conditions of the present to which emergent forms of sociality attempt to navigate?

In this chapter I take up the issue of the making, unraveling, and remaking of connections and their role in shaping urban space and economy. In situations of relative scarcity, combined with new facilities for connecting to a larger world capable of exerting extreme marginalizing effects, the critical issue is how urban residents can make new uses of what is available to them. In the end, this means how to use the city itself in different ways through the sheer remaking of the fields of social connection within it. As we have seen in the case studies, the process of remaking is not entirely a hit-and-miss affair but rather a range of instruments is involved. Sometimes social fields are pieced together as part invoked tradition, part improvisation; sometimes they are a series of inclinations or orientations to respond to contingencies in patterned ways that border on acting like discrete rationalities, yet are not as defined or structured as this term might imply. In the case studies, I discussed histories of movement, the elaboration of livelihood outside of formally structured employment and entrepreneurship, the elaboration of invisible worlds, and an array of practices that keep memory, skills, and aspirations alive through a kind of spectral haunting. I have pointed out how all of these processes gear residents to engage the city in ways not readily apparent through prevailing governance structures and policy language.

My concern throughout this investigation has been on how African cities work and on how the capacity to generate new and largely ephemeral forms of social collaboration are important in this process. If production possibilities are limited in African cities, then existent materials of all kinds are to be appropriated — sometimes through theft and looting; sometimes through the "heretical" uses made of infrastructures, languages, objects, and spaces; sometimes through social practices that ensure that available materials pass through many hands. The key here is to multiply the uses that can be made of documents, automobiles, houses, wood, or whatever, and this means the ability to put together different kinds of combinations of people with different skills, perspectives, linkages, identities, and aspirations. This multiplexity of social organization constitutes a kind of perceptual system, a way of seeing that then engages the urban environment in such a way that single items, objects, and experiences are put to many otherwise unanticipated uses.

If residents are to make new use of existent materials and resources, then they must in some sense delink themselves from the familiar social contexts in which they have been embedded. This is necessary in order for them to see differently — that is, in order to participate in social configurations that permit a different kind of cognition to take place. But then the question arises of what happens to the important sense of predictability and support provided by stable social ties. How can individuals then protect themselves from the many dangers incumbent in urban life? What becomes of regulatory structures that seek to secure the consistency necessary for people to commit themselves to long-term efforts to improve their urban environments? What happens to the sense of people being able to come up with working predictions of what is likely to ensue if they act in particular ways, and that then allow them a greater range of independent action? In other words, how can provisionality, fluidity, and stability exist in some kind of functional tandem?

These are some of the critical questions that I have attempted to address through the case studies, and that I return to here in this final discussion. Here, I try to speak more theoretically about the locations of such tentative balances, and how they increasingly express themselves within a transurban world — a world that situates urban Africa within both a more expansive and more narrow field of reference.

Proliferating Connections

Conventional understandings of urban Africans often tend to portray them as reluctant participants in urbanization with no real desire to come to or be in the city in the first place. Regardless of whether their behavior reflects it, they prefer to think of their important influences continuing to be rooted in rural ways of life. African urbanists often can be heard to ask: "If there were a real desire for urbanization, wouldn't a shared interest exist in the future of the city?" "Wouldn't individuals see themselves as citizens of an entire city, rather than of discrete quarters or networks?" "Wouldn't this identification lead to the elaboration of some overarching sense of belonging or operation that exceeds the confines of parochial neighborhoods or extended family systems?"[2]

Yet, there is an apparent "promiscuity" of participation in the city. City life, especially at the economic margins, propels an incessant opportunism to make use of all kinds of knowledge, relationships, and positions in multiple social networks in order to access some kind of opportunity to consolidate one's position. Here, a practice of being what one needs to be at any given moment enters into an ongoing tension with needing to be someone specific. Here, different social arrangements and temporalities are mutually reinforced and undermined. Individuals thus conclude that the only way to consolidate a niche or identity in the city is to constantly be different things for different networks. As a result, stability — in social ties and neighborhood relations and location — have more options to reproduce themselves. They are also more prone to disruption by a wide variety of sources and events.

An ethos of conviviality often seems to predominate in urban life, managing to bring about some sense of commonality — the sense of all being here in the city together. As Achille Mbembe suggests, this conviviality is an almost baroque exaggeration of mutual familiarity, where the powerful and powerless are separated only by the extent to which their most banal aleatory functions become the subject of speculation and spectacle.[3]

In situations of hardship, the determination to survive at all costs would seem to intensify people's vulnerability and make them less willing to collaborate with each other. Although we have certainly witnessed just how brutal African everyday life can be, the largely urban practice of deflating pretentiousness and authority through gossip and through the speedy circulation of impressions and information makes everyone, the rulers and the ruled, somehow known to each other. In practice, this sense of conviviality compensates for the vast discrepancies in access to resources and power. It convinces people that such discrepancies do not fundamentally deter anyone from approaching the city as a resource that could be used in many different ways. The structures of glaring inequality may remain and dominate, yet they don't completely suppress various efforts to act as if indifferent to them.

Conviviality is also a means of implicating others in one's own project of survival. It motivates them to get involved in some way whether they want to or not, for the recent contingencies of structural adjustment reiterate a deep-seated sensibility in many African societies that everything and everyone can be remade. This remaking is tolerable because everyone can, theoretically, be included and no one is exempt. Indeed, such remaking has historically operated as a means of inclusion.[4]

If events and actions are, then, to be linked and coordinated, sometimes new forms of linkage have to occur. This is especially the case in cities that have been hard hit by various forms of disintegration and "collapsed modernism." In Freetown, Monrovia, Brazzaville, and Kinshasa, shadowy youth clubs have emerged that are purposely mobilized as consorts of strangers. By appearing to belong to no clearly identified quarter, political faction, or religious group, they also pretend to make themselves available for almost any unspoken task to various competing elite in an effort to become beholden to no one. These are people with no prior connections but who cement some kind of tie to each other by staging operations at public events. For example, diffuse gangs of young adolescents have used musical events in Kinshasa to strip naked and attack police, who in turn, having come to believe the popular mythologies about the power of young virgins, are uncertain whether to flee or to kill. In Brazzaville, smaller gangs have been known to make elaborate plans of sneaking into fancy hotel ballrooms, where they shout down speeches and disrupt various social functions.

In many of these clubs, rules are established obligating young men and women to constantly exchange partners. This practice is believed not only to be a form of protection against HIV, but also ensures a more general protection. In highly divided cities, this sexual practice symbolically means that no quarter of the city can penetrate or disrupt the activities of the group, because all parts of the city have slept with each other. Each known neighborhood must be represented in the club before its activities can be set in motion but there can only be one representative from each quarter involved because each member must embody the entirety of a specific territory.

There are also discursive practices associated with delinking individuals from affiliations that are considered to slow down the individual pursuit of flexibility and success and, by default, reiterate the value of these affiliations. Take, for example, the notion of *thiof* in Dakar. This concept appropriates the Wolof word for fish, which is a staple of the Senegalese daily diet. In its new connotation, the concept refers to a substantial set of unwritten rules for what an individual has to do to become successful, or at least appear to be. Most of these "rules" specify the contents of one's lifestyle — the kinds of products one must own; the places one must spend one's leisure time.

The rules also deal with how one is supposed to behave and talk. Most important, thiof concerns how a person is to get others to do their bidding and circumvent the constrictions imposed by local cultural norms, social organizations, and politics. Thiof, then, is not only a practice increasingly incorporated into various aspects of the public realm but also implicitly reinforces the salience and reinvigoration of traditional family and religious ties for those who fail in their efforts to be thiof.

At the same time, the proliferation of connections across discrete social contexts and boundaries can provoke the reenclosure of collective life within intimate spaces of regeneration and raise the possibilities of new forms of subjection. These forms of subjection arise through the sense of an endless exchangeability and recomposition of identity.[5] They also arise through the provision of an endless number of local spaces where individuals, groups, and communities can be whatever they want.

Because of these dangers, urban Africans are being drawn to forms of religious expression and affiliation that are increasingly transnational in character. These affiliations grow as conventional forms of community life and solidarity become increasingly unreliable and precarious sources of support. Pentecostalism, for example, has had a major impact in urban Africa and emphasizes a complete break from the past. Birgit Meyer talks about the conflicts between Pentecostalism and a renewed nationalism, which seeks to reconstruct a sense of cultural continuity that was interrupted by colonialism.[6]

Pentecostalism downplays relinking to a past as a methodology of renewal and development. Instead, it emphasizes that the past is to be understood as the source of present difficulties: one must identify it so as to let it go. What is to be let go of is the ongoing influence of the extended family whose demands get in the way of realizing modern individual identities. These family influences are seen as the source of an almost occult power capable of detracting individuals from potential deliverance into an individualized independence. By identifying the extended family as the past that must be exceeded, a particularly local domain of power is identified as the most salient to an individual's prospects in life. Identifying the extended family as bad nevertheless identifies it as something powerful. As the believer must always be in the process of getting past the past, the reality of kin relations is acknowledged. Ways to negotiate the gap between this reality of kinship relations and the aspirations for greater individual autonomy are also elaborated.[7]

In her research in Nigeria, Ruth Marshall-Fratani also discusses how Pentecostalism protects against the insecurities associated with both the dissolution and persistence of outmoded support systems. Pentecostalism provides new spiritual and material networks that go beyond local, regional, ethnic, and social class considerations.[8] Indeed, it serves as a map for navigating a more globalized world. Again, we see another instance here of the domestication of tradition and modernity.

In its focus on being "born again," Pentecostalism seeks to mediate situations where individuals have great difficulties managing multiple identities — familial, professional, regional, and modern. Networking across transnational trajectories is not simply an abstract concept, but is concretely made instrumental through thousands of interdenominational groups, missions, ministries, retreats, and friendship networks, in addition to its comprehensive use of media, from video and audio tapes to radio and television shows.

In addition, in Pentacostalism individual adherence to collective tenets and cultural forms is played down, and the responsibility for salvation is placed in the believer's own hands. An individual can attain a sense of belonging and of being embedded in something local as long as they can imagine themselves as part of a larger "community of sentiment" without location or boundaries. This act of imagination is cultivated through the importance placed on reading or watching and discussing various religious pamphlets, magazines, and videos.[9] In other words, the sense of the local is attained through a concrete practice shared with others, who are people both near and far. There are no specific spaces in which such a sense of belonging or locality is confined.

Building a community of sentiment relies on delocalizing messages and media. This does not mean that Pentecostalism is disengaged from local contexts and histories. On the contrary, the impediments of salvation and the problems of everyday life are clearly situated as the responsibility of local actors and their wayward practices. As the state's enactment of power is popularly understood to take place through sorcery and evil spirits, Pentecostalism is an instrument for fighting this evil.[10] As Marshall-Fratani points out, Pentecostalism claims a redemptive vision of citizenship in which the ability to govern the self is linked to a larger power capable of influencing the conduct of others.[11]

Mbembe claims, albeit with many disputes, that the postcolonial situation is largely one where subjects are enclosed in a claustrophobic game: the state makes the basis of people's diverse histories, practices, and identities a piece in a game of pretended nationhood. Citizens must then implicitly participate in the surface authority, legitimacy, and majesty of the state in order to get back some sense of who they are. Otherwise, there is no space in which these identities can make themselves known and operate.[12] Because Pentecostalists have recourse to an "outside"—in the transnational character of Pentecostal affiliation—it is possible to avoid being trapped in the implosive circuit that Mbembe describes.

Given Pentecostalism's transnational character, with its reliance on various delocalized media and forms of community, the state has a difficult time cracking down on religious expression and affiliation. It is difficult for the state to appropriate either the message or instruments of religion for its own purposes. At the same time, the transnational character of Pentecostalism is premised on its ability to overcome boundaries and differences in national identity, class composition, and religious belief.

As Marshall-Fratani points out, if Nigeria is to be won for Jesus, what happens to the fact that half of the country is Muslim? Certainly the state at some point would have to establish limits in how far and through what means Nigeria is to be won for Jesus. For years, Nigeria has been a hotbed of religious conflict, with many incidents of violent riots across its cities.[13] Increasingly the ante is being upped, especially as several Nigerian states have adopted Muslim Sharia law. The transnational character, so crucial to Pentecostal instrumentality, can reinvigorate state power, which then would require a counternationalistic response. This is a process that risks an escalating spiral of violence, and the space in which devotees can operate would become restricted. This restriction in turn would lead to more parochial orientations and practices when such parochialism is the very thing many who come to Pentecostalism seek to overcome.

As such, defending individual or collective identities has little use. Rather, efforts should be focused on what identities can be in a constant state of movement, and how to anticipate and recognize such changes. Here, an urban practice that attempts to open up spaces of maneuver and creativity tries to do simultaneously two very different but related things: first, politics becomes a matter of constituting a generic identity without privilege and without any specific terms other than itself. It is thus capable of putting together distinct singularities into a collective collaboration, but also able to maintain their distinction. Second, such tactics aim to make the specificity of identity just that: untranslatable, nonexchangeable, highly local, and unable to be "hooked up" or "phased in" to a larger world of comparisons and substitutes.[14]

This is, of course, a utopian urban practice. It is a practice aimed at resisting the new forms of subjection that attempt to get identities to always become part of some new superidentity. It is also aimed, conversely, at resisting attempts to ghettoize identities away from participating in surprising and potentially disruptive collaborations with those identities with which they would never be expected to collaborate. But such a utopian practice is implicitly being experimented with, and is embedded within the urban practices of groups across the continent, as the case studies in this volume have shown. To reinforce this point, I will briefly discuss an example of such experimentation.

Yopougon: Assembling the Commons   Yopougon II is one of the largest submunicipalities of the city of Abidjan. It is also one of the city's more cosmopolitan quarters. As such, it is the site from which many new forms of spiritual practice emerge. One such grouping broke away from a large branch of the Celestial Church in another suburb, Point Bouêt. This group combined an ecstatic Christianity with the already largely syncretic trappings of the Mami Water cults that predominate along the West African coast. Instead of forming a new church, the group preferred to travel across different neighborhoods, where they usually appeared at wakes, funerals, and naming ceremonies. Although for purposes of description this group could be considered a sect, it made no substantial efforts to institutionalize itself outside of its appearances at key life-stage ceremonies. The event described below is one of many appearances I witnessed of this "nomadic" sect over the period of 1993 to 1995.

In early 1994, a large and diverse crowd gathered at the wake of a prominent academic in Abidjan. The marking of death at wakes and funerals has the function of reaffirming social ties across nearly all cultures, and the wake here was no different in this effect. What stands out in this instance is the particular ways in which such ties were marked and used. Because the academic was a lapsed Catholic, his eldest daughter was concerned that the wake should have some kind of spiritual presence. She had heard about the new-form Celestial mission and the wonders they were capable of performing, and so she arranged to have a group of about twenty of their members officiate at the wake.

At the beginning of the wake, a space was marked in the yard at the family compound where the event was being held. Devotees of the sect were to offer gifts to specific spirits/gods with whom they expressed a particular association. These spirits/gods were, in turn, part of a larger pantheon of divinities to which the sect paid obeisance. The presiding "priest" noted each devotee's affiliation with a particular spirit. From his position, the priest made a series of markings in the ground, which made up a kind of tally indicating which spirit was aligned with which devotee. More important, these markings also provided some rough indication of how these particular devotees would subsequently position themselves with the larger crowd, the majority of whom were of course not members of the sect.

After some time, the priest called the entire crowd to order. He proceeded to give a lengthy narrative of the events and circumstances that led to the academic's death. The story, however, was recited in terms of the conflicts, affiliations, intrigues, and general activities experienced by the pantheon of spirits, divinities, and their "secular" associates. As particular devotees will call on and identify with specific spirits, their devotion is construed as lending "support" for the behavior of specific spirits. Devotion is thus a resource for spirits.

Accordingly, the devotee is complicit in the activities of given spirits. If particular transactions among these spirits are seen as responsible for specific events, such as a death, then the devotees are coresponsible for these events. Devotees, who may have nothing in common but their shared devotion, are thus seen as fundamentally associated. Their activities and agendas are linked, regardless of what they may know about the other.

The priest's narration mapped the interactions among spirits that "produced" the conditions or causes through which the academic died. This narrative is not viewed as providing an exhaustive account; rather, it establishes a general frame through which others gathered at the wake, both members and nonmembers of the sect, might orient themselves to the event. The priest then asked the relevant spirits to now become present and to use the marking of death as an opportunity to reconcile any lingering antagonisms.

After the priest was finished, the crowd engaged in many hours of conversation, and in many different combinations. The conversations situated the death in terms of a larger series of actions and actors and enabled those gathered to situate themselves in the event. The situating was to be done in such a way so that those present could "collectively" start making the necessary adjustments in their behaviors and reflections so that subsequent deaths might be avoided.

Such situating may have been the explicit objective of this exercise. Perhaps of greater importance is the complex circulation of information, inquiries, assays, seduction, speculation, and proposals for alliances and deals that occurred as a by-product. Such circulation occurs, in part, because the priest calls for sect members and nonmembers alike to lend protection to the household members of the deceased and thereby reduce the vulnerability that the death brings. This reduction of vulnerability for household members is to be accomplished by placing them in a new "neighborhood" of spiritual alignments.

These references to spiritual planes and alignments act as a catalyst to the construction of another narrative. It is a narrative that attempts to take those gathered "beyond" the death by implicating everyone in it. The academic had been killed in a car accident; something that occurs with alarming frequency in Abidjan. Yet, the story does not end there.

The academic's driver, also killed in the accident (and perhaps its "target"), was the brother of a former associate of the expresident's wife who had been involved in a massive corruption scheme that forced him to spend several years of exile in Liberia. He had returned without fanfare to Abidjan the night before the accident. This event coincided with the first visit in twenty years of the former president to his wife's village. The story mushrooms with coincidences and connections as almost each person present at the wake contributes additional pieces to the puzzle, charts out the interconnections of seemingly disparate events, and eventually locates themselves and specific actions on their part to one or more aspects of the event.

Members of the sect, with the map of the priest in mind, move through the crowd. They assess the various directions in which the narrative is going. They steer specific persons in the crowd into conversation with each other for the purpose of moving the narrative along in ways that might facilitate the spiritual realignments that they explicitly seek. By now everyone is being implicated by and oriented to these series of events. The process forces all of them to think carefully about what they have done and what they are doing. Even those individuals attending the wake who made disparaging remarks about the process at the beginning, find themselves carried along. In the meantime, those gathered begin to find out a lot they did not know about each other. There are intensely intimate conversations among strangers. There are direct outpourings of plans, intentions, and aspirations among social categories whose interaction would otherwise be highly regulated. Older adults are listening to the ramblings of children they would never otherwise allow themselves to listen to. Groups of middle age men are asking advice from young female adolescents. Important dignitaries are making plans to support the initiatives of street traders.

In other words, the common social arrangements of Abidjan are being momentarily upended. As a sense of commonality is affirmed, there is the recognition that opening up potentially more viable courses of individual action require realignments between self and others, and others and others. Such realignments will not be the exclusive products of one's own doing or control; rather, these realignments also require facilitating new abilities in others to act correctly and expediently. This is a process that is being defined to the crowd as the need for spiritual intervention. Members of the sect see it as their job to provide the right kind of spiritual intervention, and they are busy bringing different combinations of people together without necessarily doing anything else to insert themselves into what is subsequently discussed.

Existing social ties are also reconfirmed. Further, an outward-looking practice of remaking those ties is cultivated at the same time. The death of an individual thus provides a locus for those gathered to be enjoined in a sense of community, one that exceeds the sense of common loss. This sense of commonality is brought about through several ways of intersecting markedly different events and actors, and no one should leave feeling excluded or exculpated. Enjoined in a common sense, those gathered thus have a platform on which to do things differently with various others. And they can do things differently without having to feel that they have to give up something or leave something behind. In other words, the wake acts as an arena for enabling those gathered to explore new exteriors and new "neighborhoods" for the day-to-day agendas of seeking security and opportunity.

In Yopougon we can see how spiritual practice is capable of relocating individual actors within a different frame of identity and recognition. This relocation enables them to understand their relationships with other actors and events in new ways. The scope of everyone's links to each other is broadened: actors speak and deal with each other in ways that otherwise would be impossible. Such unanticipated interaction can become a rehearsal for new ways of navigating complex urban relationships and for constructing a sense of commonality that goes beyond parochial identities.

In all of these contexts and illustrations there is a work in progress. It is the work of making and grappling with cities, which are both nodes in a globalized geography of flows and also arbitrary administrative designations for a collection of highly localized spaces and quarters. These are works in progress that, in small and tentative ways, try to make a concrete urban life in the in-between.

Intersecting Urban Futures

Urban associational life in Africa has taken many forms and assumed different functions. It has been shaped by various political and economic influences. At times, solidarity was invented as a by-product of the need for otherwise disconnected persons to pool resources.[15] Associations also became instruments that enabled groups of neighbors to put together larger spaces of operation within the larger city — that is, as a means of developing external networks.[16] Associations could act as vehicles of intensified ethnic identification, especially when they were able to control where and how their members worked. Often, associations provided direct economic support to their members for a set time period, from which members were progressively weaned. Here, solidarity becomes a mechanism to support an individual's need to act with increasing measures of autonomy.[17]

Associations also could be political creations: when neighborhoods were not ethnically segregated, service provisioning as a means of cultivating political support was limited because these amenities benefited individuals. Politicians had little motivation to rally around better service provision if they wanted to solidify a following based on the long-term loyalty of a specific group. Hence, forging group support was played out through political patronage.[18] Perhaps more important, associations were instruments for helping connect modern and traditional spheres, and also for managing the effects that such interconnections had on the city.[19]

Now, throughout the world, the internal structure of localities becomes more fragmented. At the same time, networks of collaboration and belonging extend across broader and more differentiated spaces.[20] The capacity for sustained and coordinated actions among diverse populations across territory increases. The local foundations of solidarity and cooperation become more precarious and fragile. Governance, discipline, and control are no longer a function of subsuming diverse peoples and situations under the rubric of territorial proximity or totalizing institutions capable of legislating or administering all facets of daily life.

Throughout much of the southern part of the world, not only in Africa, localities experience heightened levels of instability. Accelerated population shifts occasioned by migration, demographic change, the dispersion of economic resources, and the relocation of growth are major factors in this instability. Instability is also intensified by the proliferation of more singular survival strategies pursued by local residents forced into more opportunistic and ad hoc behaviors. Globalization, economic deregulation, migration, and weakened political states all contribute to a growing uncertainty as to people's identities, motivations, and likely courses of action. This uncertainty may be the case even when people have lived together all of their lives.[21] It could be argued that such uncertainty means that internal cohesion has become more stringently held to as a defense against an unknown "out there." But an overly urgent concern on the part of communities with localized forms of cohesion is often unable to stop a downward spiral into breaking into levels of fragmentation.[22]

Poor communities face particular difficulties in juggling efforts to attain social cohesion and expand economic opportunities. Reciprocity, sharing resources, social cooperation, familial or community obligations, highly codified moral prescriptions, and open-ended information flow may be vital elements in preserving a sense of coherence under conditions of scarcity or social vulnerability. But there is also a need to be opportunistic and provisional. Individuals must often guard information, circumvent the behavioral implications of their beliefs and morals, and take steps to undermine the capacities of others. This undermining gives rise to economies of compensation. The objective of such economies is to generate opportunities for some form of gain, access, and income.

In any cursory scrutiny of poor communities, it is clear that there is social cooperation around the amelioration of misfortune for some. There are also economies based on intensifying misfortune for others. For example, in the Manenberg Township of Cape Town, gang members generously provide job and educational opportunities, food, protection, and even emotional support to scores of households in return for professions of loyalty. At the same time, they terrorize those households that refuse such professions.

The lack of health care, income, bonds, stability, cohesion, and mobility gives rise to many practices to make up for these lacks. These compensations in turn provide jobs, status, and earnings for specific members of a community. All community members simultaneously act as competitors and coconspirators in survival. Those without predictable and institutionally available resources use their profession or withholding of loyalty to others, who are perceived as more powerful, as a means of survival. Crises occasioned by a shifting economy of loyalties, obligations, betrayals, and deceit bring about seemingly endless compensations for these crises. The compensations frequently put together a different set of social ties. Because of its compensatory status, such an economy does not truly institutionalize itself into predictable behaviors and consequences. This is a situation that leads to further crises.

To undermine the authority of others becomes an important means of establishing authority for oneself. Because this is a "negative" strategy — focusing on what it can take away, rather than what it can give — those employing this strategy tend to be anxious about how long their authority will last. In their extreme, compensations generalize this anxiety throughout the social field. Bonds are broken and repaired, and are repaired in ways that tend to draw others into the game. No matter what they are, actions will be construed as a threat to someone. There is no capacity to allow things to "slide" — for individuals to say, "this doesn't have anything to do with me, my livelihood, or life chances." At the same time, the actions of others are not allowed or enabled to be sufficiently persuasive in terms of affecting broader change. Instead, one must defend against them.

Lines of Sight Given increasing levels of uncertainty, African residents "invest" heavily in opportunities to be socially visible in a variety of ways that are not organized in terms of formal associations. This investment is a critical aspect of making lives in urban quarters. The task is to find ways to situate oneself in order to assess what is happening in one's environs: who is talking to whom, who is visiting whose house, who is riding in the same car, who is trading together or buying from each other.

Public space is "filled," then, not simply with actors who seek to reconfirm social ties or legitimate everyday practices and attitudes; rather, there are also public actions that exist in order to create impressions that certain social realities, alliances, loyalties, and political and economic activities are taking place — regardless of whether or not they are taking place in actuality. For example, evening markets are often improvised, not so much to actually buy and sell things but to mark a place where people can mingle with and observe each other outside of the pressures and obligations that usually mark most other social events. "Working" assessments are made of potential opportunities and prevailing realities. A potential network of relations is maintained that need not be activated right away but that exists in some immanent state for future mobilization when necessary.[23]

For example, it is well known that Igbo Nigerians are major economic players in the inner city of Johannesburg, with interests in narcotics, money laundering, computer fraud, mobile phones, real estate, and beauty products and hair care. Every mid-afternoon, on a block in the center of the city, several thousand Nigerians mill publicly in the street. While a common assumption is that they are plying their drug trade, this is only incidentally the case. Most Nigerians involved in the array of provisional and frequently illicit trades have taken over the majority of the area's hotels as residential centers and thus usually purchase their meals from women who sell cooked food in the streets.

This purchase of the main mid-afternoon meal, however, serves many different purposes. First, it is a way for the Nigerians to demonstrate their capacity to mobilize a public presence. This space, Quartz Street between Kotze and Pretoria streets, becomes one of the few places where public life attains such density — thus iterating the Nigerians as a distinct sociality within the city, with distinct capacities for mobilization and coherence. This display becomes a display of impunity, pointing to the insufficiency of

South Africans to not only effectively deal with them, but also their own deficit of public action. Second, this publicity becomes a means of mutual witnessing. In other words, it is a means of Nigerians from many different walks of life, with different skills, patrons, trades, allegiances, and aspirations, to circulate and to exchange information. They also watch the various meetings of patrons—who arrive in luxury cars with their respective "lieutenants"—that take place on the balconies of several bars that overhang the street.

An investment in positions, and of using formal organizations as a vehicle through which to put together more short-term, informal ways of collaborating, has much to do with the difficulties involved for residents trying to orient themselves to changing local conditions. More than ever, localities need more diverse links with the larger world. These links maximize sites of opportunity and resources. At the same time, such heterogeneity can also undermine civility and a shared sense of belonging. For as links to the outside world are diversified, so are the inequities present within communities. Such inequities foster substantial disruptions in the way localities once understood, and perhaps tolerated, internal differences and disparities in wealth and power. Sudden and inexplicable accumulations, opportunities, or losses generate additional confusions as to who is doing what to whom, who has access to what, and to what extent these changes are attributable to things not being what they appear to be.[24]

Households, extended families, social networks, or neighborhoods are frequently uncertain as to just what is causing their lives to be the way they are. As a result, they take into consideration people and situations with which they once coexisted at a distance but never really paid attention to. Unclear as to what constrains their life chances, distant factors now may be relevant. When an enlarged plurality of events, people, and situations is seen as having something to do with how everyday life is lived, the universe of who one trusts, affiliates with, and is loyal to can also narrow.

Each group attached to a particular point of view, history, and identity must assume its rightness to the exclusion of others. In addition, they must be capable of insulating points of view, histories, and identities from counterfactuals or differing perspectives. Yet, different groups must often operate in close proximity to each other. They are often forced to become competitors in what are, for the most part, shrinking economies and public sectors. Nevertheless, these groups keep their eye out for each other and watch each other closely. Through this process of scrutinizing each other closely, substantial similarities among them may develop.

On the other hand, this "keeping the other in one's gaze" becomes increasingly problematic when major and distinct groups seem to be proceeding along diverging paths. For example, a study of family change in Nigeria concludes that little, if any, convergence in family trends between the Hausa on one side and the Yoruba and Igbo on the other has taken place in the past two decades. The socialization of marriage, childbearing, and childrearing behaviors remains critical to the self-valuation of the Hausa. On the other hand, increasing rates of delayed marriage, nucleated family structures, reduced fertility, and shorter postpartum sexual abstinence demonstrate that both Yoruba and Igbo are responding to prevailing socioeconomic processes.[25] The increasing divergence among trajectories makes it more difficult to identify some common ground.

Efforts to attain a balance between social cohesion and opportunity are not easily governed. The prescription of particular practices, incentives, or penalties that would unequivocally bring about such balance is practically impossible in localities with little formal employment, education, and human resource provision.

The Dilemmas of Social Integration   Given the nature of both colonial and postcolonial rule, solidarity has often taken shape through an interpenetration of domains and sectors rather than through the consolidation of citizenship within well-defined and well-managed institutions and social spheres. In other words, the interweaving of different strands of life brings together different social positions and identities in ways that force them to deal with each other but not necessarily take responsibility for each other. Traditional authorities, soldiers, bureaucrats, patrons, clients, households, religious figures, traders, and healers can't truly operate without dealing with each other.[26] These identities, however, largely function as markers for fluid transactions in a social environment that can be at times both excessively static and provisional. What is important is not that identities — such as local headman, prefect, shaykh, and so forth — act as enclosed domains of specific responsibilities, behaviors, or functions, but rather that the designations of identities help both insiders and outsiders track the many kinds of exchanges that are taking place among individuals and groups who not only alternate distinct identities but contradict them as well.

Such entanglements are not universal either within or across African cities. They do, however, show up as some kind of legacy in specific domains and quarters across the continent, if not farther afield: in the early settlement of colonial cities, some quarters manifested a fairly straightforward reproduction of village life; other quarters were simply transition zone for highly mobile labor; and still others reflected an intricate interlacing of trends, identities, and influences.

Valdo Pons conducted an important work of urban ethnography some forty years ago in Stanleyville (now Kisangani in the Democratic Republic of the Congo).[27] In this work, Pons documented how the process of adapting to the city entailed a great deal of trial and error and of making mistakes that were sometimes tolerated and that at other times became the occasion for argument. In fact, tolerance and dispute were both necessary for adaptation.

Pons showed that the character of quarters and their contributions to the overall urban system were quite heterogeneous. He focused on a quarter known as Avenue 21. There, a large number of the residents came from ethnic groups without close rural-urban links and with low fertility rates. As a result, most social interaction was not subject to the pressures or controls from networks of well-defined institutional relations either within or beyond the city. This is not to say that these social relations didn't pay attention to these established networks; indeed, residents would usually claim that what they did was in adherence to the norms of these networks. Because their adherence was, for the most part, simulated, the quarter could operate according to norms that were in reality much more flexible than the established ones and were open to various interpretations.

Variability thus played a big part in generating the agreed-on principles and meanings that pieced together local urban culture. The variations in what different residents knew about that culture and in their judgments about what aspects of their lives this culture affected were also significant. Quarters were not closed systems removed from each other, and thus the emerging distinctions in character among quarters became resources for working out various everyday-life dilemmas faced by different sets of residents living in different kinds of quarters.

During the colonial period, immigrants largely settled in locations approximating where they first arrived in the city. Accordingly, the ethnic composition of some quarters was clearly associated with social features and patterns of behavior that had become factors of internal differentiation for the country as a whole. This is particularly the case in situations where an urban labor force was recruited from specific regions, or where certain opportunities in the city were cultivated on the basis of what local societies were doing or subjected to in their regions of origin.

For example, mine workers may have been drawn from specific regions and assigned specific quarters in the city based on their occupation. Small-scale traders in food may have come from other regions, carrying out their activities on the periphery of the city. Administrators and police were often drawn from still other regions and assigned to specific residential zones. This process of territorialization was then reinforced by the selective ways the city acted on different regions.

The colonial city consolidated different functions, characters, and operating practices within different quarters. It then attempted to regulate the interactions among them. In some instances, fostering homogenous ethnic quarters facilitated carrying out specific urban functions. This was especially the case where colonial administrators didn't want workers to settle in the city on a permanent basis. In other instances it was more important to dilute ethnic solidarity and emphasize occupational and/or social class identities. Space had then to be cultivated for an intermixing of people from different regions and ethnic groups.

The relative importance of ethnicity, class, assimilation, and urbanization thus depended on the places and situations where these attributes were invoked and supported. In addition, different attributes could be mobilized as ways of countering the territorial arrangements imposed by colonial administrations, or as ways of breaking up settlements established autonomously by Africans. Different instruments of identity had different spaces and occasions of operation. Differences in the degree to which affiliations and everyday practices were determined by ethnic consolidation were contingent on several factors, including the historical circumstances under which specific migrants came to the city; the degree to which ethnic groups were dispersed across the city; the character of urban-rural linkages; and the position of migrants and ethnic groups within the labor system and urban economy.

Even at this time in the colonial history of Stanleyville, a particular constellation of factors didn't necessarily produce the same outcome. The process of identity making and exchange as fundamental aspects of emerging urban social relations was just that — a continuous process of making and exchanging. People did have their identities — different moral regimes, governance systems, and economic practices were associated with different quarters. Still, the urbanizing experiences of everyday life were not brought under the complete control of these regimes, systems, or practices. Residents from all walks of life increasingly "tried out" different ways of being and doing things in the city. Regularities were sought and often institutionalized. At the same time, very little that was tried was completely discarded or given up.

Operational memory was thus spatialized. In other words, African residents came to work out specific places and domains for being specific things and for working out what were often contradictory needs and aspirations. There were places to "keep tradition alive" and there were places to be "modern," places to be a "kinsman" and places to be a cosmopolitan urban "dweller," as well as more textured and subtle combinations of these primarily artificial polarities. This process of spatializing memory, options, and alternatives had a large affect on making African use of the city as dynamic as possible.[28]

There were limits, however, on how strict or thorough such spatializing could be. After all, different facets of African everyday life and identity had to nurture each other under often rigid colonial and postcolonial controls and economic limitations. Urban quarters across the region continue to express concerns that to delink religious life from the political, the political from the entrepreneurial, or the familial from the public may weaken African urban societies. In cities facing many different kinds of crises, this interdependency means that the resolution of any particular difficulty within one sector is potentially availed the influences and resources of any other.

On the other hand, the intermeshing of sectors may not create sufficient space for changes to take hold in how individual spheres of activity operate, be they religious, political, economic, familial, and so forth. Without this space, it may be difficult to generate new forms of independent action and innovation that could be brought to the larger public sphere. If changes in how local politics operate are seen as having substantial effects on how religion, business, family life, and community affairs are practiced, people will be cautious about bringing about such political change. This is because too many dimensions of life may be at stake. Accordingly, independent action is limited.

What is important in this dilemma of sociality is that independent action and social interdependency are still related to each other; still have something to do with each other. In contrast, contemporary modalities of urban governance in Europe and North America often seem to pull apart interdependency and autonomy, responsibilities and rights, and community and individuality, rendering them as parallel, nonintersecting conditions. An individual can be connected to various networks and institutions, yet still find themselves ultimately on their own and responsible for their own welfare. Individuals and groups can chart out courses of independent action and still find themselves hemmed in on all sides of interlocking mechanisms of institutional control with little room to maneuver. Yet moves toward both social interdependency and individuation are presently being intensified.

On Keeping Futures in Play   Many urban communities in Africa exist within what Michael Rowlands has labeled "temporal inconsistencies."[29] To simplify his point, communities live simultaneously in a traditional and a modern world. On the one hand, many African urban residents live in an unyielding sameness of making do and surviving through a limited range of activities, the content of which does not substantially change over time. Small improvements may be made to provide shelter. The household may succeed in feeding itself, but not much more. The site of residence may basically be far removed from much external scrutiny. As a result, people are allowed to practice their survival with a large measure of autonomy, especially because institutional affiliations are minimal. Few services are provided, and in many cases tenants have had no contact with public officials or even landowners for long periods of time. To put it bluntly, residents live a "ghettoized" existence.

On the other hand, the minimal features of this existence come to provide a context for economic activities, almost always unconventional and frequently illicit, that are often far-reaching in their scope and highly flexible and sophisticated in their organization. These activities take the actors who drive them far out into the external world, often covering great distance and crossing many different social networks. So while a given community may look substantially cut off from the larger world, at the same time and within a different sense of time the community has the potential of reaching that larger world. It is true that such a sense of the larger world is usually the purview or privilege of small numbers. Nevertheless, it operates through and alongside the very constrictions of the ghettoization that otherwise would seem to dominate.

Tradition is invoked as an instrument to deal with the increasing fluidity and uncertainty in people's lives. As such, it becomes an aspect of the very contemporary contest over whose interests are more important or powerful. In order for it to make its point, what is traditional or referred to as "traditional" in local struggles must become increasingly "modern" or "nonconventional" in how it makes it claims, organizes loyalty, and puts its point across.

In many quarters development is adamantly refused, for development is read as forcing residents to make visible what it is they do in order to survive. Whatever benefits may accrue, the feeling is that the risks may be too high; that development is just a ploy to displace and uproot the limited foothold residents have managed to secure for themselves. Those with contacts protect their reach and diversity through the fact that there are residents whose perhaps limited readings of their situation reproduce a highly ghettoized existence.

At the same time, ambiguities in the organization of social life at the local level may contribute to enhancing the speed and mobility of transactions, resources, and alliances. If no clear roles and channels of exchange are institutionalized or are forced to be as opportunistic as possible, and almost everyone is available to do something out of the ordinary, things can happen very fast, if not necessarily efficiently. It is a process of keeping communities on their toes. Despite the fact that communities may have to repiece solidarity and coherence together on almost a day-to-day basis, an aspiration to put together a richly textured translocal social life is often at work in these survival practices.

African urban communities largely "remain on their toes"—ready to move across incessantly rearranged and intermeshed sectors and identities, yet with a sense that any position, space, or experience is not irrevocably networked into a specific constellation of meanings. Rather, that which is assembled retains a fundamental sense of detachment, delinked from various governance partnerships. In this way, each element or "contributor" maintains a certain autonomy and independence of maneuver without being subsumed into some larger, consensual objective or trajectory. With such autonomy, the connections unfolding this "assemblage" are sustained in what Alain Pottage calls a process of provocation and anticipation—each position or component challenging the others through nonprogrammed maneuvers; each position or component becoming flexible enough to roll with the challenges.[30] In this way, specific and cohesive spaces for specific tasks, operations, and collaborations can emerge from the very process of being inverted, dispersed, and interchanged.

In all of the case studies and examples explored herein, there is a push to acquire capacities to converse with and engage globally reworked urban formations. But this capacity is sought on terms emanating from both a deep-seated memory of a broad range of tactical engagements with the urban over time and a desire to evacuate everything that came before. There is desire to belong and to define the terms of belonging, but not necessarily in the spaces or the ways that the prevailing paradigms and operations of urban development would normatively consign them. There is, rather, a desire to keep open the reality that African cities are places where anything might happen, while at the same time expand the scope of what actually does happen, as well as pay a less severe price for such a potentiality. As such, urban sociality must go beyond strict demarcations of the formal and informal, becoming and belonging, visibility and invisibility, and normative and dysfunctional, and use the possibilities of one to change the apprehension and use of the other. In this way, particular social experiments or provisional formations are not targeted either as the purveyors of development or subversion, and thus are not subject to the implications or responsibilities that these designations imply.

Translocal Opportunities and the Cohesion of Place   As we have seen, development processes usually stir up internal conflicts. Mitigating these conflicts, in part, means extending and diversifying networks external to individual localities. The availability of larger numbers of heterogeneous external networks has many different implications. On the one hand, if sectors, interests, populations, and groups don't get along, the availability of an expanded range of external linkages reduces their need to deal with each other.

The exception to this is when access to contacts, opportunities, and resources explicitly mandates specific levels of local cooperation. Less contact does not necessarily spell out a good or a bad outcome. Just because distinct groups share what has administratively or politically been designated a common locality does not necessarily mean that they have to deal with each other. It does not mean that dealing with each other at some point will produce benefits for all.

The strength of any community is not only reflected in the degree of interchange among differences or social harmony, it is also reflected in a community's ability to be indifferent to different groups acting on their differences. Local conflicts usually ensue, as we have seen previously, when groups feel that they have to take what other groups are doing into consideration. Conflicts ensue when the actions of others are necessarily interpreted as having something inevitably to do with one's life chances or situation.

The availability of external networks increasingly provides a vehicle of solidarity that does not rely on concepts of territoriality. As such, it is much more flexible. It is possible for groups to be convinced that they are rooted in the world, and that they have a sense of belonging no matter where they might be located. Such convictions make it possible for groups to share space with those who are different from them. Without a sense of "rooted-ness" that goes beyond a specific locality or territory, those differences have a greater chance of becoming an incessant source of threat.[31]

In some circumstances, groups limit what they do because they know that they have to deal with another group with whom they share interests, territory, membership, or common location. As a result, violence and manipulation may be constrained. At the same time, enterprise, initiative, and creativity may also find themselves diminished.

On the other hand, the availability of external linkages supportive of the interests, agendas, and operations of local groups may harden their "negotiating" position when dealing with others. The availability of external linkages may lessen the extent to which they take into consideration the other's experience and viewpoint. Groups may refuse to "play" if they don't get their way.

Furthermore, actors may assume one point of view or position within a local context, but then take a very different position outside the locality. As I pointed out earlier, it is quite common in urban African politics for elite actors to assume a particular position within a local context, and then do completely the opposite when dealing outside it. This versatility can potentially be a strategic maneuver capable of strengthening the position of localities within diverse external networks.

At the same time, community participation can be impeded, and important understandings of local dynamics on the part of community residents confounded. This duplicity is especially dangerous where community leaders or patrons claim to be operating in the interest of specific constituencies. Complicity among these elite in external networks for the purpose of their own self-aggrandizement or enrichment tends to foster antagonisms. These antagonisms tend to be expressed as a matter of intergroup conflict rather than as recognition of elite duplicity.

In general, however, if a locality is to cultivate external networks, much of the exploration of possible niche markets, affiliations, alliances, resources, and knowledge inputs will take place informally. For the critical challenge is how to recognize the identity of a single locality in many different localities. Alliances with finance capital in one locality do not rule out alliances to popular citizens' movements in another. Investing in business in a "foreign" city does not necessarily mean a diversion of funds away from businesses at "home." Localities have an increasing number of ways to affiliate with all of the different things going on in all of the different localities of the world. Given this, what are all of the various things a locality can say about itself that can be used to explore a wide range of productive relationships?

Instead of a locality looking at where it is and how it got there, the challenge is to use all available pathways and networks as vehicles to make a locality known to wider audiences. Here it is also important that these potential audiences agree that there is something worth paying attention to. At the same time, it is also important that "the something" is not just one thing. In other words, the more the locality can project itself as a plurality of positive features, the more angles it has to actually forge concrete connections with external networks and places.

This strategy of urban development goes beyond contemporary notions of fiscal performance. An obsession with fiscal performance tends to reduce diversities in social production to the homogenizing calculus of monetary indicators. Instead, it is a strategy that uses the dematerialization represented by global financial markets (for example, the derivatives of money-making derivatives) and flows to carve out multiple relocations of the locality throughout the wider world.

Globalization is not about what localities can attract but where they can go; where they can "find" themselves. As Jordi Borja indicates, the viability of cities largely rests on their ability to act on information regarding international markets, the flexibility of their commercial and productive structures and their capacity to enter networks of various dimensions and complexities.[32] These capacities are more important than geographical location, past positions within national or international economies, accumulated capital, or natural resources.

The elaboration of leading-edge strategies is not to subsume all aspects of local economies to the predominance of securing a specific niche in an internationalized urban hierarchy. Rather, such strategies provide opportunities for localities to establish footholds in other localities, engage in diverse markets and investments, and secure points of articulation and "breakthroughs" for an equally differentiating local economy. In other words, local economic development in cities rethinks local resources and resourcefulness in new ways in order to foster context-specific articulations to global urbanizing and economic trends. This is a very different orientation than the prevailing tendency of generating high and medium technology and small- and medium-scale enterprises as some standardized panacea to urban difficulties.

This sense of reaching far beyond the locality in order to achieve the locality is also a different way of thinking about local democracy. Local politics usually entails who gets what under what circumstances. Efforts are directed to lessening the social distance among different identities, groups, and circumstances. Often, development is slowed down by virtue of the uncertainty it raises as to who will benefit or who might gain undue advantage over another. When cultivating external networks becomes an important task, no member of a locality can be theoretically excluded. Granted, vast disparities exist in terms of the kinds of networks and resources to which specific groups and individuals have access. There are also disparities as to the kinds of leverage that mobilizing those networks potentially have over local everyday life. Yet, it is rare that any African urban resident is without some kind of external network that can be plied or mobilized in some way.

Throughout urban Africa, in fact, apparent disparities between districts are often rebalanced through the differences of investment placed in external ties. Middle-class districts may have a more solid anchorage in local power and accumulation structures, yet poorer communities, often by necessity, can possess a greater and more diverse range of external contacts outside the city that might accrue particular benefits and advantages in the overall urban system. During the recent history of economic crisis and structural adjustment, middle-class families often confronted greater difficulties feeding themselves than many living in poorer districts.

Cultivating networks is not by itself sufficient grounds for local viability. Especially now, the fate of localities as a whole is often enjoined to those residents and sectors whose networks are the most solidified. Nevertheless, an enlarged space is opened up for local initiatives undertaken at "home." Public authorities can potentially appropriate such an enlargement of a space for local initiatives as an excuse to withdraw from certain responsibilities. In addition, an increasing number of public relationships are threatened with privatization. Still, intensified local activism adds synergy to local capacities and makes institution building better suited to local realities.

Reconnecting Cities As cities everywhere become increasingly heterogeneous, the implications of heightened interest rates and energy costs, trade regimes, and redirected flows of commodities, bodies, knowledge, and influence will be differentially reflected and embodied by different populations and territories within the same city. The African urban peoples will, as is already happening, find places of operation far beyond the region itself. While these differentiated impacts — and subsequent compensations, advantages, and so forth — still occur within the semblance of a coherent time-space system (i.e., the "city" designated with a name, with relational proximity) the elaboration of policy and governance practices becomes increasingly difficult. Urban institutions, because they must deal with a heterogeneity of local populations, have to strengthen this heterogeneity while at the same time keep the "differences" conversant with each other — that is, mutually implicated and cross-subsidized.

On top of this, the cityscape of a national territory is, in the words of John Browder and Brian Godfrey, a "mosaic of fragmented social spaces," with cities differentially articulated to global and national forces and to each other, and with a plurality of local models arising from this very disarticulation.[33] This is a long way from the so-called urban convergence model, which predicts a progressive homogenization of urban form and governance across the globe. For even within the same subregion, cities can be linked in radically different ways to national, regional, and global markets, as well as different modes of production and spatial organization.

Regionally configured development and governance frameworks are increasingly seen as the most appropriate means of organizing the productive forces of an urban economy so as to overcome intraregional competition, fragmentation, and disarticulation.[34] Cities, especially those in some form of geographical proximity, should not compete but rather identify ways of complementing each other. Thickening such complementary interactions is seen as capable of sustaining new forms of comparative advantage for regional clusters or the conurbation of cities as a whole. The need for regional network frameworks may be clear, with their expanded and more open-ended requirements for defining and bringing coherence to the city.

But it is not clear whether the kinds of clustering, articulations, overlaps, complementarity, specialization, and negotiations called for can be a matter of intentional planning. Articulations must be practiced and based on the highly singular ways in which local populations manage to cross and interpenetrate divides of all kinds. How diverse populations operating within a city are motivated to do this is not clear, particularly because this navigation may rely on increasing stealth and dissimulation. One aspect of the ever-increasing size of cities is that existing and still proliferating spatial divides may begin to fold in on each other as the management of urban infrastructures begins to confront substantial limits to their environmental sustainability, as well as to their regulatory, surveillance, and policing systems. This "folding in," as already evidenced in many situations, establishes new and sometimes prolonged, bitter, and probably necessary periods of contestation over space, resources, and rights.

As the practices of different urban worlds intersect, new, provisional, and often ephemeral urban worlds are made. Urban Africa demonstrates that the theorization of global change has paid insufficient attention to the social practices through which diverse "socialities," brought into greater proximity, concretely operate within these engagements and what is then done with them. Increasingly, urban economies are focusing on how intersections are actually practiced and performed. What practices can be deployed in order to navigate the intersections, to compel specific dispositions from them, or to direct them into being resources for specific projects or aspirations?[35] What happens to the traces and effects of these intersections after they occur—if and when it is possible to mark an ending?

In an era of new geographies, the instruments through which peoples can be constituted in or attached to particular places of belonging—as well as the terms through which peoples and identities can emerge onto given territories—seem to be waning. For the specificity of African, European, Asian, or Latin American urban realities, and the sensibilities and histories to which they give rise, are spread out—they have both infiltrated other places and have also been infiltrated.[36] When diverse peoples, localities, and regions intersect, there is a need to narrate the intersection, to define it as an intersection of differences. The ability to produce such a narration always assumes that these diversities are already to some extent incorporated into each other, already on the same plane of communicability, whether this is a sense of intersubjective generality or a more diffuse openness to solidarity.[37]

The very possibilities of narrating intersections must proceed from the heterogeneous possibilities, events, and futures potentially derivable from the intersection itself—that is, what could be made or what is being made that does not enter the terms of recognition.[38] This is the case even when specific modalities for narrating and controlling these intersections—determining what they will mean, what they will be used for—are subject to those able to display inordinate power. The possibilities for making worlds are not exhausted by these modalities.[39] In its proliferation of political sites, of actions upon actions, the very display of the efficacy of the capacities of those who are stronger implicitly opens up opportunities for the basis of their authority to be questioned, if not circumvented.[40]

Cities are sometimes sites of substantial intersections. As such they are more than the infrastructures, codes, and inputs necessary to manage population sizes and built environments. They are full of unanticipated associations, visions, confluence, noise, and things to consume — none of which are easily used or useful. At the same time, there remain the "necessary" orders, rules, habits, habitats, and institutions. What is dynamic about this configuration is the space in-between these excessive expenditures and the widening proficiency of power to engineer stability and stasis. On the one hand, there are no locations outside the ravenous accumulations of a capitalist system that accelerates feelings of loss and uselessness. What we may discover to be joyous, wise, and festive may also glow with awesome contamination. On the other hand, efforts to ward off the dangers of excess by encompassing the city with some form of "global" overview, as with the surveillance of modern policing or satellite imaging, inevitably fail as an instrument of total control at a distance.[41]

For as African cities increasingly suggest, the city in general is a nebulous world where security operatives, freedom fighters, terrorists, corporate raiders, gangsters, rebels, activists, militants, presidents, smugglers, communication technicians, hackers, accountants, consultants, and priests are all like each other but not the same thing. As of yet, we have no language to adequately understand these "like" relations — yet the relations are the important thing, and not the clear definition of the identities. It is in navigating these murky relations — operating in a world with incessant criss-crossing of identifications, allegiances, and collaborations — that new spaces of urban economy are being made.

A Concluding Word In this book I have attempted to examine some important dimensions of African urban life — the ways in which public spheres are pieced together, orientations toward city life are developed, livelihood is secured, and social action is engendered and managed. In doing so, I have also attempted to provide a theoretical basis for promoting a sense of the "multiplex" in African urban development, by which I mean the ability to negotiate among locally and externally generated urban development knowledge and to enhance the impact of African experiences and contributions to the consolidation of urban knowledge in general.

Where most African cities may be headed is perhaps more uncertain than ever. We are now more aware of the convergence of diverse powers, the character of this convergence, and the kinds of power that are converged. The large uncertainty that remains, however, can be attributed to the fact that much remains unknown about how African cities work. We know that there are often remarkable forces of dynamism and transformation. We know that there are equally remarkable blockages and resistance. Somewhere in the middle, the particular details of individual everyday lives exist. African urban futures are caught up in the delicate maneuvers of African urban actors to navigate through the twists and turns of events that most feel they only barely control, if at all.

François Woukoache's film *Fragments of Life* tells three stories of individuals living in a quarter of Yaounde. In the first story a college student looking for a job, after having put up a steady resistance to a local crew of inept thieves, gets drawn into transporting illicit goods across the city. In the second story a girl decides to take revenge on a police commissioner who had her father killed some seven years before after standing up to the "honor" of his wife. The third tale involves a couple reunited after years of a mysterious separation when, unbeknownst to the returning man, his daughter falls into an inexplicable coma. These three stories represent just some of the fragments of thousands of daily stories where urban actors find their lives suddenly transformed. Immersed in daily struggles to make a living and to survive the economic chaos and political manipulations around them, some unexpected directions are opened up; some are survived and some are not.

In his film's narratives, Woukoache intermittently returns to a particularly haunting image. In the depth of the night a young couple sits transfixed in the wreck of yellow taxi. A woman is holding the wheel as if steering the car through nights where anything might and does happen. Nearby, young prostitutes are selling their wares. A sorcerer's circle has been drawn to hold the sacrifices of several men induced into hysterical trances by a witch. Small vendors line the scene, selling cigarettes and prepared food. People spill in and out of the bars. Fancy cars discharge well-dressed men who disappear into the quarter on "special missions." Others return home after the several-hour walk from their places of work.

Throughout these activities, the couple in the taxi remains vigilant. Eyes wide open without blinking, they look like zombies whose souls have been stolen. Perhaps they have seen just too much, and they are frozen. Unable to make sense of anything around them, they are caught in an endless position of "wait and see": don't do anything until it becomes just a little more clear what it is that is really safe to do; what is really worth doing. The taxi, even if its engine were intact and could be driven away, is not positioned for a quick escape. It is turned to the quarter, not away. The couple's backs are not turned on where they have come from. They remained positioned to see everything. And in seeing everything, there is a burdensome knowledge to bear.

What is this knowledge? What do they really see? The filmmaker keeps returning to them, as a device to connect his three stories and three lives, but also as a kind of closing argument about what in the end can be said about the urban forces at work. If the knowledge is too much to handle, there are plenty of places in the quarter's webs of alleys and lanes where rest might be taken; where one could hide out yet still find some way of making do. Still, night after night, the couple is behind the wheel. The windshield is long gone, but the lights still work and are on. They are ready to take what they know and get away. Even if the car is not moving, perhaps they are on the road, somewhere. Perhaps the only way to deal with the real powers — whatever they are, as so many names have been applied to them — is to stare them down or to open oneself up to them completely, still and silent. It is another night; and they are still navigating the city — without map, without motion. They are ready to face the music. In this and all other African cities, the music is relentless.

Notes

Introduction: Remaking African Cities

1 Sony Labou Tansi, *The Antipeople* (New York: Marion Boyers Press, 1988).
2 Dominique Malaquais, *Architecture, pouvoir et dissidence au Cameroun* (Paris: CERI, Karthala, 2002).
3 Michel Ágier, "Between War and City: Towards an Urban Anthropology of Refugee Camps," *Ethnography* 3 (2002): 317–42; Achille Mbembe, "Necropolitics," *Public Culture* 15 (2003): 12–40.
4 See Krishno Dey and David Westendorff, eds., *Their Choice or Yours: Global Forces or Local Voices?* (Geneva: United Nations Research Institute for Social Development, 1996); Celestin Monga, *The Anthropology of Anger: Civil Society and Democracy in Africa* (Boulder: Lynne Rienner, Publishers, 1996); Aili Mari Tripp, *Changing the Rules: The Politics of Liberalization and the Urban Informal Economy in Tanzania* (Berkeley: University of California Press, 1997); Filip De Boeck, "Beyond the Grave: History, Memory, and Death in Postcolonial Zaire," in *Memory and the Postcolony: African Anthropology and the Critique of Power*, ed. Richard Werbner (London: Zed, 1998); Donald Moore, "Subaltern Struggles and the Politics of Place: Remapping Resistance in Zimbabwe's Eastern Highlands," *Cultural Anthropology* 13 (1998): 344–82; Christian Lund, "Precarious Democratization and Local Dynamics in Niger: Micropolitics in Zinder," *Development and Change* 32 (2001): 845–69; Adeline Masquelier, "Behind the Dispensary's Prosperous Façade: Imagining the State in Rural Niger," *Public Culture* 13 (2001): 267–91.
5 E. A. Brett, "The Participation Principle in Development Projects: The Costs and Benefits of Participation," *Public Administration and Development* 16

(1996): 5–19; Carole Rakodi, "Order and Disorder in African Cities: Governance, Politics, and Urban Land Development Processes," in *Under Siege: Four African Cities: Freetown; Johannesburg; Kinshasa; Lagos*, ed. Okwui Ewenzor (Ostfildern-Ruit, Germany: Harje Cantz Publishers, 2003).

6 Yusuf Bangura, "Economic Restructuring, Coping Strategies, and Social Change: Implications for Institutional Development in Africa," *Development and Change* 25 (1994): 785–827; Peter Schübeler, *Participation and Partnership in Urban Infrastructure Management* (Washington, D.C.: Urban Management Program, World Bank, 1996).

7 Ali El-Kenz, "Youth and Violence," in *Africa Now: People, Politics, Institutions*, ed. Stephen Ellis (London: James Currey; Portsmouth, NH.: Heinemann, in association with the Dutch Ministry of Foreign Affairs, 1996): René Devisch, "Frenzy, Violence, and Ethical Renewal in Kinshasa," *Public Culture* 7 (1995): 593–629; Mamadou Diouf, H. M. Fotê, and Achille Mbembe, "The Civil Status of the State in Africa," *Codesria Bulletin* 1–2 (1999): 39–47.

8 Salem Sethuraman, *Africa's Informal Economy* (Geneva: International Labor Organization, 1997); International Labor Organization, *Jobs for Africa: A Policy Framework for an Employment-Intensive Growth Strategy* (Geneva: International Labor Organization, 1998); Paul Collier and Jan Willem Gunning, "Explaining African Performance," *Journal of Economic Literature* 37 (1999): 64–111; Paul Lachance, *Africa's Real Economy and Its Development Projects: Rethinking African Development Issues* (Paris: OECD, 2000).

9 See Nazneen Kanji, "Gender, Poverty, and Economic Adjustment in Harare, Zimbabwe," *Environment and Urbanization* 7 (1995): 37–55; Annelet Harts-Broekhuis, "How to Sustain a Living: Urban Households and Poverty in a Sahelian Town of Mopti, Africa," *Africa* 67 (1997): 106–31; Claire Roberston, *Trouble Showed the Way: Women, Men, and Trade in the Nairobi Area, 1890–1990* (Bloomington: Indiana University Press, 1997); Lynne Bryden, "Tightening Belts in Accra, 1975–1990," *Africa* 69 (1999): 366–85.

10 See Van Arkadie, "The State and Economic Change in Africa," in *The Role of the State in Economic Change in Africa*, ed. Ha-Joon Chang and Robert Rowthorn (Oxford: Clarendon Press, 1995); Kenneth King, *Jua Kali Kenya: Change and Development in an Informal Economy, 1970–95* (Nairobi: East African Educational Publishers, 1996).

11 See Joseph Lugalla, *Crisis, Urbanization, and Urban Poverty in Tanzania: A Study of Urban Poverty and Survival Politics* (Lanham, Md.: University Presses of America, 1995); Kisangani Emizet, "Confronting Leaders at the Apex of the State: The Growth of the Unofficial Economy in Congo," *African Studies Review* 41 (1998): 99–137; Janet Roitman, "The Garrison-Entrepôt," *Cahiers d'etudes africaines* 150–52 (1998): 297–329.

12 Thandika Mkandawire and Charles Soludo, *Our Continent, Our Future:*

African Perspectives on Structural Adjustment (Dakar: Codesria; Trenton, N.J.: Africa World Press, 1998).

13 Ivor Chipkin, "Functional and Dysfunctional Communities: The Making of National Citizens," *Journal of Southern African Studies* 29 (2003): 63–82.

14 Thandika Mkandawire, "Incentives, Governance, and Capacity Development in Africa," in *Capacity for Development: New Solutions to Old Problems,* ed. Sakiko Fukuda-Parr, Carlos Lopes, and Khalid Malik (London: Earthscan; New York: United Nations Development Program, 2002). See also Club du Sahel/OECD and the Municipal Development Program, "Managing the Economy Locally in Africa: Assessing Local Economies and Their Prospects," available at http://webnet1.oecd.org/pdf/M00020000/M00020 320.0pdf.

15 This is a notion developed by Juan Obarrio in "History as Geopolitics in the Postcolony: The Mozambican Case," presented at "Portuguese/African Encounters Congress 2002," the Watson Institute, Brown University, April 25–29, 2002.

16 Juan Obarrio, "The Spirit of the Laws in Mozambique," *Public Culture* 15, no. 4 (2004, forthcoming).

17 See Mayamba Thierry Nlandu, "Kinshasa: When Illiterate and Literate Move beyond Political Democracy," available at http://i-p-o.org/congdem2.htm; Kevin Hetherington, "Phantasmagoria/Phantasm Agora: Movements Out of Time and the Language of Seeing," *Space and Culture* 11–12 (2002): 24–41.

18 Pheng Cheah, "Spectral Nationality: The Living on [sur-vie] of the Postcolonial Nation and Neocolonial Globalization," *boundary* 2 26 (1999): 225–52.

19 See Brad Weiss, "Thug Realism: Inhabiting Fantasy in Urban Tanzania," *Cultural Anthropology* 17 (2002): 93–128; Filip De Boeck, "Kinshasa: Tales of the 'Invisible City' and the Second World," in *Under Siege: Four African Cities: Freetown; Johannesburg; Kinshasa; Lagos,* ed. Okwui Ewenzor (Ostfildern-Ruit, Germany: Harje Cantz Publishers, 2003).

20 The majority of the most cogent of these summaries have been reviewed in Chris Rogerson, "Globalization or Informalization: African Urban Economies in the 1990s," in *The Urban Challenge in Africa: Growth and Management of Its Large Cities,* ed. Carole Rakodi (Tokyo: United Nations University Press, 1997). Other significant works include Janet MacGaffrey, *Entrepreneurs and Parasites: The Struggle for Indigenous Capitalism in Zaire* (Cambridge: Cambridge University Press, 1988); Carlos Maldonado, "The Underdogs of the Urban Economy Join Forces: Results of an ILO Programme in Mali, Rwanda, and Togo," *International Labour Review* 128 (1989): 65–84; John Dawson, "The Relevance of the Flexible Specialisation Paradigm for Small-Scale Industrial Restructuring in Ghana," *Bulletin of the Institute of Development Studies* 23 (1992): 34–38; Crispin Grey-Johnson, "The African Informal Sector at the Crossroads: Emerging Policy Options," *African*

Development 18 (1992): 65–91; David Simon, *Cities, Capital, and Development: African Cities in the World Economy* (London: Belhaven: 1992); Christian Peters-Berries, *Putting Development Policies into Practice: The Problems of Implementing Policy Reforms in Africa* (Geneva: International Labor Organization, 1993); King, *Jua Kali Kenya*; Jean Loup, *Employment, Unemployment, and the Informal Economy of Yaounde and Antananarivo: A New Survey Method for the Employment Market Applied to Sub-Saharan Africa* (Paris: L'institut français scientifique pour le développement en coopération, 1996); Meine Pieter Van Dijk, "The Urban Informal Sector as New Engine for Development: Theoretical Developments since 1972," *Asien afrika lateinamerka* 24 (1996): 177–92; Sethuraman, *Africa's Informal Economy*; Salem Sethuraman, *Urban Poverty and the Informal Sector: A Critical Assessment of Current Strategies* (Geneva: International Labor Organization, 1997); Tripp, *Changing the Rules.*

21 Guy Mhone, *The Impact of Structural Adjustment on the Urban Informal Sector in Zimbabwe* (Geneva: International Labor Organization, 1995).

22 Kanji, "Gender, Poverty, and Economic Adjustment in Harare, Zimbabwe."

23 Sara Berry, "Stable Prices, Unstable Values: Some Thoughts on Monetization and the Meaning of Transactions in West African Economies," in *Money Matters: Instability, Values, and Social Payments in the Modern History of West African Communities*, ed. Jane Guyer (Portsmouth, N.H.: Heinemann; London: James Currey, 1995).

24 Stephen Ellis and Janet MacGaffey, "Research on Sub-Saharan Africa's Unrecorded International Trade: Some Methodological and Conceptual Problems," *African Studies Review* 39 (1996): 19–41; Achille Mbembe, "At the Edge of the World: Boundaries, Territoriality, and Sovereignty in Africa," *Public Culture* 12 (2000): 259–84.

25 Michel Serres, *Genesis* (Ann Arbor: University of Michigan Press, 1995). This point has also been widely discussed in terms of the intersection of urban lives through the various infrastructural circuits, both physical and social, that transverse urban space; see most particularly Michel Maffesoli, *Time of Tribes: The Decline of Individualism in Mass Society* (London: Sage, 1996); Nigel Clark, "Botanizing on the Asphalt? The Complex Lives of Cosmopolitan Bodies," *Body and Society* 6 (2000): 12–33.

26 Paula Donnelly-Roark, Karim Ouedrago, and Xiao Ye, "Can Local Institutions Reduce Poverty? Rural Decentralization in Burkina Faso," World Bank, 2001, available at http://econ.worldbank.org/files2402_wps2677.pdf.

27 Jacques Ranciére, *Disagreements: Philosophy and Politics* (Minneapolis: University of Minnesota Press, 1998).

28 François Constantin, "La transnationalité, de l'individu à l'Etat: A propos des modes populaires d'action internationale en Afrique orientale," in *Les individus dans les relations internationales*, ed. Michel Girard (Paris, Economica, 1994).

29 Janet MacGaffey, Vwakyanakazi Mukohya, Walu Engundu, Makwala M. Mavambu ye Beda, and Brooke G. Schoepf, eds., *Real Economy of Zaire: The Contribution of Smuggling and Other Unofficial Activities to National Wealth* (Philadelphia: University of Pennsylvania Press, 1991); Jean-François Bayart, Stephen Ellis, and Beatrice Hibou, eds., *The Criminalization of the State in Africa* (Indianapolis: Indiana University Press; London: James Currey, 1999); Observatoire Geopolitique des Drogues, *World Geopolitics of Drugs Annual Report 1997/98*; Bio Goura Soulé and Cyril Obi. "Prospects for Trade between Nigeria and Its Neighbors," OECD, Paris, 2001, available at http://webnet1.oecd.org/pdf/M00018/M00018169.pdf; Charles Gore and David Pratten, "The Politics of Plunder: The Rhetorics of Order and Disorder in Southern Nigeria," *African Affairs* 102 (2003): 211–40.

30 See, for example, Bruce Fetter, *The Creation of Elizabethville 1910–1940* (Stanford: Stanford Univeristy Press, 1976); Richard Roberts, *Warriors, Merchants, and Slaves: The State and Economy in the Middle Niger Valley, 1700–1914* (Stanford: Stanford University Press, 1987); and P. Pels, *A Politics of Presence: Contacts between Missionaries and Waluguru in Late Colonial Tanganyika* (London: Routledge, 1998).

31 John Illife, *The Africans* (Cambridge: Cambridge University Press, 1995); J. D. Y. Peel, "Urbanization and Urban History in West Africa," *Journal of African History* 21 (1980): 269–77.

1 The Informal: The Projet de Ville in Pikine, Senegal

1 Sethuraman, *Urban Poverty and the Informal Sector.*

2 Ellis and MacGaffey, "Research on Sub-Saharan Africa's Unrecorded International Trade"; Donna Flynn, "'We Are the Border': Identity, Exchange, and the State along the Benin-Nigeria Border," *American Ethnologist* 24 (1997): 311–30.

3 Dennis Rondinelli and John Karsada, "Job Creation Needs in Third World Cities," in *Third World Cities: Problems, Policies, and Prospects,* ed. John Karsada and Alan Parnell (London: Sage, 1993); International Labor Organization, *Decent Work and the Informal Economy* (Geneva: ILO, 2002).

4 Renato Aguilar and Mario Carlos Zejan. "Income Distribution and the Labor Market in Angola," *Development Southern Africa* 11 (1994): 341–50.

5 Caroline Moser, Alicia Herbert, and Roza Makonnen, *Urban Poverty in the Context of Structural Adjustment: Recent Evidence and Policy Responses* (Washington, D.C.: Urban Development Division, World Bank (1993); Peter Evans, ed., *Livable Cities? Urban Struggles for Livelihood and Sustainability* (Berkeley: University of California Press, 2002).

6 Rogerson, "Globalization or Informalization?"

7 Charles Gore, *Social Exclusion and Africa South of the Sahara: A Review of the Literature* (Geneva: International Institute for Labor Studies, 1994).

8 Kinuthia MacHaria, *Social and Political Dynamics of the Informal Economy in African Cities: Nairobi and Harare* (Washington, D.C.: University Press of America, 1997).

9 Sethuraman, *Africa's Informal Economy.*

10 Ibid.

11 International Labor Organization, Jobs and Skills Program for Africa, *African Employment Report 1992* (Addis Ababa: ILO, 1992).

12 Gore, *Social Exclusion and Africa South of the Sahara.*

13 Richard Maclure, *Overlooked and Undervalued: A Synthesis of Educational Research Network for West and Central Africa, Reviews on the State of Education and Research in West and Central Africa* (Washington, D.C.: Support for Analysis and Research in Africa, United States Agency for International Development, 1997).

14 Claire Robertson, "Women Entrepreneurs? Trade and Gender Division of Labor in Nairobi," in *African Entrepreneurship: Theory and Reality*, ed. Anita Spring and Barbara McDade (Gainesville: University Press of Florida, 1998).

15 Judith Krieger, "Entrepreneurs and Family Well-Being: Agriculture and Trading Households in Cameroon," in *African Entrepreneurship: Theory and Reality*, ed. Anita Spring and Barbara McDade (Gainesville: University Press of Florida, 1998).

16 John Sender and Sheila Smith, *Poverty, Class, and Gender in Rural Africa: A Tanzanian Case Study* (London: Routledge, 1990).

17 Rogerson, "Globalization or Informalization?"

18 Claire Robertson, "Traders and Urban Struggle: Ideology and the Creation of a Female Militant Underclass in Nairobi, 1960–1990," *Journal of Women's History* 4 (1993): 9–42.

19 Tripp, *Changing the Rules.*

2 The Invisible: Winterveld, South Africa

1 Mahmood Mamdani, *Citizen and Subject: Contemporary Africa and the Legacy of Late Colonialism* (Princeton: Princeton University Press, 1996).

2 Catherine Coquery-Vidrovitch, "The Process of Urbanization in Africa," *African Studies Review* 34 (1991): 1–98.

3 André Horn, "How Many People Are There in Winterveld? What a Proper Census Should Show," *Urban Forum* 8 (1996): 117–32.

4 National Building Research Institute, *Winterveld: A Population Survey* (Pretoria, NBRI, 1981).

5 Teddy Matsetela, "The Informal Sector in the Political Economy of Winterveld" (master's thesis, University of Witwatersrand, 1979).

6 Settlement Planning Services, *Southern Odi-Moretele Development Appraisal: Volume 2: Technical Appendices* (Pretoria: SPS, 1991).

7 NBRI, *Population Survey.*
8 Van Zyl, Attwell and de Kock, "Winterveld Structure Plan," Johannesburg, 1984.
9 NBRI, *Population Survey.*
10 Republic of Bophuthatswana, *Winterveld: A Socio-Economic Survey and Preliminary Development Guideline* (Mbatho: Republic of Bophuthatswana, 1987).
11 Centre for Development and Enterprise, *Displaced Urbanization: Definition, Methodology, and Eight Locality Studies* (Johannesburg: CDE, 1997).
12 Van Zyl, Attwell and de Kock "Winterveld Structure Plan."
13 The exchange rate has changed significantly since that time; in 2000 US$1 = R7, approximately.
14 Joint Government Investigation, "Proposed Upgrading Strategy 1981."
15 Development Bank of Southern Africa, *Winterveld Agency Program Report* (Midrand: DBSA, 1987).
16 Joint Government Investigation, *Proposed Upgrading Strategy.*
17 Commission for Justice and Peace, Archdiocese of Pretoria and the Winterveld Action Committee of the Pretoria Council of Churches, "A Profile of Winterveld," December 1983.
18 Development Bank of Southern Africa, *Winterveld Agency Program Report.*
19 Assessments of the Development Bank of Southern Africa, focus group of February 3, 1997.
20 Development Bank of Southern Africa, *Winterveld Agency Program Report.*
21 Ibid.
22 National Building Research Institute, *Winterveld: A Socio-Economic Survey* (Pretoria: NBRI, 1989).
23 African Medical and Research Foundation and the Northwest Province Department of Human and Social Welfare, *Baseline Survey of Winterveld: An Informal Urban Settlement* (Pretoria: AMRF, 1994).
24 Markdata (PTY) LTD, *The Displaced Urbanization of the Apartheid Era: Its Current Consequences, A Focused Interview Survey in Six Areas* (Johannesburg: Markdata, 1997).
25 Settlement Planning Services, *Southern Odi-Moretele Development Appraisal; Volume 1: Household Socio-Economic Conditions* (Pretoria: SPS, 1991).
26 Centre for Development and Enterprise, *Displaced Urbanization.*
27 Based on my counting of enterprises marked with signs.
28 National Building Research Institute, *Winterveld: A Socio-Economic Survey.*
29 Ibid.
30 Barbara Harriss-White, "Informal Economic Order: Shadow States, Private Status States, States of Last Resort, and Spinning States — a Speculative Discussion on South Asian Case Material," QEH working paper, QEHWUS06, Oxford University, 1997.

31 Jean-Phillipe Platteau, "Behind the Market Stage Where Real Societies Exist: The Role of Private and Public Order Institutions," *Journal of Development Studies* 35 (1994): 533–78.

32 Maxine Reitzes and Sivuyile Bam, "One Foot In, One Foot Out: Immigrants and Civil Society in the Winterveld," research report no. 51, Social Policy Series, Center for Policy Studies, Johannesburg, 1996.

33 Much of this information stems from the ethnographic work of Paul Thulare of the Centre for Policy Studies, who conducted fieldwork among Mozambican residents in Winterveld during 1996, which in turn formed the basis of much of the report compiled by Reitzes and Bam, "One Foot In."

34 Development Bank of Southern Africa, focus group of February 3, 1998.

35 This is the point of view expressed by the Northwest Province Department of Local Government and Housing.

36 This financial information is derived from the document "A Report on the Financial Viability of Winterveld TRC," which was prepared by the Northwest Province Department of Local Government, Housing, Planning and Development exclusively for my research for this chapter.

37 Palmer Development Group, "Financial and Institutional Overview of Water Supply Arrangements in Urban Areas," a report for the Water Research Commission, Pretoria, 1993.

38 Palmer Development Group, "Winterveld: Case Study of Informal Water Supply Arrangements," a report for the Water Research Commission, Pretoria, 1994.

3 The Spectral: Assembling Douala, Cameroon

1 Roger Simon, Mario DiPaolantonio, and Mark Clamen, "Remembrance as Praxis and the Ethos of the Inter-Human," *Cultural Machine* 4 (2000), available at http://culturemachine.tees.ac.uk/Cmach/Backissues/j004/Articles/Simon.htm.

2 Avery Gordon, *Ghostly Matters: Haunting and the Sociological Imagination* (Minneapolis: University of Minnesota Press, 1996).

3 Alice Conklin, *A Mission to Civilize: The Republican Idea of Empire in France and West Africa, 1895–1930* (Stanford: Stanford University Press, 1997); James Ferguson, *Expectations of Modernity: Myths and Meanings of Urban Life on the Zambian Copperbelt* (Berkeley: University of California Press, 1999); Brian Raftopolous and Tsueneo Yoshikuni, eds., *Sites of Struggle: Essays in Zimbabwe's Urban History* (Harare: Weaver Press, 1999): Filip De Boeck, "Borderland Breccia: The Mutant Hero and the Historical Imagination of a Central-African Diamond Frontier," *Journal of Colonialism and Colonial History* 1 (2000): 1–44.

4 Nicholas Thomas, *Colonialism's Culture* (Princeton: Princeton University Press, 1994).

5 Malam, interview by author, New Bell, Douala, July 17, 2002.

4 Movement: The *Zawiyyah* as the City

1 Nikolas Papastergiadis, *The Turbulence of Migration* (Cambridge: Polity Press, 2000).

2 Uma Kothari, "Migration and Chronic Poverty," working paper no. 16, Institute for Development Policy and Management, University of Manchester, 2002. Gunnar Malmberg, "Time and Space in International Migration," in *International Migration, Immobility, and Development: Multidisciplinary Perspectives*, ed. Tomas Hammar, Grete Brochman, Kristof Tamas, and Thomas Faist (Oxford: Berg, 1997).

3 Phil Marfleet, "Migration and the Refugee Experience," in *Globalisation and the Third World*, ed. Ray Kiely and Phil Marfleet (London: Routledge, 1998).

4 Christine Oppong, "African Family Systems and Socio-Economic Crisis," in *Family, Population, and Development in Africa*, ed. Aderanti Adepoju (London: Zed, 1997).

5 Aderanti Adepoju, "Regional Integration, Continuity, and Changing Patterns of Intraregional Migration in Sub-Saharan Africa," in *International Migration into the Twenty-First Century*, ed. Mohamed Abubakr Siddique (Aldershot: Edward Elgar Publishing, 2000).

6 Regarding subsistence needs, see Jean-Marie Cour and Serge Snrech. *Preparing for the Future: A Vision of West Africa in the Year 2020. West African Long-Term Prospective Study* (Paris: OECD/Club du Sahel, 1998).

7 Savina Ammassari and Richard Black, *Harnessing the Potential of Migration and Return to Promote Development: Applying Concepts to West Africa* (Sussex: Sussex Centre for Migration Research, University of Sussex, 2001).

8 Dennis Cordell, Joel Gregory, and Victor Peché, *Hoe and Wage: A Social History of a Circular Migration System in West Africa* (Boulder: Westview, 1996).

9 John Hanson, "Islam, Migration, and the Political Economy of Meaning: *Fergo Nioro* from the Senegalese River Valley, 1862–1890," *Journal of African History* 35 (1994): 37–60.

10 Thomas Faist, *The Volume and Dynamics of International Migration and Transnational Social Spaces* (Oxford: Clarendon, 2000).

11 Jörgen Carling, "Migration in the Age of Involuntary Immobility: Theoretical Reflections and Cape Verdean Experiences," *Journal of Ethnic and Migration Studies* 28 (2002): 3–42.

12 Luis Eduardo Guarnizo and Michael Smith, "The Locations of Transnationalism," in *Transnationalism from Below*, ed. Michael Smith and Luis Eduardo Guarnizo (New Brunswick, N.J.: Transaction, 1998).

13 Oliver Bakewell, "Returning Refugees or Migrating Villages? Voluntary Repatriation Programmes in Africa Reconsidered," *New Issues in Refugee Research*, working paper 15, United Nations High Commission on Refugees, 2000; Saskia Van Hooyweghen, "Sovereignty in Postcolonial Tanzania," *New Issues in Refugee Research*, working paper 49, United Nations High Commission on Refugees, 2001.

14 Jeff Crisp, "Africa's Refugees: Patterns, Problems, and Policy Challenges," *Journal of Contemporary African Studies* 18 (2000): 157–68.

15 Mariane Ferme, *The Underneath of Things: Violence, History, and the Everyday in Sierra Leone* (Berkeley: University of California Press, 2001).

16 Mervyn Hiskett, *The Development of Islam in West Africa* (London: Longman, 1984).

17 Robert Launay and Benjamin Soares, "The Formation of an 'Islamic Sphere' in French Colonial West Africa," *Economy and Society* 28 (1999): 497–519.

5 Reconciling Engagement and Belonging: Some Matters of History

1 David Anderson and Richard Rathbone, "Urban Africa: Histories in the Making," in *Africa's Urban Past*, ed. David Anderson and Richard Rathbone (Portsmouth, N.H.: Heinemann; Oxford: James Currey, 2000).

2 William Bascom, "The Urban African and His World," in *Perspectives on the African Past*, ed. M. A. Klein and G. W. Johnson (Boston: Little, Brown, 1972).

3 J. R. Rayfield, "Theories of Urbanization and the Colonial City in West Africa," *Africa* 44 (1974): 163–85.

4 A. J. Christopher and James Tarver, "Urbanization During Colonial Days in Sub-Saharan Africa," in *Urbanization in Africa*, ed. James Tarver (Westport, Conn.: Greenwood Press, 1994).

5 H. Max Miller and Ram Singh, "Urbanization during Postcolonial Days," in *Urbanization in Africa*, ed. James Tarver (Westport, Conn.: Greenwood Press, 1994).

6 Jerry Erbach and John Gaudet, *Urbanization Issues and Development in Sub-Saharan Africa* (Washington, D.C.: Africa Bureau, United States Agency for International Development, 1998).

7 Ademolou Salau, "The Urban Process in Africa: Observations on the Points of Divergence from the Western Experience," *African Urban Studies* 4 (1979): 27–34.

8 Anthony O'Connor, *The African City* (New York: Africana Publishing Company, 1983).

9 Keith Hart, *Political Economy of West African Agriculture* (Cambridge: Cambridge University Press, 1982).

10 O'Connor, *The African City*.

11 Abdou Salam Fall, "Migrants' Long Distance Relationships and Social Networks in Dakar," *Environment and Urbanization* 10 (1998): 135–45.

12 David T. Goldberg, " 'Polluting the Body Politic': Racist Discourse and Urban Location," in *Racism, the City, and the State*, ed. Malcolm Cross and Michael Keith (London: Routledge, 1993).

13 Anthony King, *Urbanism, Colonialism, and the World Economy: Cultural and Spatial Foundations of the World Urban System* (London: Routledge, 1991).

14 Ibid.

15 Fred Cooper, "Conflict and Connection: Rethinking Colonial African History," *American Historical Review* 99 (1994): 1530.

16 Ralph Austen and Rita Headrick, "Equitorial Africa under Colonial Rule," in *History of Central Africa*, vol. 2, ed. David Birmingham and Phyllis Martin (London: Longman, 1983).

17 Ibid.

18 Mamadou Diouf, "The French Colonial Policy of Assimilation and the Civility of the Originaires of the Four Communes (Senegal): A Nineteenth Century Globalization Project," *Development and Change* 29 (1998): 671–96.

19 Fred Cooper, *Decolonization and the African Society: The Labor Question in French and British Africa* (Cambridge: Cambridge University Press, 1996).

20 Anthony Hopkins, *An Economic History of West Africa* (New York: Columbia University Press, 1973).

21 Ibid.

22 Pels, *A Politics of Presence*.

23 Jane Guyer, "Introduction: The Currency Interface and Its Dynamics," in *Money Matters: Instability, Values, and Social Payments in the Modern History of West African Communities*, ed. Jane Guyer (Portsmouth, N.H.: Heinemann; Oxford: James Currey, 1995).

24 Ibid.

25 Wambui Mwangi, "Conquest: The East African Currency Board, the Rupee Crisis, and the Problem of Colonialism in the East African Protectorate," a paper presented at the annual meeting of the African Studies Association, Philadelphia, November 11, 1999.

26 Cooper, *Decolonization and the African Society*.

27 Hopkins, *An Economic History of West Africa*.

28 Ibid.

29 Ibid.

30 Ayodeji Olukoju, "The Cost of Living in Lagos, 1914–1945," in *Africa's Urban Past*, ed. David Anderson and Richard Rathbone (Portsmouth, N.H.: Heinemann; Oxford: James Currey, 2000).

31 Cooper, *Decolonization and the African Society*.

32 Ibid.

33 Bruce Kapferer, "Structural Marginality and the Urban Social Order," *Urban Anthropology* 7 (1978): 287–317.

34 Ibid.

35 Ibid.

36 Fred Cooper, "Urban Space, Industrial Time, and Wage Labor in Africa," in *Struggle for the City: Migrant Labor, Capital, and the State in Urban Africa*, ed. Fred Cooper (Beverly Hills: Sage, 1983), 35.

37 Ibid.

38 Richard Joseph, "Settlers, Strikers, and *Sans Travail*: The Douala Riots of September 1945," *Journal of African History* 15 (1974): 669–87.

39 Ibid.

40 Hopkins, *An Economic History of West Africa.*

41 Cooper, *Decolonization and the African Society.*

42 Austen and Headrick, "Equitorial Africa under Colonial Rule."

43 Hopkins, *An Economic History of West Africa.*

44 Jim Glassman and Abdi Samatar "Development Geography and the Third-World State," *Progress in Human Geography* 21 (1997): 164–98.

45 Cooper, *Decolonization and African Society.*

46 Ibid., 458–61.

47 Ibid.

48 Hopkins, *An Economic History of West Africa.*

49 Gwendolyn Wright, *The Politics of Design in French Colonial Urbanism* (Chicago: University of Chicago Press, 1991).

50 Ibid.

51 Odile Goerg, "From Hill Station (Freetown) to Downtown Conakry (First Ward): Comparing French and British Approaches to Segregation in Colonial Cities at the Beginning of the Twentieth Century," *Canadian Journal of African Studies* 32 (1998): 1–31.

52 King, *Urbanism, Colonialism, and the World Economy.*

53 Phyllis Martin, *Leisure and Society in Colonial Brazzaville* (Cambridge: Cambridge University Press, 1995).

54 Joseph Uyanga, "Urban Planning Strategy in Nigeria: The Institutional Policy Perspective," *African Urban Studies* (1979): 49–58.

55 Wright, *The Politics of Design in French Colonial Urbanism.*

56 Akin Mabogunje, "Urban Planning and the Post-Colonial State in Africa: A Research Overview," *African Studies Review* 33 (1990): 121–203.

57 Regarding the validation of historical processes, see Mouriba Touré, "Population, Urbanization, and Migration in Africa," in *Population Growth and Sustainable Development,* ed. African Development Bank (Abidjan: African Development Bank, 1994).

58 Michael Cohen, *Urban Policy and Political Conflict in Africa: A Study of the Ivory Coast* (Chicago: University of Chicago Press, 1974).

59 Richard Stren, "Institutional Arrangements," in *Strengthening Local Government in Sub-Saharan Africa,* ed. Economic Development Institute (Washington, D.C.: World Bank, 1989).

60 Mabogunje, "Urban Planning and the Post-Colonial State," 123.

61 Mamdani, *Citizen and Subject.*

62 D. M. Boswell, "Personal Crisis and the Mobilization of a Social Network," in *Social Networks in Urban Situations: Analyses of Personal Relationships in Central African Towns,* ed. J. Clyde Mitchell (Manchester: Manchester University Press, 1969).

63 René Clignet, "Urbanization and Family Structure in the Ivory Coast," *Comparative Studies in Society and History* 8 (1966): 385–401.

64 Terrence Ranger, *Dance and Society in Eastern Africa, 1890–1970: The Beni Ngoma* (Berkeley: University of California Press, 1975).

65 Jean La Fontaine, *City Politics: A Study of Leopoldville, 1962–63.* (London: Cambridge University Press, 1970).

66 Patrick Cole, *Modern and Traditional Elites in the Politics of Lagos* (London: Cambridge University Press, 1975).

67 William Hanna, and Judith Hanna, *Urban Dynamics in Black Africa*, 2nd ed. (New York: Aldine, 1981).

68 Lawrence Frank, "Ideological Competition in Nigeria: Urban Populism versus Ethnic Nationalism," *Journal of Modern African Studies* 17 (1974): 433–52.

69 Tripp, *Changing the Rules*.

70 Karen Hansen, "Budgeting against Uncertainty: Cross-Class and Transethnic Redistribution Mechanisms in Urban Zambia," *African Urban Studies* 21 (1985): 65–73.

71 Lugalla, *Crisis, Urbanization, and Urban Poverty in Tanzania*, 118.

72 Ibid.

73 World Bank, *Adjustment in Africa: Reforms, Results, and the Road Ahead* (Washington, D.C.: World Bank, 1994).

74 Based on household interviews conducted in eight cities on a project comparing local governance strategies conducted by the African NGO Habitat Caucus.

75 Josephine Olu Abiodun, "The Challenges of Growth and Development in Metropolitan Lagos," in *The Urban Challenge in Africa: Growth and Management of Its Large Cities*, ed. Carole Rakodi (Tokyo: United Nations University Press, 1997).

76 Peter Geschiere, *The Modernity of Witchcraft: Politics and the Occult in Postcolonial Africa* (Charlottesville: University of Virginia Press, 1997).

77 Ian Hamilton Grant, "At the Mountain of Madness: The Demonology of the New Earth and the Politics of Becoming," in *Deleuze and Philosophy: The Difference Engineer*, ed. Keith Ansell-Pearson (New York: Routledge, 1997).

78 Geschiere, *The Modernity of Witchcraft*; Harry West, "Creative Destruction and Sorcery of Construction: Power, Hope, and Suspicion in Post-War Mozambique," *Cahiers d'études africaines* 37 (1997): 675–98.

79 Coquery-Vidrovitch, "The Process of Urbanization in Africa."

80 Eleanor Fapohunda, "Urban Women's Roles and Nigerian Government Development Strategy," in *Sex Roles, Population, and Development in West Africa: Studies on Work and Demographic Issues*, ed. Christine Oppong (London: Heinemann, 1987); Jane Guyer, "Feeding Yaounde," in *Feeding African Cities*, ed. Jane Guyer (Manchester: Manchester University Press, 1987); Robertson, "Traders and Urban Struggle"; and Akosua Ampoto, "Controlling and Punishing Women in Ghana," *Review of African Political Economy* 56 (1994): 102–10.

81 Emmanuel Akyeampong, "Sexuality and Prostitution among the Akan of the Gold Coast, c. 1650–1950," *Past and Present* 156 (1997): 144–73; Carole Levin, Daniel Maxwell, Margaret Amar-Klemesu, Marie Ruel, and Saul Morris, "Working Women in an Urban Setting: Traders, Vendors, and Food Security in Accra," *World Development* 27 (1997): 1977–96.
82 Beth Ahlberg, "Is There a Distinct African Sexuality? A Response to Caldwell," *Africa* 64 (1994): 220–42.
83 Yvette Monga, "A Historical Perspective on African Entrepreneurship: Lessons from the Duala Experience in Cameroon," *African Entrepreneurship: Theory and Reality*, ed. Anita Spring and Barbara McDade (Gainesville: University Press of Florida, 1998).
84 John Caldwell, I. O. Orubuloya, and Pat Caldwell, "The Destabilization of the Traditional Yoruba Sexual System," *Population and Development Review* 17 (1991): 229–62.
85 Robertson, *Trouble Showed the Way.*
86 Ibid.
87 Ibid.
88 Ibid., 73.
89 Martin, *Leisure and Society in Colonial Brazzaville.*
90 La Fontaine, *City Politics.*
91 Martin, *Leisure and Society in Colonial Brazzaville.*
92 David Clark, "Unregulated Housing, Vested Interest, and the Development of Community Identity in Nairobi," *African Urban Studies* 3 (1979): 33–46.

6 The Production and Management of Urban Resources

1 Richard Stren, *Urban Research in the Developing World; Volume 2: Africa* (Toronto: Centre for Urban and Community Studies, University of Toronto, 1994); Patricia McCarney, *Cities and Governance: New Directions in Latin America, Asia, and Africa* (Toronto: Centre for Urban and Community Studies, University of Toronto, 1996).
2 Richard Stren and Rodney White, eds., *African Cities in Crisis: Managing Rapid Urban Growth* (Boulder: Westview, 1986).
3 Franklin Cardy, "Environment and Forced Migration: A Review," in *Human Impact on the Environment: Sustainable Development in Africa*, ed. Michael B. K. Darkoh and Apollo Rwomire (Oxford: Ashgate, 2002).
4 Musifiky Mwanasali, "The View from Below," in *Greed and Grievance: Economic Agendas in Civil Wars*, ed. Mats Berdal and David Malone (Boulder: Lynne Rienner Publishers, 1999); Mark Duffield, "Post-Modern Conflict: Warlords, Post-Adjustment States, and Private Protection," *Civil Wars* 1 (1998): 66–102.
5 Ferguson, *Expectations of Modernity*, 232.
6 Bucyalimwe Mararo, "Land, Power, and Ethnic Conflict in Masisi, 1940s–1994," *International Journal of African Historical Studies* 30 (1997): 503–37.

7   Christine Tacoli, "Changing Rural-Urban Interactions in Sub-Saharan Africa and Their Impact on Livelihoods: A Summary," *Working Paper Series on Rural-Urban Interactions and Livelihood Strategies*, no. 7, London, 2002. International Institute for Environment and Development, London, 2002.

8   Deborah Bryceson, "Sub-Saharan Africa: Betwixt and Between," de-agrarian-isation and rural employment research project, African Studies Centre, University of Leiden, 1999; Deborah Bryceson, "Multiplex Livelihoods in Rural Africa: Recasting the Terms and Conditions of Gainful Employment," *Journal of Modern African Studies* 40 (2002): 1–28; Elizabeth Francis, *Making a Living: Changing Livelihoods in Rural Africa* (London: Routledge, 2000).

9   Berry, "Stable Prices, Unstable Values."

10 Liz Alden Wiley, "Reconstructing the African Commons," *Africa Today* (2001): 77–99.

11 Tacoli, "Changing Rural-Urban Interactions."

12 Sally Findley, "Migration and Family Interaction in Africa," in *Family, Population, and Development in Africa*, ed. Aderanti Adepoju (London: Zed, 1997).

13 Mirjam de Bruijn, Rijk van Dijk, and Dick Foeken, eds., *Mobile Africa* (Leiden: Brill, 2001); Gertrude Schrieder and Bèatrice Knerr, "Labour Migration as a Social Security Mechanism for Smallholder Households in Sub-Saharan Africa," *Oxford Development Studies* 28 (2000): 223–36.

14 Arjan de Haan, Johann Kirsten, and Juliana Rwelamira, "Migration and Rural Assets: Evidence from Surveys in Three Semi-Arid Regions in South Africa, India, and Botswana," Poverty Research Unit, Institute of Development Studies, University of Sussex, 2000, available at http://www.sussex.ac.uk/Unites/PRU/migrationandruralassets.pdf.

15 Ton Dietz and Fred Zaal, "The Provisioning of African Cities, with a Case Study of Ouagadougou," in *Re-Aligning Government, Civil Society, and the Market: New Challenges in Urban and Regional Development. Essays in Honour of G. A. de Bruijne*, ed. Isa Baud, Johan Post, Leo de Haan, and Ton Dietz (Amsterdam: AGIDS, 2001); Adriana Allen, "Environmental Planning and the Management of the Periurban Interface," paper presented at the conference "Rural-Urban Encounters: Managing the Environment of the Periurban Interface," London, November 9–10, 2001.

16 Bryceson, "Sub-Saharan Africa."

17 Sara Berry, "Tomatoes, Land, and Hearsay: Property and History in Asante in the Time of Structural Adjustment," *World Development* 25 (1997): 1225–41; Kate Meagher, *The Bargain Sector: Economic Restructuring and the Nonfarm Sector in the Nigerian Savannah* (Aldershot: Ashgate, 2001).

18 Tim Kelsall, "Governance, Local Politics, and Districtization in Tanzania: The 1998 Arumeru Tax Revolt," *African Affairs* 99 (2000): 533–51.

19 Thomas Reardon, "Using Evidence of Household Income Diversification to Inform Study of the Rural Nonfarm Labor Market in Africa," *World Development* 25 (1997): 735–48.

20 Christopher B. Barrett, Thomas Reardon, and Patrick Webb, "Nonfarm Income Diversification and Household Livelihood Strategies in Rural Africa: Concepts, Dynamics, and Policy Implications," *Food Policy* 25 (2001): 315–31.

21 Reardon, "Using Evidence of Household Income Diversification."

22 Jennifer Leavy and Howard White, "Rural Labour Markets and Poverty in Sub-Saharan Africa," Institute of Development Studies, University of Sussex, 2000, available at http://www.ids.ac.uk.ids.pvty/pdf-files/rurallabourinssa.pdf.

23 World Bank, "Living on Fragile Lands: Inclusion, Innovation, and Migration," in *World Development Report 2003: Sustainable Development in a Dynamic Economy* (Washington, D.C.: World Bank, 2003).

24 Central Intelligence Agency, *World Fact Book 1998* (Washington, D.C.: GPO, 1998).

25 Food and Agricultural Organization of the United Nations, *HIV/AIDS, Agriculture, and Food Security in Mainland and Small Island Countries of Africa: Twenty-Second Regional Conference for Africa, Cairo, 4–8 February 2002* (Rome: FAO, United Nations, 2002).

26 Hasan Solomon, "Emigration Dynamics in Southern Africa," Unit of African Studies Working Papers, University of Pretoria, 2000.

27 Jens Andersson, "Reintegrating the Rural-Urban Connection: Migration Practices and Sociocultural Dispositions of Buhera Workers in Harare," *Africa* 71 (2001): 81–111.

28 Harri Englund, "The Village in the City, the City in the Village: Migrants in Lilongwe," *Journal of Southern African Studies* 28 (2002): 137–59.

29 Ferguson, *Expectations of Modernity*; Barth Chukwuezi, "Through Thick and Thin: Igbo Rural-Urban Circularity, Identity, and Investment," *Journal of Contemporary African Studies* 19 (2001): 55–66.

30 Ibrahim Elbadawi and Benno Ndulu, "Long Run Development and Sustainable Growth in Sub-Saharan Africa," in *New Directions in Development Economics*, ed. M. Lundahl and B. Ndulu (London: Routledge, 1996).

31 Economic Commission for Africa. *African Economic Report 1998* (Addis Ababa: Economic Commission for Africa, 1998).

32 Collier and Gunning, "Explaining African Economic Performance."

33 Economic Commission for Africa, *African Economic Report 1998*.

34 African Development Bank Group, *African Development Report, 1998* (Abidjan: African Development Bank, 1998).

35 Ibid.

36 Ibid.

37 Ibid.

38 Collier and Gunning, "Explaining African Economic Performance."

39 Ibid.

40 Jean-Paul Azam and Christian Morrison, *The Political Feasibility of Adjust-*

ment in Côte d'Ivoire (Paris: Development Centre, OECD, 1994); Deryke Belshaw, Peter Lawrence, and Michael Hubbard, "A Decade of Structural Adjustment in Uganda: Agricultural Tradables, Rural Poverty, and Macroeconomic 'success,'" in *The Market Panacea: Agrarian transformation in the LDC's and Former Socialist Economies*, ed. Max Spoor (London: International Technology Publications, 1994).

41 Economic Commission for Africa, *Economic Report on Africa 1998.*

42 Lou Schalpen and Peter Gibbon, with Paul Ove Pederson. *Africa's Real Private Sector* (Copenhagen: Centre for Development Research, 2001).

43 Economic Commission for Africa, *Economic Report on Africa 1999* (Addis Ababa: Economic Commission for Africa, 1999).

44 Ernest Aryeety and Machiko Nissanke, "Asia and Africa in the Global Economy: Economic Policies and External Performance in South-East Asia and Sub-Saharan Africa," a paper presented at the conference "Asia and Africa in the Global Economy," United Nations University–African Economic Research Consortium, Tokyo, August 3–4, 1998.

45 Mkandawire and Soludo, *Our Continent, Our Future.*

46 Ibid.

47 W. F. Banyikwa, "The Making of a Hybrid Millionaire City: Dar es Salaam, Tanzania," *African Urban Quarterly* 4 (1989): 228–51.

48 Adrien Wood and Jörg Mayer, *Africa's Export Structure in Comparative Perspective* (Geneva: United Nations Conference on Trade and Development, 1998); B. Lynne Salinger, "Productivity, Comparative Advantage, and Competitiveness in Africa," African Economic Policy Discussion Paper, no. 35, Equity and Growth through Economic Research Program, United States Agency for International Development, Washington, D.C., 2001.

49 World Bank, *World Development Report 1999: Entering the Twenty-First Century* (Washington, D.C.: World Bank, 1999).

50 Wilbert Goonaratne and Robert Obudho, eds., *Contemporary Issues in Regional Development Policy: Perspectives from Eastern and Southern Africa* (Aldershot: Averbury, 1997).

51 Catherine Farvacque-Vitkovic and Luc Godin, *The Future of African Cities: Challenges and Priorities for Urban Development* (Washington, D.C.: World Bank, 1998).

52 Ibid.

53 Demba Niang, Bouna Warr, Laurent Bossard, and Jean-Marie Cour, "The Local Economy of St. Louis and the Senegal River Delta," Club du Sahel, OECD, and the Municipal Development Program, 1997, available at http://wblnoo18.worldbank.org/ . . ./$File/D98471a.doc.

54 Ibid.

55 Farvacque-Vitkovic and Godin, *The Future of African Cities.*

56 African Regional Office, World Bank, "Project Appraisal Document in a Proposed Credit in the Amount of SDR 12.9 Million (U.S. 18 Million Equiv-

alent) to the Republic of Guinea for a Third Urban Development Project in the Support of the First Phase of the Third Urban Development Program," World Bank, Washington, D.C., 1999.

57 Alain Dubresson, "Abidjan: From the Public Making of a Modern City to the Urban Management of a Metropolis," in *The Urban Challenge in Africa: Growth and the Management of Its Large Cities*, ed. Carole Rakodi (Tokyo: United Nations University Press, 1997).

58 Farvacque-Vitkovic and Godin, *The Future of African Cities*; Odd-Helge Fjelstad and Joseph Semboja, "Dilemmas of Fiscal Decentralisation: A Study of Local Government Taxation in Tanzania," *Forum for Development Studies* 27 (2000): 7–41.

59 Margaret Peil, *Lagos: The City Is the People* (Boston: G. K. Hall and Co., 1991).

60 Alain Durand-Lasserve, "Researching the Relationship between Economic Liberalisation and Changes to the Land Markets and Land Prices," in *Methodology for Land and Housing Market Analysis*, ed. Garth Jones and Peter Ward (London: UCL, 1991).

61 Akin Mabogunje, "Urban Land and Urban Management Policies in Sub-Saharan Africa," *Urban Perspectives* 4 (1994): 35–60.

62 Dessalegn Rahmato and Arkilu Kidanu, 2001. *Consultation with the Poor: A Study to Inform the World Development Report 2000/01 on Poverty and Development (National Report, Ethiopia)* (Washington, D.C.: World Bank, 2001).

63 Richard Stren, *Housing the Urban Poor in Africa: Policy, Politics, and Bureaucracy in Mombasa* (Berkeley: Institute of International Studies, University of California, 1978; James Campbell, "Urbanization, Culture, and the Politics of Urban Development in Ghana, 1875–1985," *Urban Anthropology* 23 (1994): 409–50.

64 Tunde Agbola and A. M. Jinadu, "Forced Eviction and Forced Relocation in Nigeria: The Experience of Those Evicted from Maroko in 1990," *Environment and Urbanization* 9 (1997): 271–88.

65 Ibid.

66 Jean-Luc Piermay, "Kinshasa: A Reprieved Mega City?" in *The Urban Challenge in Africa: Growth and Management of Its Large Cities*, ed. Carole Rakodi (Tokyo: United Nations University Press, 1997).

67 Ibid.

68 Peil, *Lagos*.

69 D. R. Aronson, "Capitalism and Culture in Ibadan Urban Development," *Urban Anthropology* 7 (1978): 253–64.

70 Ibid.

71 James Sidaway and Michael Power, "Sociospatial Transformations in the 'Postsocialist' Periphery: The Case of Maputo, Mozambique," *Environment and Planning A* 27 (1995): 1463–91.

72 Peil, *Lagos*.

73 J. M. Lusugga Kironde, "Access to Land by the Urban Poor in Tanzania: Some Findings from Dar es Salaam," *Environment and Urbanization* 7 (1995): 77–96; Maurizio Tiepolo, "Brazzaville: A City Profile," *Cities* 13 (1998): 117–24; Ambe Njoh, "The Political Economy of Urban Land Reform in a Post Colonial State," *International Journal of Urban and Regional Research* 22 (1998): 409–23; Tumsifu Nnkya, "Land Use Planning and Practice under the Public Land Ownership Policy in Tanzania," *Habitat International* 23 (1999): 135–55.

74 Donald Williams, "Measuring the Impact of Land Reform Policy in Nigeria," *Journal of Modern African Studies* 30 (1992): 587–608.

75 Ben Arimah, "The Determinants of Housing Tenure Choice in Ibadan, Nigeria," *Urban Studies* 34 (1997): 105–24.

76 Williams, "Measuring the Impact of Land Reform Policy in Nigeria."

77 S. B. Garba, "Public Land Ownership and Urban Land Management Effectiveness in Metropolitan Kano, Nigeria," *Habitat International* 2 (1997): 305–17.

78 Johan Post, "The Politics of Urban Planning in the Sudan," *Habitat International* 20 (1996): 121–37.

79 Cour and Snrech, *Preparing for the Future.*

80 Dubresson, "Abidjan," 276.

81 Phillipe Antoine and Aka Kouame, "Côte d'Ivoire," in *Urbanization in Africa: A Handbook*, ed. James D. Tarver (Westport, Conn.: Greenwood Press, 1994), 135–52.

82 Dubresson, "Abidjan."

83 Graham Tipple and Ken Willis, "Tenure Choice in a West African City," *Third World Planning Review* 13 (1991): 27–45; United Nations Center on Human Settlements, *An Urbanizing World: Global Report on Human Settlements, 1996* (Oxford: Oxford University Press, 1996).

84 Antoine and Kouame, "Côte d'Ivoire."

85 Alphonse Yapi-Diahou, "The Informal Housing Sector of the Metropolis of Abidjan, Ivory Coast," *Environment and Urbanization* 7 (1995): 11–29.

86 Tade Akin Aina, "The Construction of Housing for the Urban Poor in Lagos," *Habitat International* 12 (1988): 31–44.

87 Demissachew Shiferaw, "Self-Initiated Transformation of Public-Provided Dwellings in Addis Ababa, Ethiopia," *Cities* 15 (1998): 437–48.

88 Graham Tipple, David Korboe, Ken Willis, and Guy Garrod, "Who Is Building What in Urban Ghana: Housing Supply in Three Towns," *Cities* 15 (1998): 399–416.

89 Ibid, 405.

90 Peil, *Lagos*, 72.

91 Ibid.

92 Personal communication, Babatunde Ahonsi, program officer, Ford Foundation, Lagos.

93 Vincent Ogu, "The Dynamics of Informal Housing in a Traditional West

African City: The Benin City Example," *Third World Planning Review* 20 (1998): 419–38.

94 Ibid., 430.

95 Uche Ikejiofor, "The God That Failed: A Critique of Public Housing in Nigeria, 1975–1995," *Habitat International* 23 (1999): 177–88.

96 Ambe Njoh, "The State, Urban Development Policy, and Society in Cameroon," *Cities* 16 (1999): 117–24.

97 Winnie Mitullah and Kivutha Kibwana, "A Tale of Two Cities: Policy, Law, and Illegal Settlements in Kenya," in *Illegal Cities: Law and Urban Change in Developing Countries*, ed. Edesio Fernandes and Ann Varley (London: Zed, 1998).

98 Ibid.

99 World Bank, *World Development Report 1999*.

100 Salah El-Shakhs, "Toward Appropriate Urban Development Policy in Emerging Mega-Cities in Africa," in *The Urban Challenge in Africa: Growth and Management in Its Large Cities*, ed. Carole Rakodi (Tokyo: United Nations University Press, 1997).

101 Tipple et al., "Who Is Building What in Urban Ghana."

102 Graham Tipple and David Korboe, "Housing Policy in Ghana: Towards a Supply-Oriented Future," *Habitat International* 23 (1998): 245–57.

103 Berry, "Tomatoes, Land, and Hearsay."

104 Ibid.

105 Tade Akin Aina, "Land Tenure in Lagos," *Habitat International* 16 (1992): 3–15.

106 See AbdouMaliq Simone, *In Whose Image: Political Islam and Urban Practices in the Sudan* (Chicago: University of Chicago Press, 1994); Achille Mbembe and Janet Roitman, "Figures of the Subject in a Time of Crisis," in *The Geography of Identity*, ed. Patricia Yaeger (Ann Arbor: University of Michigan Press, 1996); Michael Schatzberg, "Alternative Causalities," in *Political Legitimacy in Middle Africa*, ed. Michael Schatzberg (Bloomington: Indiana University Press, 2001).

107 Neil Brenner, "Between Fixity and Motion: Accumulation, Territorial Organization and the Historical Geography of Spatial Scales," *Environment and Planning D: Society and Space* 16 (1998): 459–48.

108 This is the conclusion of a broad range of initial field study reports under the auspices of the MacArthur Foundation/Council for the Development of Social Science Research in Africa, Programme on Africa's Real Economies.

109 Jeffrey Herbst, "Responding to State Failure in Africa," *International Security* 21 (1996): 120–44.

110 Peter Lock, "Military Downsizing and Growth in the Security Industry in Sub-Saharan Africa," 1999. Available on the World Wide Web at http://www.idsa-india.org/an-dec8-10.html.

111 Béatrice Hibou, "The 'Social Capital' of the State as an Agent of Deception," in *The Criminalization of the State in Africa*, ed. Jean-François Bayart, Ste-

phen Ellis, and Béatrice Hibou (London: James Currey; Bloomington: Indiana University Press, 1999).

112 Paul Collier, "Doing Well Out of Civil War," a paper presented at conference on "Economic Agendas in Civil Wars," London, April 26–27, 1999.

113 Paul Collier, "On the Economic Consequences of Civil War," *Oxford Economic Papers* 51 (1999): 168–83; William Reno, *Warlord Politics and African States* (Boulder: Lynne Rienner Publishers, 1998).

114 Observatoire Geopolitique des Drogues, *World Geopolitics of Drugs*; Janet MacGaffey and Remy Bazenguissa-Ganga, *Congo-Paris: Transnational Traders on the Margins of the Law* (Bloomington: Indiana University Press, 2000).

115 Roitman, "The Garrison-Entrepôt."

116 Patsy Healey, Stuart Cameron, Simin Davoudi, and Ali Mandani-Pour, "Introduction: The City — Crisis, Change, and Invention," in *Managing Cities: The New Urban Context*, ed. Patsy Healey, Stuart Cameron, and Simin Davoudi, Stephen Graham, and Ali Mandani-Pour (New York: Wiley, 1995).

7 Cities and Change

1 See Neil Smith, "Homeless/Global: Scaling Places," in *Mapping the Futures: Local Cultures, Global Change*, ed. John Bird, Barry Curtis, Tim Putnam, George Robertson, and Lisa Tickner (New York: Routledge, 1993); Neil Brenner, "The Urban Question as a Scale Question: Reflections on Henri Lefebvre, Urban Theory, and the Politics of Scale," *International Journal of Urban and Regional Research* 24 (2000): 361–78.

2 At the workshop "The African Informal City," held at Gorèe Institute, Dakar, Senegal, on February 22–26, 1999, these questions were raised by Salimata Wade, Department of Geography, Chiek Anta Diop University, Dakar; Ousman Dembele, Department of Geography, University of Abidjan; Jean-Charles Tall, president of the Senegalese Association of Architects; and Bachir Olude, director of the School of Urbanization and Management, University of Benin.

3 Achille Mbembe, "Provisional Notes on the Postcolony," *Africa* 12 (2000): 259–84.

4 Emmanuel Eze, "Democracy or Consensus? A Response to Wiredu," in *Postcolonial African Philosophy*, ed. Emmanuel Eze (Oxford: Blackwell, 1997).

5 Peter Geschiere and Francis Nyamnjoh, "Capitalism and Autochthony: The Seesaw of Mobility and Belonging," *Public Culture* 12 (2000): 423–52.

6 Birgit Meyer, "Make a Complete Break with the Past: Memory and Postcolonial Modernity in Ghanaian Pentacostal Discourse," in *Memory and the Postcolony: African Anthropology and the Critique of Power*, ed. Richard Werbner (London: Zed, 1998).

7 Ibid.

8 Ruth Marshall-Fratani, "Mediating the Global and the Local in Nigerian Pentacostalism," *Journal of Religion in Africa* 28 (1998): 278–315.

9 Ibid.

10 Regarding the enactment of power, see Achille Mbembe, *On the Postcolony: Studies on the History of Society and Culture* (Berkeley: University of California Press, 2001).

11 Marshall-Fratani, "Mediating the Global and the Local in Nigerian Pentacostalism."

12 Mbembe, *On the Postcolony*. In contrast to Mbembe's critique of the postcolonial situation, and the role played by emerging national states, Thandika Mkandawire has a markedly different assessment of the extent to which national states did attempt to provide a content or character to emerging national space. Mkandawire argues incisively that states performed reasonably well in the decade of independence in terms of expediting development, not only in the delivery of development products but in attempting to transform national political and administrative apparatuses ill suited for the tasks of modernization. The scope of this work forced governments to push their budgets to the limit in order to address the costs of needed physical and social infrastructures and to configure viable social contracts in order to provide at least temporary frameworks of social cohesion. In attempting to recalibrate the financial viability of development, the political capacities of societies have been eroded, resulting in the imposition of disciplinary regimes that establish enclaves of fiscal administrative capacity distanced from real engagements with either local social processes or institutions (see Mkandawire, "Incentives, Governance, and Capacity Development in Africa").

13 Toyin Falola, *Violence in Nigeria: The Crisis of Religious Politics and Secular Ideologies* (Rochester: University of Rochester Press, 1998).

14 Brian Massumi, "The Politics of Everyday Fear," 1993, available at http://www.anu.edu.au/HRC/first_and_last works.

15 Peter Lloyd, Akin Mabogunje, and B. Awe, eds., *The City of Ibadan* (Cambridge: Cambridge University Press, 1967).

16 Sandra Barnes, "Voluntary Associations in a Metropolis: The Case of Lagos, Nigeria," *African Studies Review* 18 (1975): 75–87; Amy Patterson, "The Dynamic Nature of Citizenship and Participation: Lessons from Three Rural Senegalese Case Studies," *Africa Today* 46 (1999): 3–18; Arne Tostensen, Inge Tvedten, and Mariken Vaa, eds., *Associational Life in African Cities: Popular Responses to the Urban Crisis* (Upsala: Nordic Africa Institute, 2001).

17 Peter Garlick, *African Traders and Economic Development in Ghana* (Oxford: Clarendon, 1971).

18 Harold Wolpe, *Urban Politics in Nigeria* (Berkeley: University of California Press, 1974).

19 Joseph Gugler and William Flanagan, *Urbanization and Social Change in West Africa* (Cambridge: Cambridge University Press, 1978).

20 Enzo Mingione, *Fragmented Societies: A Sociology of Economic Life beyond the Market Paradigm* (Oxford: Basil Blackwell, 1991).

21 Zygmunt Bauman, *Postmodernity and Its Discontents* (London: Polity, 1997).

22 Arjun Appadurai, *Modernity at Large: Cultural Dimensions of Globalization* (Minneapolis: University of Minnesota Press, 1996).

23 Asef Bayat, "Uncivil Society: The Politics of 'Informal' People," *Third World Quarterly* 18 (1997): 53–72.

24 Arjun Appadurai, "Dead Certainty: Ethnic Violence in the Era of Globalization," *Public Culture* 10 (1998): 225–47.

25 Tim Heaton and Tom Hirschl, "The Trajectory of Family Change in Nigeria," *Journal of Comparative Family Studies* 30 (1999): 35–55.

26 See Janet Roitman, "The Politics of Informal Markets in Sub-Saharan Africa," *Journal of Modern African Studies* 28 (1990): 671–96; Inge Amundsen, "Afropessimism: A Response from Below?" in *Development Theory: Recent Trends*, ed. Arve Ofstad and Arne Wiig (Bergen: Christian Michelsen Institute, 1992); Victor Azarya, "Civil Society and Disengagement in Africa," in *Civil Society and the State in Africa*, ed. J. W. Harbeson, David Rothchild, and Naomi Chazan (Boulder: Lynne Rienner Publishers, 1994); Patrick Chabal and Jean-Pascal Daloz, *Africa Works: Disorder as a Political Instrument* (Oxford: James Currey, 1999).

27 Valdo Pons, *Stanleyville: An African Urban Community under Belgian Administration* (London: International African Institute, Oxford University, 1969).

28 Ibid.

29 Michael Rowlands, "Temporal Inconsistencies in Nation-Space," in *Worlds Apart: Modernity through the Prism of the Social*, ed. Daniel Miller (London: Routledge, 1995); Sandra Greene, "Sacred Terrain: Religion, Politics, and Place in the History of the Anloga (Ghana)," *International Journal of African Historical Studies* 30 (1997): 1–22; Michael Watts, "Islamic Modernities: Citizenship, Civil Society, and Islamism in a Nigerian City," in *Cities and Citizenship*, ed. James Holston (Durham: Duke University Press, 1999).

30 Alain Pottage, "Power as an Act of Contingency: Luhman, Deleuze, Foucault," *Economy and Society* 27 (1998): 1–27.

31 Peter Marden, "Geographies of Dissent: Globalization, Identity, and the Nation," *Political Geography* 16 (1997): 37–64.

32 Jordi Borja, "Cities: New Roles and Forms of Governing," in *Preparing for the Urban Future: Global Pressures and Local Forces*, ed. Michael Cohen, Blair Ruble, Joseph Tulchin, and Allison Garland (Washington, D.C.: Woodrow Wilson Center Press, 1996).

33 John Browder and Brian Godfrey, *Rainforest Cities: Urbanization, Development, and Globalization of the Brazilian Amazon* (New York: Columbia University Press, 1997).

34 Brenner, "Between Fixity and Motion."

35 David Scott, *Refashioning Futures: Criticism after Postcoloniality* (Princeton: Princeton University Press, 1999).

36 Nevzat Soguk and Geoffrey Whitehall, "Wandering Grounds: Transversality, Identity, Territoriality, and Movement," *Millenium: Journal of International Studies* 28 (1999): 675–98.

37 Regarding intersubjectivity, see Paul Ricoeur, *Hermeneutics and Human Sciences: Essays on Language, Action, and Interpretation* (Cambridge: Cambridge University Press, 1981). For a discussion on openness to solidarity, see Stuart Hall, "Identity in Question," in *Modernity and Its Futures*, ed. Stuart Hall, David Held, and Anthony McGrew (Oxford: Polity Press, 1992); and Rachel Bloul, "Beyond Ethnic Identity: Resisting Exclusionary Identification," *Social Identities* 5 (1999): 7–30.

38 Dipesh Chakrabarty, *Provincializing Europe: Postcolonial Thought in Historical Difference* (Princeton: Princeton University Press, 2000).

39 Arif Dirlik, "The Postcolonial Aura: Third World Criticism in the Age of Global Capitalism," *Critical Inquiry* 20 (1994): 328–56.

40 Regarding political sites, see Paul Paton, "Foucault's Subject of Power," *Political Theory Newsletter* 6 (1994): 60–71. On such notions of authority, see Ian Chambers, "At the End of This Sentence a Sail Will Unfurl . . . Modernities, Musics, and the Journey of Identity," in *Without Guarantees: In Honor of Stuart Hall*, ed. Paul Gilroy, Lawrence Grossberg, and Angela McRobbie (London: Verso, 2000).

41 Donatella Mazzoleni, "The City and the Imaginary," in *Space and Place*, ed. Erica Carter, James Donald, and Judith Squires (London: New Formations/ Lawrence and Wishart, 1993).

References

Abiodun, Josephine Olu. "The Challenges of Growth and Development in Metropolitan Lagos." In *The Urban Challenge in Africa: Growth and Management of Its Large Cities,* ed. Carole Rakodi. Tokyo: United Nations University Press, 1997.

Adedibu, Afolabi, and Michael Afolayan. "Socio-Economic Areas and Associated Housing Types in Ilorin, Nigeria." *African Urban Quarterly* 4 (1989): 104–14.

Adepoju, Aderanti. "Regional Integration, Continuity, and Changing Patterns of Intraregional Migration in Sub-Saharan Africa." In *International Migration into the Twenty-First Century*, ed. Mohamed Abubakr Siddique. Aldershot: Edward Elgar Publishing, 2000.

African Development Bank Group. *The African Development Report, 1998.* Abidjan: African Development Bank, 1998.

African Medical and Research Foundation and the Northwest Province Department of Human and Social Welfare. *Baseline Survey of Winterveld: An Informal Urban Settlement.* Pretoria: AMRF, 1994.

African Regional Office, World Bank. "Project Appraisal Document in a Proposed Credit in the Amount of SDR 12.9 Million (U.S. 18 Million Equivalent) to the Republic of Guinea for a Third Urban Development Project in the Support of the First Phase of the Third Urban Development Program." World Bank, Washington, D.C., 1999.

Agbola, Tunde, and A. M. Jinadu. "Forced Eviction and Forced Relocation in Nigeria: The Experience of Those Evicted from Maroko in 1990." *Environment and Urbanization* 9 (1997): 271–88.

Agier, Michel. Between War and City: Toward an Urban Anthropology of Refugee Camps. *Ethnography* 3 (2002): 317–42.

Aguilar, Renato, and Mario Carlos Zejan. "Income Distribution and the Labor Market in Angola. *Development Southern Africa* 11 (1994): 341–50.

Ahlberg, Beth. "Is There a Distinct African Sexuality? A Response to Caldwell." *Africa* 64 (1994): 220–42.

Aina, Tade Akin. "The Construction of Housing for the Urban Poor in Lagos." *Habitat International* 12 (1988): 31–44.

———. "Land Tenure in Lagos." *Habitat International* 16 (1992): 3–15.

———. "Popular Settlements in Metropolitan Lagos." *Third World Planning Review* 11 (1989): 393–415.

Akyeampong, Emmanuel. "Sexuality and Prostitution among the Akan of the Gold Coast, c. 1650–1950." *Past and Present* 156 (1997): 144–73.

Allen, Adriana. "Environmental Planning and the Management of the Periurban Interface." Paper presented at the conference "Rural-Urban Encounters: Managing the Environment of the Periurban Interface," London, November 9–10, 2001.

Ammassari, Savina, and Richard Black. *Harnessing the Potential of Migration and Return to Promote Development: Applying Concepts to West Africa.* Sussex: Sussex Centre for Migration Research, University of Sussex, 2001.

Ampoto, Akosua. "Controlling and Punishing Women in Ghana." *Review of African Political Economy* 56 (1994): 102–10.

Amundsen, Inge. "Afropessimism: A Response from Below?" In *Development Theory: Recent Trends*, ed. Arve Ofstad and Arne Wiig. Bergen: Christian Michaelson Institute, 1992.

Anderson, David, and Richard Rathbone. "Urban Africa: Histories in the Making." In *Africa's Urban Past*, ed. David Anderson and Richard Rathbone. Portsmouth, N.H.: Heinemann; Oxford: James Currey, 2000.

Andersson, Jens. "Reintegrating the Rural-Urban Connection: Migration Practices and Sociocultural Dispositions of Buhera Workers in Harare." *Africa* 71 (2001): 81–111.

Antoine, Phillipe, and Aka Kouame. "Cote d'Ivoire." In *Urbanization in Africa: A Handbook*, ed. James D. Tarver. Westport, Conn.: Greenwood Press, 1994.

Appadurai, Arjun. "Dead Certainty: Ethnic Violence in the Era of Globalization." *Public Culture* 10 (1998): 225–47.

———. *Modernity at Large: Cultural Dimensions of Globalization.* Minneapolis: University of Minnesota Press, 1996.

Arimah, Ben. "The Determinants of Housing Tenure Choice in Ibadan, Nigeria." *Urban Studies* 34 (1997): 105–24.

Arkadie, Van. "The State and Economic Change in Africa." In *The Role of the State in Economic Change in Africa*, ed. Ha-Joon Chang and Robert Rowthorn. Oxford: Clarendon Press, 1995.

Aronson, D. R. "Capitalism and Culture in Ibadan Urban Development." *Urban Anthropology* 7 (1978): 253–64.

Aryeety, Ernest, and Machiko Nissanke. "Asia and Africa in the Global Economy: Economic Policies and External Performance in South-East Asia and

Sub-Saharan Africa." Paper presented at the conference "Asia and Africa in the Global Economy," United Nations University–African Economic Research Consortium, Tokyo, August 3–4, 1998.

Austen, Ralph, and Rita Headrick. "Equatorial Africa under Colonial Rule." In *History of Central Africa* vol. 2, ed. David Birmingham and Phyllis Martin. London: Longman, 1983.

Azam, Jean-Paul, and Christian Morrison. *The Political Feasibility of Adjustment in Côte d'Ivoire.* Paris: Development Centre, OECD, 1994.

Azaraya, Victor. "Civil Society and Disengagement in Africa." In *Civil Society and the State in Africa*, ed. J. W. Harbenson, David Rothchild, and Naomi Chazan. Boulder: Lynne Rienner Publishers, 1994.

Bakewell, Oliver. "Returning Refugees or Migrating Villages? Voluntary Repatriation Programmes in Africa Reconsidered." *New Issues in Refugee Research*, working paper 15, United Nations High Commission on Refugees, 2000.

Bangura, Yusuf. "Economic Restructuring, Coping Strategies, and Social Change: Implications for Institutional Development in Africa." *Development and Change* 25 (1994): 785–827.

Banyikwa, W. F. "The Making of a Hybrid Millionaire City: Dar es Salaam, Tanzania." *African Urban Quarterly* 4 (1989): 228–51.

Barnes, Sandra. "Voluntary Associations in a Metropolis: The Case of Lagos, Nigeria." *African Studies Review* 18 (1975): 75–87.

Barrett, Christopher B., Thomas Reardon, and Patrick Webb. "Nonfarm Income Diversification and Household Livelihood Strategies in Rural Africa: Concepts, Dynamics, and Policy Implications." *Food Policy* 26 (2001): 315–31.

Bascom, William. "The Urban African and His World." In *Perspectives on the African Past*, ed. M. A. Klein and G. W. Johnston. Boston: Little, Brown, 1972.

Bastian, Misty. 1993. "Bloodhounds Who Have No Friends: Witchcraft and Locality in the Nigerian Popular Press." In *Modernity and Its Malcontents: Ritual and Power in Postcolonial Africa*, ed. Jean Comaroff and John Comaroff. Chicago: University of Chicago Press, 1993.

Bauman, Zygmunt. *Postmodernity and Its Discontents.* London: Polity, 1997.

Bayart, Jean-François. "Africa in the World: A History of Extraversion." *African Affairs* 99 (2000): 217–67.

Bayart, Jean-François, Stephen Ellis, and Béatrice Hibou, eds. *The Criminalization of the State in Africa.* Indianapolis: Indiana University Press; London: James Currey, 1999.

Bayat, Asef. "Uncivil Society: The Politics of 'Informal' People." *Third World Quarterly* 18 (1997): 53–72.

Bazenguissa-Ganga, Remy. "The Spread of Political Violence in Congo-Brazzaville." *African Affairs* 98 (1999): 37–54.

Belshaw, Deryke, Peter Lawrence, and Michael Hubbard. "A Decade of Structural Adjustment in Urganda: Agricultural Tradeables, Rural Poverty, and Macroeconomic 'success.' " In *The Market Panacea: Agrarian Transformation in the LDC's and Former Socialist Economies*, ed. Max Spoor. London: International Technology Publications, 1997.

Berry, Sara. "Stable Prices, Unstable Values: Some Thoughts on Monetization and the Meaning of Transactions in West African Economies." In *Money Matters: Instability, Values, and Social Payments in the Modern History of West African Communities*, ed. Jane Guyer. Portsmouth, N.H.: Heinemann; London: James Currey, 1995.

———. "Tomatoes, Land, and Hearsay: Property and History in Asante in the Time of Structural Adjustment." *World Development* 25 (1997): 1225–41.

Bloom, David, and Jeffrey Sachs. *Geography, Demography, and Economic Growth in Africa*. Boston: Center for International Development, Harvard University, 1998.

Bloul, Rachel. "Beyond Ethnic Identity: Resisting Exclusionary Identification." *Social Identities* 5 (1999): 7–30.

Borja, Jordi. "Cities: New Roles and Forms of Governing." In *Preparing for the Urban Future: Global Pressures and Local Forces*, ed. Michael Cohen, Blair Ruble, Joseph Tulchin, and Allison Garland. Washington, D.C.: Woodrow Wilson Center Press, 1996.

Boswell, D. M. "Personal Crisis and the Mobilization of a Social Network." In *Social Networks in Urban Situations: Analyses of Personal Relationships in Central African Towns*, ed. J. Clyde Mitchell. Manchester: Manchester University Press, 1969.

Brenner, Neil. "Between Fixity and Motion: Accumulation, Territorial Organization and the Historical Geography of Spatial Scales. *Environment and Planning D: Society and Space* 16 (1998): 459–48.

———. "The Urban Question as a Scale Question: Reflections on Henri Lefebvre, Urban Theory, and the Politics of Scale." *International Journal of Urban and Regional Research* 24 (2000): 361–78.

Brett, E. A. "The Participation Principle in Development Projects: The Costs and Benefits of Participation." *Public Administration and Development* 16 (1996): 5–19.

Browder, John, and Brian Godfrey. *Rainforest Cities: Urbanization, Development, and Globalization of the Brazilian Amazon*. New York: Columbia University Press, 1997.

Bryceson, Deborah. "Multiplex Livelihoods in Rural Africa: Recasting the Terms and Conditions of Gainful Employment." *Journal of Modern African Studies* 40 (2002): 1–28.

———. "Sub-Saharan Africa: Betwixt and Between." De-Agrarianisation and Rural Employment Research Project, African Studies Centre, University of Leiden, 1999.

Bryden, Lynne. "Tightening Belts in Accra, 1975–1990." *Africa* 69 (1999): 366–85.

Caldwell, John, I. O. Orubuloya, and Pat Caldwell. "The Destabilization of the

Traditional Yoruba Sexual System." *Population and Development Review* 17 (1991): 229–62.

Campbell, James. "Urbanization, Culture, and the Politics of Urban Development in Ghana, 1875–1985." *Urban Anthropology* 23 (1994): 409–50.

Cardy, Franklin. "Environment and Forced Migration: A Review." In *Human Impact on the Environment: Sustainable Development in Africa*, ed. Michael B. K. Darkoh and Apollo Rwomire. Oxford: Ashgate, 2002.

Carling, Jörgen. "Migration in the Age of Involuntary Immobility: Theoretical Reflections and Cape Verdean Experiences." *Journal of Ethnic and Migration Studies* 28 (2002): 3–42.

Central Intelligence Agency. *CIA World Fact Book, 1998*. Washington, D.C.: GPO, 1998.

Centre for Development and Enterprise. *Displaced Urbanization: Definition, Methodology and Eight Locality Studies*. Johannesburg: CDE, 1997.

Chabel, Patrick, and Jean-Pascal Daloz. *Africa Works: Disorder as a Political Instrument*. Oxford: James Currey, 1999.

Chakrabarty, Dipesh. *Provincializing Europe: Postcolonial Thought in Historical Difference*. Princeton: Princeton University Press, 2000.

Chambers, Ian. "At the End of This Sentence a Sail Will Unfurl . . . Modernities, Musics, and the Journey of Identity." In *Without Guarantees: In Honor of Stuart Hall*, ed. Paul Gilroy, Lawrence Grossberg, and Angela McRobbie. London: Verso, 2000.

Chant, Sylvia, and Sara Radcliffe. "Migration and Development: The Importance of Gender. In *Gender and Migration in Developing Countries*, ed. Sylvia Chant. London: Belhaven Press, 1992.

Cheah, Pheng. "Spectral Nationality: The Living on [sur-vie] of the Postcolonial Nation in Neocolonial Globalization. *boundary 2* 26 (1999): 225–52.

Chipkin, Ivor. "Functional and Dysfunctional Communities: The Making of National Citizens." *Journal of Southern African Studies* 29 (2003): 63–82.

Christopher, A. J., and James Tarver. "Urbanization during Colonial Days in Sub-Saharan Africa. In *Urbanization in Africa*, ed. James Tarver. Westport, Conn.: Greenwood Press, 1994.

Chukwuezi, Barth. "Through Thick and Thin: Igbo Rural-Urban Circularity, Identity, and Investment." *Journal of Contemporary African Studies* 19 (2001): 55–66.

Clark, David. "Unregulated Housing, Vested Interest, and the Development of Community Identity in Nairobi." *African Urban Studies* 3 (1979): 33–46.

Clark, Nigel. "Botanizing on the Asphalt? The Complex Lives of Cosmopolitan Bodies." *Body and Society* 6 (2000): 12–33.

Clignet, René. "Urbanization and Family Structure in the Ivory Coast." *Comparative Studies in Society and History* 8 (1966): 385–401.

Club du Sahel/OECD and the Municipal Development Program. "Managing the Economy Locally in Africa: Assessing Local Economies and their Pros-

pects," 2001. Available at http://webnet1.oecd.org/pdf/M00020000/M000
20320.pdf.

Cohen, Michael. *Urban Policy and Political Conflict in Africa: A Study of the Ivory Coast*. Chicago: University of Chicago Press, 1974.

Cole, Patrick. *Modern and Traditional Elites in the Politics of Lagos*. London: Cambridge University Press, 1975.

Collier, Paul. "Doing Well Out of Civil War," paper presented at the conference "Economic Agendas in Civil Wars," London, April 26–27, 1999.

———. "On the Economic Consequences of Civil War." *Oxford Economic Papers* 51 (1999): 168–83.

Collier, Paul, and Jan Willem Gunning. "Explaining African Economic Performance." *Journal of Economic Literature* 37 (1999): 64–111.

Conklin, Alice. *A Mission to Civilize: The Republic Idea of Empire in France and West Africa, 1895–1930*. Stanford: Stanford University Press, 1997.

Constantin, François. "La transnationalité, de l'individu à l'Etat: A propos des modes populaires d'action internationale en Afrique orientale." In *Les individus dans les relations internationales*, ed. Michel Girard. Paris: Economica, 1994.

Cooper, Fred. "Conflict and Connection: Rethinking Colonial African History." *American Historical Review* 99 (1994): 1516–45.

———. *Decolonization and African Society: The Labor Question in French and British Africa*. Cambridge: Cambridge University Press, 1996.

———. "Urban Space, Industrial Time, and Wage Labor in Africa." In *Struggle for the City: Migrant Labor, Capital, and the State in Urban Africa*, ed. Fred Cooper. London: New Dehli: Sage, 1983.

Coquery-Vidrovitch, Catherine. "The Process of Urbanization in Africa (from the Origins to the Beginning of Independence)." *African Studies Review* 34 (1991): 1–98.

Cordell, Dennis, Joel Gregory, and Victor Peché. *Hoe and Wage: A Social History of a Circular Migration System in West Africa*. Boulder: Westview Press, 1996.

Cour, Jean Marie, and Serge Snrech. *Preparing for the Future: A Vision of West Africa in the Year 2020, West Africa Long-Term Prospective Study*. Paris: OECD/Club du Sahel, 1998.

Crisp, Jeff. "Africa's Refugees: Patterns, Problems, and Policy Challenges." *Journal of Contemporary African Studies* 18 (2000): 157–78.

Dawson, John. "The Relevance of the Flexible Specialisation Paradigm for Small-Scale Industrial Restructuring in Ghana." *Bulletin of the Institute of Development Studies* 23 (1992): 34–38.

De Boeck, Filip. "Beyond the Grave: History, Memory, and Death in Postcolonial Congo/Zaire." In *Memory and the Postcolony: African Anthropology and the Critique of Power*, ed. Richard Werbner. London: Zed, 1998.

———. "Borderland Breccia: The Mutant Hero and the Historical Imagination of a Central-African Diamond Frontier." *Journal of Colonialism and Colonial History* 1 (2000): 1–44.

——. "Kinshasa: Tales of the 'Invisible City' and the Second World." In *Under Siege: Four African Cities: Freetown; Johannesburg; Kinshasa; Lagos,* ed. Okwui Ewenzor. Ostfildern-Ruit, Germany: Harje Cantz Publishers, 2003.

De Bruijn, Mirjam, Rijk van Dijk, and Dick Foeken, eds. *Mobile Africa.* Leiden: Brill, 2001.

De Haan, Arjan, Johann Kirsten, and Juliana Rwelamira. "Migration and Rural Assets: Evidence from Surveys in Three Semi-Arid Regions in South Africa, India, and Botswana." Poverty Research Unit, Institute of Development Studies, University of Sussex, 2000. Available at http://www.sussex.ac.uk/Units/PRU/migration_and_rural assets.pdf.

De Herdt, Tom. "Economic Action and Social Structure: 'Cambisme' in Kinshasa." *Development and Change* 33 (2002): 683–708.

Development Bank of Southern Africa. *Winterveld Agency Program Report.* Midrand: DBSA, 1987.

Devisch René. "Frenzy, Violence, and Ethical Renewal in Kinshasa." *Public Culture* 7 (1995): 593–629.

Dey, Krishno, and David Westendorff, eds. *Their Choice or Yours: Global Forces or Local Voices?* Geneva: United Nations Research Institute for Social Development, 1996.

Dietz, Ton, and Fred Zaal. "The Provisioning of African Cities, with a Case Study of Ouagadougou." In *Re-Aligning Government, Civil Society, and the Market: New Challenges in Urban and Regional Development. Essays in Honour of G.A. de Bruijne,* ed. Isa Baud, Johan Post, Leo. de Haan, and Ton Dietz. Amsterdam: AGIDS, 2001.

Diouf, Mamadou. "The French Colonial Policy of Assimilation and the Civility of the *Originaires* of the Four Communes (Senegal): A Nineteenth Century Globalization Project." *Development and Change* 29 (1998): 671–96.

Diouf, Mamadou, H. M. Fotê, and Achille Mbembe. "The Civil Status of the State in Africa." *Codesria Bulletin* 1–2 (1999): 39–47.

Dirlik, Arif. "The Postcolonial Aura: Third World Criticism in the Age of Global Capitalism." *Critical Inquiry* 20 (1994): 328–56.

Donnelly-Roark, Paula, Karim Ouedraogo, and Xiao Ye. "Can Local Institutions Reduce Poverty? Rural Decentralization in Burkina Faso." World Bank, 2001. Available at http://econ.worldbank.org/files/2402_wps2677.pdf.

Dubresson, Alain. "Abidjan: From the Public Making of a Modern City to the Urban Management of a Metropolis." In *The Urban Challenge in Africa: Growth and the Management of Its Large Cities,* ed. Carole Rakodi. Tokyo: United Nations University Press, 1997.

Duffield, Mark. "Post-Modern Conflict: Warlords, Post-Adjustment States, and Private Protection." *Civil Wars* 1 (1998): 66–102.

Durand-Lasserve, Alain. "Researching the Relationship between Economic Liberalisation and Changes to the Land Markets and Land Prices." In *Methodology for Land and Housing Market Analysis*, ed. Garth Jones and Peter Ward. London: UCL, 1994.

Economic Commission for Africa. *African Economic Report 1998*. Addis Ababa: Economic Commission for Africa, 1998.

——. *Economic Report on Africa 1999*. Addis Ababa: Economic Commission for Africa, 1999.

Elbadawi, Ibrahim, and Benno Ndulu. "Long Run Development and Sustainable Growth in Sub-Saharan Africa." In *New Directions in Development Economics*, ed. Matts Lundahl and Benno Ndulu. London: Routledge, 1996.

El-Kenz, Ali. "Youth and Violence." In *Africa Now: People, Policies, Institutions*, ed. Stephen Ellis. London: James Currey; Portsmouth, N.H.: Heinemann, in association with the Dutch Ministry of Foreign Affairs, 1996.

Ellis, Stephen, and Janet MacGaffey. "Research on Sub-Saharan Africa's Unrecorded International Trade: Some Methodological and Conceptual Problems." *African Studies Review* 39 (1996): 19–41.

El-Shakhs, Salah. "Towards Appropriate Urban Development Policy in Emerging Mega Cities in Africa." In *The Urban Challenge in Africa: Growth and Management of Its Large Cities*, ed. Carole Rakodi. Tokyo: United Nations University Press, 1997.

Emizet, Kisangani. "Confronting Leaders at the Apex of the State: The Growth of the Unofficial Economy in Congo." *African Studies Review* 41 (1998): 99–137.

Englund, Harri. "The Village in the City, the City in the Village: Migrants in Lilongwe." *Journal of Southern African Studies* 28 (2002): 137–59.

Erbach, Jerry, and John Gaudet. *Urbanization Issues and Development in Sub-Saharan Africa*. Washington, D.C.: Africa Bureau, US AID, 1998.

Evans, Peter, ed. *Livable Cities? Urban Struggles for Livelihood and Sustainability*. Berkeley: University of California Press, 2002.

Eze, Emmanuel. "Democracy or Consensus? A Response to Wiredu." In *Postcolonial African Philosophy*, ed. Emmanuel Eze. Oxford: Blackwell, 1997.

Faist, Thomas. *The Volume and Dynamics of International Migration and Transnational Social Spaces*. Oxford: Clarendon, 2000.

Fall, Abdou Salam. "Migrants' Long Distance Relationships and Social Networks in Dakar." *Environment and Urbanization* 10 (1998): 135–45.

Falola, Toyin. *Violence in Nigeria: The Crisis of Religious Politics and Secular Ideologies*. Rochester: University of Rochester Press, 1998.

Fapohunda, Eleanor. "Urban Women's Roles and Nigerian Government Development Strategy." In *Sex Roles, Population, and Development in West Africa: Studies on Work and Demographic Issues*, ed. Christine Oppong. London: Heinemann, 1987.

Farvacque-Vitkovic, Catherine, and Lucien Godin, 1998. *The Future of African Cities: Challenges and Priorities for Urban Development*. Washington: D.C.: World Bank, 1998.

Ferguson, James. *Expectations of Modernity: Myths and Meanings of Urban Life on the Zambian Copperbelt*. Berkeley: University of California Press, 1999.

Ferme, Marianne. *The Underneath of Things: Violence, History, and the Everyday in Sierra Leone*. Berkeley: University of California Press, 2001.

Fetter, Bruce. *The Creation of Elizabethville, 1910–1940*. Stanford: Stanford University Press, 1976.

Findley, Sally. "Migration and Family Interaction in Africa." In *Family, Population, and Development in Africa London*, ed. Aderanti Adepoju. London: 1997.

Fjelstad, Odd-Helge, and Joseph Semboja. "Dilemmas of Fiscal Decentralisation: A Study of Local Government Taxation in Tanzania." *Forum for Development Studies* 27 (2000): 7–41.

Flynn, Donna. " 'We are the Border': Identity, Exchange, and the State along the Benin-Nigeria Border." *American Ethnologist* 24 (1997): 311–30.

Food and Agricultural Organization of the United Nations. *HIV/AIDS, Agriculture and Food Security in Mainland and Small Island Countries of Africa: Twenty-Second Regional Conference for Africa, Cairo, 4–8 February 2002*. Rome: FAO, United Nations, 2002.

Francis, Elizabeth. *Making a Living: Changing Livelihoods in Rural Africa*. London: Routledge, 2000.

Frank, Lawrence. "Ideological Competition in Nigeria: Urban Populism versus Ethnic Nationalism." *Journal of Modern African Studies* 17 (1974): 433–52.

Freund, Bill. "Contrasts in Urban Segregation: A Tale of Two African Cities, Durban (South Africa) and Abidjan (Côte d'Ivoire)." *Journal of Southern African Studies* 27 (2001): 527–46.

Garba, S. B. "Public Land Ownership and Urban Land Management Effectiveness in Metropolitan Kano, Nigeria." *Habitat International* 2 (1997): 305–17.

Garlick, Peter. *African Traders and Economic Development in Ghana*. Oxford: Clarendon, 1971.

Geschiere, Peter. *The Modernity of Witchcraft: Politics and the Occult in Postcolonial Africa*. Charlottesville: University of Virginia Press, 1997.

Geschiere, Peter, and Francis Nyamnjoh. "Capitalism and Autochthony: The Seesaw of Mobility and Belonging." *Public Culture* 12 (2000): 423–52.

Glassman, Jim, and Abdi Samatar. "Development Geography and the Third-World State." *Progress in Human Geography* 21 (1997): 164–98.

Goerg, Odile. "From Hill Station (Freetown) to Downtown Conakry (First Ward): Comparing French and British Approaches to Segregation in Colonial Cities at the Beginning of the Twentieth Century." *Canadian Journal of African Studies* 32 (1998): 1–31.

Goldberg, David T. " 'Polluting the Body Politic': Racist Discourse and Urban Location." In *Racism, the City, and the State*, ed. Malcolm Cross and Michael Keith. London: New York: Routledge, 1993.

Goonaratne, Wilbert, and Robert Obudho, eds. *Contemporary Issues in Re-*

gional Development Policy: Perspectives from Eastern and Southern Africa. Aldershot: Averbury, 1997.

Gordon, Avery. *Ghostly Matters: Haunting and the Sociological Imagination.* Minneapolis: University of Minnesota Press, 1996.

Gore, Charles. *Social Exclusion and Africa South of the Sahara: A Review of the Literature.* Geneva: International Institute for Labor Studies, 1994.

Gore, Charles, and David Pratten. "The Politics of Plunder: The Rhetorics of Order and Disorder in Southern Nigeria." *African Affairs* 102 (2003): 211–40.

Grant, Iain Hamilton. "At the Mountain of Madness: The Demonology of the New Earth and the Politics of Becoming." In *Deleuze and Philosophy: The Difference Engineer,* ed. Keith Ansell-Pearson. London: Routledge, 1997.

Greene, Sandra. "Sacred Terrain: Religion, Politics, and Place in the History of the Anloga (Ghana)." *International Journal of African Historical Studies* 30 (1997): 1–22.

Grey-Johnson, Crispin. "The African Informal Sector at the Crossroads: Emerging Policy Options." *African Development* 18 (1992): 65–91.

Guarnizo, Luis Eduardo, and Michael Smith. "The Locations of Transnationalism." In *Transnationalism from Below,* ed. Michael Smith and Luis Eduardo Guarnizo. New Brunswick: Transaction, 1998.

Gugler, Joseph, and William Flanagan. *Urbanization and Social Change in West Africa.* Cambridge: Cambridge University Press, 1978.

Guyer, Jane. *An African Niche Economy: Farming to Feed Ibadan, 1968–88.* Edinburgh: Edinburgh University Press for the International African Institute, London, 1998.

———. "Feeding Yaounde." In *Feeding African Cities,* ed. Jane Guyer. Manchester: Manchester University Press, 1987.

———. "Introduction: The Currency Interface and Its Dynamics." In *Money Matters: Instability, Values, and Social Payments in the Modern History of West African Communities,* ed. Jane Guyer. Portsmouth, N.H.: Heinemann; Oxford: James Currey, 1995.

Hall, Stuart. "Identity in Question." In *Modernity and Its Futures,* ed. Stuart Hall, David Held, and Anthony McGrew. Oxford: Polity Press, 1992.

Hanna, William, and Judith Hanna. *Urban Dynamics in Black Africa.* 2nd ed. New York: Aldine, 1981.

Hansen, Karen. "Budgeting against Uncertainty: Cross-Class and Transethnic Redistribution Mechanisms in Urban Zambia." *African Urban Studies* 21 (1985): 65–73.

Hanson, John. "Islam, Migration, and the Political Economy of Meaning: *Fergo Nioro* from the Senegalese River Valley, 1862–1890." *Journal of African History* 35 (1994): 37–60.

Harriss-White, Barbara. "Informal Economic Order: Shadow States, Private Status States, States of Last Resort, and Spinning States—A Speculative Discussion on South Asian Case Material." QEH working paper QEHWPS06, Oxford University, 1997.

Hart, Keith, *Political Economy of West African Agriculture*. Cambridge: Cambridge University Press, 1982.

Harts-Broekhuis, Annelet. "How to Sustain a Living: Urban Households and Poverty in a Sahelian Town of Mopti, Africa." *Africa* 67 (1997): 106–31.

Healey, Patsy, Stuart Cameron, Simin Davoudi, Stephen Graham, and Ali Mandani-Pour. "Introduction: The City — Crisis, Change, and Invention." In *Managing Cities: The New Urban Context*, ed. Patsy Healey, Stuart Cameron, Simin Davoudi, Stephen Graham, and Ali Mandani-Pour. New York: Wiley, 1995.

Heaton, Tim, and Tom Hirschl. "The Trajectory of Family Change in Nigeria." *Journal of Comparative Family Studies* 30 (1999): 35–55.

Herbst, Jeffrey. "Responding to State Failure in Africa." *International Security* 21 (1996): 120–44.

Hetherington, Kevin. "Phantasmagoria/Phantasm Agora: Movements Out of Time and the Language of Seeing." *Space and Culture* 11-12 (2002): 24–41.

Hibou, Béatrice. *The Political Economy of the World Bank's Discourse: From Economic Catechism to Missionary Deeds and (Misdeeds)*. Paris: Centre d' Etude et de Recherches Internationales, 2000.

———. "The 'Social Capital' of the State as an Agent of Deception." In *The Criminalization of the State in Africa*, ed. Jean-François Bayart, Stephen Ellis, and Béatrice Hibou. London: James Currey; Bloomington: Indiana University Press, 1999.

Hiskett, Mervyn. *The Development of Islam in West Africa*. London: Longman, 1984.

Hopkins, Anthony. *An Economic History of West Africa*. New York: Columbia University Press, 1973.

Horne, André. "How Many People Are There in Winterveld? What a Proper Census Should Show." *Urban Forum* 8 (1997): 117–32.

Ikejiofor, Uche. "The God That Failed: A Critique of Public Housing in Nigeria, 1975–1995." *Habitat International* 23 (1999): 177–88.

Illife, John. *The Africans*. Cambridge: Cambridge University Press, 1995.

International Labor Organization. *Decent Work and the Informal Economy*. Geneva: ILO, 2002.

———. *Jobs for Africa: A Policy Framework for an Employment-Intensive Growth Strategy*. Geneva: ILO, 1998.

International Labor Organization, Jobs and Skills Program for Africa. *African Employment Report 1992*. Addis Ababa: ILO, 1992.

Joseph, Richard. "Settlers, Strikers, and *Sans Travail*: The Douala Riots of September 1945." *Journal of African History* 15 (1974): 669–87.

Kanji, Nazneen. "Gender, Poverty, and Economic Adjustment in Harare, Zimbabwe." *Environment and Urbanization* 7 (1995): 37–55.

Kapferer, Bruce. "Structural Marginality and the Urban Social Order." *Urban Anthropology* 7 (1978): 287–320.

Kelsall, Tim. "Governance, Local Politics, and Districtization in Tanzania: The 1998 Arumeru Tax Revolt." *African Affairs* 99 (2000): 533–51.

King, Anthony. *Urbanism, Colonialism, and the World Economy: Cultural and Spatial Foundations of the World Urban System.* London: Routledge, 1991.

King, Kenneth. *Jua Kali Kenya: Change and Development in an Informal Economy, 1970–95.* Athens: University of Ohio Press, 1996.

Kironde, J. M. Lussuga. "Access to Land by the Urban Poor in Tanzania: Some Findings from Dar es Salaam." *Environment and Urbanization* 7 (1995): 77–96.

Kothari, Uma. "Migration and Chronic Poverty." Working paper no. 16, Institute for Development Policy and Management, University of Manchester, 2002.

Krieger, Judith. "Entrepreneurs and Family Well-Being: Agriculture and Trading Households in Cameroon." In *African Entrepreneurship: Theory and Reality*, ed. Anita Spring and Barbara McDade. Gainesville: University of Florida Press, 1998.

Lachance, Paul. *Africa's Real Economy and Its Development Projects: Rethinking African Development Issues.* Paris: OECD, 2000.

La Fontaine, Jean. *City Politics: A Study of Leopoldville, 1962–63.* London: Cambridge University Press, 1970.

Launay, Robert, and Benjamin Soares. "The Formation of an 'Islamic Sphere' in French Colonial West Africa." *Economy and Society* 28 (1999): 497–519.

Leavy, Jennifer, and Howard White. "Rural Labour Markets and Poverty in Sub-Saharan Africa." Institute of Development Studies, University of Sussex, 2000. Available at http://www.ids.ac.uk/ids/pvty/pdf-files/rurallabourinssa.pdf.

Levin, Carole, Daniel Maxwell, Margaret Amar-Klemesu, Marie Ruel, and Saul Morris. "Working Women in an Urban Setting: Traders, Vendors, and Food Security in Accra." *World Development* 27 (1999): 1977–96.

Lloyd, Peter, Akin Mabogunje, and B. Awe, eds. *The City of Ibadan: A Symposium on Its Structure and Development.* Cambridge: Cambridge University Press, 1967.

Lock, Peter. "Military Downsizing and Growth in the Security Industry in Sub-Saharan Africa," 1999. Available at http://www.idsa-india.org/an-dec8-10.html.

Lubkemann, Stephen. "The Transformation of Transnationality among Mozambican Migrants in South Africa." *Canadian Journal of African Studies* 34 (2000): 41–63.

Lufadeju, F. O. "The Role of Shelter in Economic Development in Africa." *African Urban Quarterly* 2 (1987): 193–201.

Lugalla, Joseph. *Crisis, Urbanization, and Urban Poverty in Tanzania: A Study of Urban Poverty and Survival Politics.* Lanham, Md.: University Presses of America, 1995.

Loup, Jean. *Employment, Unemployment, and the Informal Economy of Yaounde and Antananarivo: A New Survey Method for the Employment Market Applied to Sub-Saharan Africa*. Paris: L'Institut français scientifique pour le développement en coopération, 1996.

Lund, Christian. "Precarious Democratization and Local Dynamics in Niger: MicroPolitics in Zinder." *Development and Change* 32 (2001): 845–69.

Mabogunje, Akin. "Urban Land and Urban Management Policies in Sub-Saharan Africa." *Urban Perspectives* 4 (1994): 35–60.

——. "Urban Planning and the Post-Colonial State in Africa: A Research Overview." *African Studies Review* 33 (1990): 121–203.

MacGaffey, Janet. *Entrepreneurs and Parasites: The Struggle for Indigenous Capitalism in Zaire*. Cambridge: Cambridge University Press, 1988.

MacGaffey, Janet, Vwakyanakazi Mukohya, Walu Engundu, Makwala M. Mavambu ye Beda, and Brooke G. Schoepf. *Real Economy of Zaire: The Contribution of Smuggling and Other Unofficial Activities to National Wealth*. Philadelphia: University of Pennsylvania Press, 1991.

MacGaffey, Janet, and Remy Bazenguissa-Ganga. *Congo-Paris: Transnational Traders on the Margins of the Law*. Bloomington: Indiana University Press, 2000.

MacHaria, Kinuthia. *Social and Political Dynamics of the Informal Economy in African Cities: Nairobi and Harare*. Washington, D.C.: University Press of America, 1997.

Maclure, Richard. *Overlooked and Undervalued: A Synthesis of Educational Research Network for West and Central Africa, Reviews on the State of Education and Research in West and Central Africa*. Washington, D.C.: Support for Analysis and Research in Africa, United States Agency for International Development, 1997.

Maffesoli, Michel. *Time of Tribes: The Decline of Individualism in Mass Society*. London: Sage, 1996.

Malaquais, Dominique. *Architecture, pouvoir et dissidence au Cameroun*. Paris: CERI, Karthala, 2002.

Maldonado, Carlos. "The Underdogs of the Urban Economy Join Forces: Results of an ILO Programme in Mali, Rwanda, and Togo." *International Labour Review* 128 (1989): 65–84.

Malmberg, Gunnar. "Time and Space in International Migration." In *International Migration, Immobility, and Development: Multidisciplinary Perspectives*, ed. Tomas Hammar, Grete Brochman, Kristof Tamas, and Thomas Faist. Oxford: Berg, 1997.

Mamdani, Mahmood. *Citizen and Subject: Contemporary Africa and the Legacy of Late Colonialism*. Princeton: Princeton University Press, 1996.

Mararo, Bucyalimwe. "Land, Power, and Ethnic Conflict in Masisi, 1940s–1994." *International Journal of African Historical Studies* 30 (1997): 503–37.

Marden, Peter. "Geographies of Dissent: Globalization, Identity, and the Nation." *Political Geography* 16 (1997): 37–64.

Marfleet, Phil. "Migration and the Refugee Experience." In *Globalisation and the Third World*, ed. Ray Kiely and Phil Marfleet. London: Routledge, 1998.

Markdata (PTY) LTD. *The Displaced Urbanization of the Apartheid Era: Its Current Consequences; A Focused Interview Survey in Six Areas*. Johannesburg: Markdata, 1997.

Marshall-Fratani, Ruth. "Mediating the Global and the Local in Nigerian Pentacostalism." *Journal of Religion in Africa* 28 (1998): 278–315.

Martin, Phyllis. *Leisure and Society in Colonial Brazzaville*. Cambridge: Cambridge University Press, 1995.

Martinez, Luis. *The Algerian Civil War, 1990–1998*. New York: Columbia University Press, 2000.

Massumi, Brian. "The Politics of Everyday Fear." 1993. Available at http://www.anu.edu.au/HRC/first_and_last works.

Masquelier. Adeline. "Behind the Dispensary's Prosperous Façade: Imagining the State in Rural Niger." *Public Culture* 13 (2001): 267–91.

Matsetela, Teddy. "The Informal Sector in the Political Economy of Winterveld." Master's thesis, University of Witwatersrand, 1979.

Mazzoleni, Donatella. "The City and the Imaginary." In *Space and Place*, ed. Erica Carter, James Donald, and Judith Squires. London: New Formations/ Lawrence and Wishart, 1993.

Mbembe, Achille. "At the Edge of the World: Boundaries, Territoriality, and Sovereignty in Africa." *Public Culture* 12 (2000): 259–84.

———. "Necropolitics." *Public Culture* 15 (2003): 12–40.

———. *On the Postcolony: Studies on the History of Society and Culture*. Berkeley: University of California Press, 2001.

———. "Provisional Notes on the Postcolony." *Africa* (1992): 3–27.

Mbembe, Achille, and Janet Roitman. "Figures of the Subject in a Time of Crisis." In *The Geography of Identity*, ed. Patricia Yaegar. Ann Arbor: University of Michigan Press, 1996.

McCarney, Patricia. *Cities and Governance: New Directions in Latin America, Asia, and Africa*. Toronto: Centre for Urban and Community Studies, University of Toronto, 1996.

Meagher, Kate. *The Bargain Sector: Economic Restructuring and the Non-Farm Sector in the Nigerian Savannah*. Aldershot: Ashgate, 2001.

Meyer, Birgit. "Make a Complete Break with the Past: Memory and Postcolonial Modernity in Ghanaian Pentacostal Discourse." In *Memory and the Postcolony: African Anthropology and the Critique of Power*, ed. Richard Werbner. London: Zed, 1998

Mhone, Guy. *The Impact of Structural Adjustment on the Urban Informal Sector in Zimbabwe*. Geneva: International Labor Organization, 1995.

Miller, H. Max, and Ram Singh. "Urbanization during Postcolonial Days." In *Urbanization in Africa*, ed. James Tarver. Westport, Conn.: Greenwood Press, 1994.

Mingione, Enzo. *Fragmented Societies: A Sociology of Economic Life beyond the Market Paradigm*. Oxford: Basil Blackwell, 1991.

Mitullah, Winnie, and Kivutha Kibwana. "A Tale of Two Cities: Policy, Law, and Illegal Settlements in Kenya." In *Illegal Cities: Law and Urban Change in Developing Countries*, ed. Edesio Fernandes and Ann Varley. London: Zed, 1998.

Mkandawire, Thandika. "Incentives, Governance, and Capacity Development in Africa." In *Capacity for Development: New Solutions to Old Problems*, ed. Sakiko Fukuda-Parr, Carlos Lopes, and Khalid Malik. London: Earthscan: New York: UNDP, 2002.

———. "Social Policy in a Development Framework: United Nations Research Institute on Social Development," 2001. Available at ftp://ftpserver.unicc.org/unrisd/outgoing/pp/spd/mkandawi.pdf.

Mkandawire, Thandika, and Charles Soludo. *Our Continent, Our Future: African Perspectives on Structural Adjustment*. Dakar: Codesria; Trenton, N.J.: Africa World Press, 1998.

Monga, Celestin. *The Anthropology of Anger: Civil Society and Democracy in Africa*. Boulder: Lynne Rienner Publishers, 1996.

Monga, Yvette. "A Historical Perspective on African Entrepreneurship: Lessons from the Duala Experience in Cameroon." In *African Entrepreneurship: Theory and Reality*, ed. Anita Spring and Barbara McDade. Gainesville: University Press of Florida, 1998.

Moore, Donald. "Subaltern Struggles and the Politics of Place: Remapping Resistance in Zimbabwe's Eastern Highlands." *Cultural Anthropology* 13 (1998): 344–82.

Moser, Caroline, Alicia Herbert, and Roza Makonnen. *Urban Poverty in the Context of Structural Adjustment: Recent Evidence and Policy Responses*. Washington, D.C.: Urban Development Division, World Bank, 1993.

Mwanasali, Musifiky. "The View from Below." In *Greed and Grievance: Economic Agendas in Civil Wars*, ed. Mats Berdal and David Malone. Boulder: Lynne Rienner Publishers, 1999.

Mwangi, Wambui. Conquest: The East African Currency Board, the Rupee Crisis, and the Problem of Colonialism in the East African Protectorate." Paper presented at the annual meeting of the African Studies Association, Philadelphia, November 11, 1999.

National Building Research Institute. *Winterveld: A Population Survey*. Pretoria: NBRI, 1981.

———. *Winterveld: A Socio-Economic Survey*. Pretoria: NBRI, 1989.

Niang, Demba, Bouna Warr, Laurent Bossard, and Jean-Marie Cour. "The Local Economy of St. Louis and the Senegal River Delta." Club du Sahel, OECD, and the Municipal Development Program, 1997. Available at http://wblnoo18.worldbank.org/ . . ./$File/D98471a.doc.

Njoh, Ambe. "The Political Economy of Urban Land Reform in a Post Colonial

State." *International Journal of Urban and Regional Research* 22 (1998): 409–23.

——. "The State, Urban Development Policy, and Society in Cameroon." *Cities* 16 (1999): 117–24.

Nlandu, Mayamba Thierry. "Kinshasa: When Illiterate and Literate Move beyond Political Democracy," 2000. Available at http://i-p-o.org/congdem2 .htm.

Nnkya, Tumsifu. "Land Use Planning and Practice under the Public Land Ownership Policy in Tanzania." *Habitat International* 23 (1999): 135–55.

Obarrio, Juan. "History of Geopolitics in the Postcolony: The Mozambican Case." Presented at the "Portuguese/African Encounters Conference 2002," the Watson Institute, Brown University, April 25–29, 2002.

——. "The Spirit of the Law in Mozambique." *Public Culture* 15, no. 4 (2004, forthcoming).

O'Brien, Susan. "Spirit Discipline: Gender, Islam, and Hierarchies of Treatment in Postcolonial Northern Nigeria." *Interventions* 3 (2001): 222–41.

Observatoire Geopolitique des Drogues. *World Geopolitics of Drugs: Annual Report 1997/1998*. Paris: OGD, 1998.

O'Connor, Anthony. *The African City*. New York: Africana Publishing Company, 1983.

Ogu, Vincent. "The Dynamics of Informal Housing in a Traditional West African City: The Benin City Example. *Third World Planning Review* 20 (1998): 419–38.

Olukoju, Ayodeji. "The Cost of Living in Lagos 1914–1945." In *Africa's Urban Past*, ed. David Anderson and Richard Rathbone. Portsmouth, N.H.: Heinemann; Oxford: James Currey, 2000.

Oppong, Christine. "African Family Systems and Socio-Economic Crisis." In *Family, Population, and Development in Africa*, ed. Aderanti Adepoju. London: Zed, 1997.

Palmer Development Group. "Financial and Institutional Overview of Water Supply Arrangements in Urban Areas." Report for the Water Research Commission, Pretoria, 1993.

——. "Winterveld: Case Study of Informal Water Supply Arrangements." Report for the Water Research Commission, Pretoria, 1994.

Papastergiadis, Nikolas. *The Turbulence of Migration: Globalisation, Deterritorialization, and Hybridity*. Cambridge: Polity Press, 2000.

Paton, Paul. "Foucault's Subject of Power." *Political Theory Newsletter* 6 (1994): 60–71.

Patterson, Amy. "The Dynamic Nature of Citizenship and Participation: Lessons from Three Rural Senegalese Case Studies." *Africa Today* 46 (1999): 3–18.

Peel, J. D. Y. "Urbanization and Urban History in West Africa." *Journal of African History* 21 (1980): 269–77.

Peil, Margaret. *Lagos: The City Is the People*. Boston: G. K. Hall, 1991.

Pels, Peter. *A Politics of Presence: Contacts between Missionaries and Waluguru in Late Colonial Tanganyika*. London: Routledge, 1998.

Peters-Berries, Christian. *Putting Development Policies into Practice: The Problems of Implementing Policy Reforms in Africa*. Geneva: International Labor Organization, 1993.

Piermay, Jean-Luc. "Kinshasa: A Reprieved Mega City?" In *The Urban Challenge in Africa: Growth and the Management of Its Large Cities*, ed. Carole Rakodi. Tokyo: United Nations University Press, 1997.

Platteau, Jean-Phillipe. "Behind the Market Stage Where Real Societies Exist: The Role of Private and Public Order Institutions." *Journal of Development Studies*, 36 (1994): 533–78.

Pons, Valdo. *Stanleyville: An African Urban Community Under Belgian Administration*. London: International African Institute, Oxford University, 1969.

Post, Johan. "The Politics of Urban Planning in the Sudan." *Habitat International* 20 (1996): 121–37.

Pottage, Alan. "Power as an Act of Contingency: Luhman, Deleuze, Foucault." *Economy and Society* 27 (1998): 1–27.

Raftopolous, Brian, and Tsueneo Yoshikuni, eds. *Sites of Struggle: Essays in Zimbabwe's Urban History*. Harare: Weaver Press, 1999.

Rahmato, Dessalegn, and Arkilu Kidanu. "Consultation with the Poor: A Study to Inform the World Development Report 2000/01 on Poverty and Development (National Report, Ethiopia)," World Bank, Washington, D.C., 2001.

Rajchman, John. *Constructions*. Cambridge: MIT Press, 1998.

Rakodi, Carole. "Order and Disorder in African Cities: Governance, Politics, and Urban Land Development Processes." In *Under Siege: Four African Cities: Freetown; Johannesburg; Kinshasa; Lagos*, ed. Okwui Ewenzor. Ostfildern-Ruit, Germany: Harje Cantz Publishers, 2003.

Rancière, Jacques. *Disagreements: Philosophy and Politics*. Minneapolis: University of Michigan Press, 1998.

Ranger, Terrence. "Dance and Society in Eastern Africa, 1890–1970: The Beni Ngoma." Berkeley: University of California Press, 1975.

Rayfield, J. R. "Theories of Urbanization and the Colonial City in West Africa." *Africa* 44 (1974): 163–85.

Reardon, Thomas. "Using Evidence of Household Income Diversification to Inform Study of the Rural Nonfarm Labor Market in Africa." *World Development* 25 (1997): 735–48.

Reitzes, Maxine, and Sivuyile Bam. "One Foot In, One Foot Out: Immigrants and Civil Society in the Winterveld." Research report no. 51, Social Policy Series, Center for Policy Studies, Johannesburg, 1996.

Reno, William. *Warlord Politics and African States*. Boulder: Lynne Rienner Publishers, 1998.

Republic of Bophuthatswana. *Winterveld: A Socio-Economic Survey and Preliminary Development Guideline*. Mbatho: Republic of Bophuthatswana, 1989.

Ricoeur, Paul. *Hermeneutics and Human Sciences: Essays on Language, Action, and Interpretation.* Cambridge: Cambridge University Press, 1981.

Roberts, Richard. *Warriors, Merchants, and Slaves: The State and Economy in the Middle Niger Valley 1700–1914.* Stanford: Stanford University Press, 1987.

Robertson, Claire. "Traders and Urban Struggle: Ideology and the Creation of a Female Militant Underclass in Nairobi, 1860–1990." *Journal of Women's History* 4 (1993): 9–42.

——. *Trouble Showed the Way: Women, Men, and Trade in the Nairobi Area, 1890–1990.* Bloomington: Indiana University Press, 1997.

——. "Women Entrepreneurs? Trade and the Gender Division of Labor in Nairobi." In *African Entrepreneurship: Theory and Reality*, ed. Anita Spring and Barbara McDade. Gainseville: University Press of Florida, 1998.

Rogerson, Chris. "Globalization or Informalization? African Urban Economies in the 1990s." In *The Urban Challenge in Africa: Growth and Management of Its Large Cities*, ed. Carole Rakodi. Tokyo: United Nations University Press, 1997.

Roitman, Janet. "The Garrison-Entrepôt." *Cahiers d'ètudes africaines* 150–52 (1998): 297–329.

——. "The Politics of Informal Markets in Sub-Saharan Africa." *Journal of Modern African Studies* 28 (1990): 671–96.

Rondinelli, Dennis, and John Kasarda. "Job Creation Needs in Third World Cities." In *Third World Cities: Problems, Policies, and Prospects*, ed. John Karsada and Alan Parnell. London: Sage, 1993.

Rowlands, Michael. "Temporal Inconsistencies in Nation-Space." In *Worlds Apart: Modernity through the Prism of the Social*, ed. Daniel Miller. London: Routledge, 1995.

Salau, Ademoula. "The Urban Process in Africa: Observations on the Points of Divergence from the Western Experience." *African Urban Studies* 4 (1979): 27–34.

Salinger, B. Lynne. "Productivity, Comparative Advantage, and Competitiveness in Africa." African Economic Policy Discussion Paper, no. 35, Equity and Growth through Economic Research Program, United States Agency for International Development, Washington, D.C., 2001.

Schafer, Loveness. "True Survivors: East African Refugee Women." *Africa Today* 49 (2003): 29–50.

Schalpen, Lou, and Peter Gibbon, with Paul Ove Pedersen. *Africa's Real Private Sector.* Copenhagen: Centre for Development Research, 2001.

Schatzberg, Michael. "Alternative Causalities." In *Political Legitimacy in Middle Africa*, ed. Michael Schatzberg. Bloomington: Indiana University Press, 2001.

Schrieder, Gertrude, and Béatrice Knerr. "Labour Migration as a Social Security Mechanism for Smallholder Households in Sub-Saharan Africa." *Oxford Development Studies* 28 (2000): 223–36.

Schübeler, Peter. *Participation and Partnership in Urban Infrastructure Management*. Washington, D.C.: Urban Management Program, World Bank, 1996.

Scott, David. *Refashioning Futures: Criticism after Postcoloniality*. Princeton: Princeton University Press, 1999.

Scott, James. *Seeing like a State*. New Haven: Yale University Press, 1998.

Sender, John, and Sheila Smith. *Poverty, Class, and Gender in Rural Africa: A Tanzanian Case Study*. London: Routledge, 1990.

Serres, Michel. *Genesis*. Ann Arbor: University of Michigan Press, 1995.

Sethuraman, Salem. *Africa's Informal Economy*. Geneva: International Labor Organization, 1997.

——. *Urban Poverty and the Informal Sector: A Critical Assessment of Current Strategies*. Geneva: International Labor Organization, 1997.

Settlement Planning Services. *Southern Odi-Moretele Development Appraisal; Volume 1: Household Socio-Economic Conditions*. Pretoria: SPS, 1991.

——. *Southern Odi-Moretele Development Appraisal; Volume 2: Technical Appendices*. Pretoria: SPS, 1991.

Shiferaw, Demissachew. "Self-Initiated Transformation of Public-Provided Dwellings in Addis Ababa, Ethiopia." *Cities* 15 (1998): 437–48.

Sidaway, James, and Michael Power. "Sociospatial Transformations in the 'Post-socialist' Periphery: The Case of Maputo, Mozambique." *Environment and Planning A* 27 (1995): 1463–91.

Simon, David. *Cities, Capital, and Development: African Cities in the World Economy*. London: Belhaven, 1992.

Simon, Roger, Mario DiPaolantonio, and Mark Clamen. "Remembrance as Praxis and the Ethos of the Inter-Human." *Cultural Machine* 4, available at http://culturemachine.tees.ac.uk/Cmach/Backissues/j004/Articles/Simon.htm.

Simone, AbdouMaliq. *In Whose Image? Political Islam and Urban Practices in the Sudan*. Chicago: University of Chicago Press, 1994.

Smith, Neil. "Homeless/Global: Scaling Places." In *Mapping the Futures: Local Cultures, Global Change*, ed. John Bird, Barry Curtis, Tim Putnam, George Robertson, and Lisa Tickner. New York: Routledge, 1993.

Soguk, Nevzat, and Geoffrey Whitehall. "Wandering Grounds: Transversality, Identity, Territoriality, and Movement." *Millenium: Journal of International Studies* 28 (1999): 675–98.

Solomon, Hasan. "Emigration Dynamics in Southern Africa." Unit of African Studies working papers, University of Pretoria, 2000.

Soulè, Bio Goura, and Cyril Obi. "Prospects for Trade between Nigeria and Its Neighbors," OECD, Paris, 2001. Available at http://webnet1.oecd.org/pdf/M00018000/M00018169.pdf.

Stren, Richard. *Housing the Urban Poor in Africa: Policy, Politics, and Bureaucracy in Mombasa*. Berkeley: Institute of International Studies, University of California, 1978.

——. "Institutional Arrangements." In *Strengthening Local Government in*

Sub-Saharan Africa, ed. the Economic Development Institute. Washington, D.C.: World Bank, 1989.

——. *Urban Research in the Developing World; Volume 2: Africa*. Toronto: Centre for Uban and Community Studies, University of Toronto, 1994.

Stren, Richard, and Rodney White, eds. *African Cities in Crisis: Managing Rapid Urban Growth*. Boulder: Westview, 1986.

Sylvester, Christine. *Producing Women and Progress in Zimbabwe*. Portsmouth, NH.: Heinemann, 2000.

Tacoli, Christine. "Changing Rural-Urban Interactions in Sub-Saharan Africa and Their Impact on Livelihoods: A Summary." *Working Paper Series on Rural-Urban Interactions and Livelihood Strategies*, no. 7, London, 2002. London: International Institute for Environment and Development.

Tansi, Sony Labou. *The Antipeople*. New York: Marion Boyers Press, 1988.

Thomas, Nicholas. *Colonialism's Culture*. Princeton: Princeton University, 1994.

Tiepolo, Maurizio. "Brazzaville: A City Profile." *Cities* 13 (1998): 117–24.

Tipple, Graham, and Ken Willis. "Tenure Choice in a West African City." *Third World Planning Review* 13 (1991): 27–45.

Tipple, Graham, and David Korboe. "Housing Policy in Ghana: Towards a Supply-Oriented Future." *Habitat International* 23 (1998): 245–57.

Tipple, Graham, David Korboe, Ken Willis, and Guy Garrod. "Who Is Building What in Urban Ghana: Housing Supply in Three Towns." *Cities* 15 (1998): 399–416.

Tostensen, Arne, Inge Tvedten, and Mariken Vaa, eds. *Associational Life in African Cities: Popular Responses to the Urban Crisis*. Upsala: Nordic Africa Institute, 2001.

Touré, Mouriba. "Population, Urbanization, and Migration in Africa." In *Population Growth and Sustainable Development*, ed. African Development Bank. Abidjan: African Development Bank, 1994.

Tripp, Aili Mari. *Changing the Rules: The Politics of Liberalization and the Urban Informal Economy of Tanzania*. Berkeley: University of California Press, 1997.

United Nations Center on Human Settlements. *An Urbanizing World: Global Report on Human Settlements*. Oxford: Oxford University Press, 1996.

Uyanga, Joseph. "Urban Planning Strategy in Nigeria: The Institutional Policy Perspective." *African Urban Studies* 4 (1979): 49–58.

van Dijk, Meine Pieter. "The Urban Informal Sector as New Engine for Development: Theoretical Developments since 1972." *Asien afrika lateinamerka* 24 (1996): 177–92.

Van der Winden, Bob. *A Family of the Musseque: Survival and Development in Postwar Angola*. Tampa: WorldView Publishing, 1998.

Van Hoyweghen, Saskia. "Sovereignty in Postcolonial Tanzania." *New Issues in Refugee Research*, working paper 49, United Nations High Commission on Refugees, 2001.

Van Zyl, Attwell and de Kock. "Winterveld Structure Plan." Johannesburg 1984.

Watts, Michael. "Islamic Modernities: Citizenship, Civil Society, and Islamism in a Nigerian City." In *Cities and Citizenship*, ed. James Holston. Durham: Duke University Press, 1999.

Weiss, Brad. "Thug Realism: Inhabiting Fantasy in Urban Tanzania." *Cultural Anthropology* 17 (2002): 93–128.

West, Harry. "Creative Destruction and Sorcery of Construction: Power, Hope, and Suspicion in Post-War Mozambique." *Cahiers d'études africaines* 37 (1997): 675–98.

Wiley, Liz Alden. "Reconstructing the African Commons." *Africa Today* 48 (2001): 77–99.

Williams, Donald. "Measuring the Impact of Land Reform Policy in Nigeria." *Journal of Modern African Studies* 30 (1992): 587–608.

Wolpe, Harold. *Urban Politics in Nigeria*. Berkeley: University of California Press, 1974.

Women's Commission for Refugee Women and Children. "You Cannot Dance If You Cannot Stand: A Review of the Rwanda Women's Initiative and the United Nations High Commissioner for Refugees' Commitment to Gender Equality in Post-conflict Societies," UNHCR *Review*, 2001. Available at http://www.womenscommission.org/pdf/rwi_ass.pdf.

Wood, Adrian, and Jörg Mayer. *Africa's Export Structure in Comparative Perspective*. Geneva: United Nations Conference on Trade and Development, 1998.

World Bank. *Adjustment in Africa: Reforms, Results, and the Road Ahead*. Washington, D.C.: World Bank, 1994.

———. "Living on Fragile Lands: Inclusion, Innovation, and Migration." In *World Development Report 2003: Sustainable Development in a Dynamic Economy*. Washington, D.C.: World Bank, 2002.

———. *World Development Report 1999: Entering the Twenty-first Century*. Washington, D.C.: World Bank, 1999.

Wright, Gwendolyn. *The Politics of Design in French Colonial Urbanism*. Chicago: University of Chicago Press, 1991.

Yapi-Diahou, Alphonse. "The Informal Housing Sector of the Metropolis of Abidjan, Ivory Coast." *Environment and Urbanization* 7 (1995): 11–29.

Employment: characteristics of urban colonial, 154–60; nonfarm, 180–81; public sector, 9, 25; and the right to survival, 169–70; youth opportunities for, 42

Eshu, 64

Ethnicity, and politics, 39, 57, 101–3, 167. *See also* Social identity

Exception, states of, 211

Family and household economies: business relations, 10; ethnic relations, 101, 230–31; labor and migration, 180–82; and land use, 197; and practices of settlement, 101–3, 141–42; and social tensions, 93, 102, 218; support systems, 6, 11, 171–72

Feyman, 106–7

Fonds d'investissement et de développement économique et social des Territoires d'Outre-Mer (FIDES), 155

Formality: and development partnerships, 106; as economic organization, 25; and employment, 6, 184; and housing policies, 203, 205–7; and informal collaboration, 80, 228

Fourth Urban Project of the World Bank, 30

Fragments of a Life, 242

Freetown, 216

FRELIMO: 198

Frey, 51–54, 57–60. *See also* Customary authority

Geographies: and new intersections, 188, 121; relations of material and immaterial, 7, 18; translocal, 184, 236; and underregulated spaces, 94; urban complementarities, 239–40

Globalization: and African trade, 24, 210; characteristics of, in Africa, 184–89, 225; as urban resource, 237–38

Global Urban Research Initiative (GURI), 179

Gorèe (Dakar), 146

Groupements d'Intérêt Economique, 43

Guédiawaye (Dakar), 31, 59

Harare, 183

Hausa, 224

Hip hop, in Pikine, 44, 59. *See also* Youth

Ibadan, 167

Igbo, 167, 227, 229

Ikoyi (Lagos), 195

Informality: and associational life, 227–29; and economy, 24–25, 76–77; and illegal status, 206–7; and land use, 193–201; in Pikine, 13; and shelter, 202–7; and spaces of operation, 24, 211; as tactic, 14, 22; and unconventional trade, 209–12; and urban survival, 168–71. *See also* Social identity

Informal sector: dynamics of, 6, 25–27; as economic category, 9, 24

Infrastructure: costs, 8; deficits of, 32; developments in late colonialism, 155–57; development projects in Douala, 98–100; politics of, 89–91, 179; spectral dimensions of, 109–11

International Monetary Fund, 185

Invisibility: and family politics, 103; as political force, 63, 66, 208–9; as tactic, 14, 22, 65; trading networks, 79; in Winterveld, 13. *See also* Clandestinity

Islam: and identity, 16; and land use (*wakf*), 194; as platform of global engagement, 133; Quranic training and children, 57; Shar'ia law, 220; Sufi traditions, 36, 118, 125; urban citizenship, 148. *See also* Sufi orders

119–23; rural to urban, 140–42; 181–82, 230–31; workers in Winterveld, 77. *See also* Movement; Rural areas; Urbanization

Mission d'Aménagement et Equipement Terrains Urbains et Ruraux, 97, 106

Mombasa, 153

Monetization: and attributions of value, 149; and the parceling of social life, 148–49

Monrovia, 216

Mouride, 40–42, 45–46

Movement: Africa as space of, 118; in Jidda, 13–14; self-reproducing logic of, 120; as social practice, 22, 119, 122; urban mobility, 62, 93, 101. *See also* Migration

Muslim Brotherhood, 126

Mutaçion, 115

Nairobi, 27, 138, 158, 174–75, 177, 206–7

Ndebele, 77

New Bell (Douala), 95, 154

Nongovernmental organizations, 12, 17, 56, 106. *See also* Local associations

Nouadibhou, 17

Ouagadougou, 212

Pan-African Congress, 82

Pentacostalism, 218–20

Peul, 62

Pikine, 13, 24, 28–34, 38–39, 42, 44, 46, 52, 56–57, 59–60, 133

Planning: colonial, 160–62; limits of participatory, 103–4; postcolonial, 162–68, urban, 35. *See also* Local governance; Urbanization

Popular neighborhoods, 176, 193, 227. *See also* Local associations

Port Bouêt (Abidjan), 201

Port Gentile, 17

Port Harcourt, 167

Postcolonial cities, 6, 18

Practices: ephemeral, 21; of resource distribution, 4; spiritual, 223–24; of urban conviviality, 216; of urban social formation, 3, 7, 9, 23, 67, 220. *See also* Collaboration

Pretoria, 63, 71, 76

Projet de ville, 21–29, 32–34, 38, 48–51, 56–57, 59–60, 133. *See also* Pikine

Prostitution, and women's urban trade, 174–75. *See also* Women's economic activities

Provisionality: economic logic of, 15, 120; and social formation, 14, 170; and urban survival, 158, 226, 240

Relational webs, 7. *See also* Collaboration

Repair, economies of, 46

Rural areas, 141–42; changing dimensions of, 179–84; and colonial export economies, 149–50; and women's labor, 27. *See also* Migration

Qaddriyah, 125

Santhiaba (Dakar), 57–62

Sanusiyya, 125

Schaub, Didier, 111, 115

Shangaan, 77–78

Shelter: characteristics of urban Africa, 192, 201–7; costs and standards of, 204–6; and public sector investments, 201, 204–6; self-built, 202–3; and sociality, 142–43; spontaneous settlements, 100. *See also* Planning; Urban services

Social diversity, as resource and impediment, 69, 90–91, 106, 158

Social identity: attributions of, 27, 36, 101–3, 157–58; ethnicity and politics, 39; fluid compositions of, 62, 120, 229–31, 235–36; and religious expression, 220; and urban development, 81, 143–45, 212, 215–16, 241. *See also* Associational life; Local associations
Social integration, 229–33
Social multiplexity, and the organization of urban perception, 214–15, 241. *See also* Social identity
Social solidarity, 37, 93. *See also* Local associations; Social identity; Urban residents
Sorcery, 172–73
Soshanguve, 71, 76, 79–80
Sow, N'deye Ami, 47
Spectrality, 214; and counterreality, 9, 14, 22; in Douala, 13; as urban circulation, 92–94; values, 8
Spiritualism: and citizenship in Senegal, 146; and economic practice in Winterveld, 77–79; in Nigeria, 218–20; in Yopougon, 222–24
Stanleyville (Kisangani), 230–33
States: and land policies, 199–200; and local development, 49; post-independence, and development, 7; and regulation, 8, 187; and shelter provision, 201–2; and social welfare, 8. *See also* Local governance
St. Louis (Senegal), 146
Structural adjustment: and African trade, 24; impact on public life, 6, 8–9; and macroeconomics, 185–86. *See also* Macroeconomic policies
Subsidiarity, 189. *See also* Decentralization
Sufi orders (*tariqa*), 40, 44, 46, 123, 125–26, 130
Sumegné, Joseph Francis, 112, 115
Symbolic economies, 93, 166

Taxation, 190–192. *See also* Local governance
Thiof, 217
Tidiane, 40, 42, 46, 124–25, 128–29
Touba, 40
Trade liberalization, 24
Transitional populations, 94. *See also* Movement
Translocal, topographies, 184, 234–37
Transnational networks: and illicit economies, 211; and Pentacostalism, 219–20
Treichville (Abidjan), 201
Tswana, 71–73
Twelve tribes, 129–33

Unconventional trade, 18, 25, 61, 78, 107, 128, 209–12; in Jidda, 131–32
UNESCO Managing Social Transformations Program (MOST), 52
Union des Frères de Yeubmel, 52
Union des Opératrices de la Pêche Artisanale de la Grand Côte, 58
United Nations Local Agenda 21 Program, 29
Urban cultures: and shared politics, 212; and social identity, 230–31
Urban fringe, 67
Urban governance: general characteristics of, in Africa, 178–79; and shared urban cultures, 212, 232. *See also* Local governance; Planning
Urbanization: African modes of, 3, 10–11, 17, 215, 230–33, 238; articulations of, to ethnic practices, 165–67; consolidation versus hybridity, 10; and engagement, 139–40; and macroeconomic policy, 187–88, 237; and management, 193, 198
Urban modernity, 36–37, 54, 95–96, 100, 157–58, 162–65

Urban Popular Economy Program of Environmental Action Development in the Third World, 33–34, 51–52, 54

Urban residents: and shelter, 206–7; and spectrality, 95; and strategies of social connection, 11–13, 16, 65, 93, 137, 169, 171, 225–26, 238

Urban-rural linkages, 140–43, 183–184. *See also* Migration; Rural areas

Urban segregation, 161–63

Urban services, 27, 43, 50–52; water in Winterveld, 86–91. *See also* Water politics

Urban unrest: 152–54

Victoria Island, 195

Visibility, politics of, 65–66, 69–70, 227–28

Warfare and economy, 8

Water politics: in Douala, 104–5; in Winterveld, 86–90; in Yeumbel South, 51–55

Winterveld, 13, 63, 67–69, 70–80, 82–87, 89, 90, 92, 134

Winterveld Action Committee, 73

Winterveld Crisis Committee, 82–83, 88–89, 134–35

Winterveld Development Authority, 73

Winterveld Development Foundation, 75

Winterveld Presidential Lead Project, 86–91

Wolof, 62

Women's economic activities, 25, 27, 57–61, 172–74

World Bank, 191

Woukoache, François, 242

Yaounde, 242

Yeumbel South (Dakar), 51–55

Yopougon (Abidjan), 221, 224

Yoruba, 64, 197, 229

Youth: access to influence, 33, 41–42, 57–58, 104–5; and social reproduction, 3, 6, 26. *See also* Hip hop

Zawiyyah, 118, 123–25, 128, 131–33

Zone Nylon (Douala), 96–100, 102–3, 105–7

AbdouMaliq Simone is the assistant director of
the graduate program in international affairs
at the New School University.

Library of Congress Cataloging-in-Publication Data

Simone, AbdouMaliq
For the city yet to come : changing African life
in four cities / AbdouMaliq Simone.
p. cm.
Includes bibliographical references and index.
ISBN 0-8223-3434-8 (cloth : alk. paper)
ISBN 0-8223-3445-3 (pbk.: alk. paper)
I. Cities and towns — Africa. 2. Sociology, Urban —
Africa. 3. Social change — Africa. I. Title.
HT148.A2S52 2004
307.76'096 — dc22   2004007449